AN EVIL CRADLING

Brian Keenan was born in Belfast in 1950 and after
completing a degree in English literature at Coleraine
University he worked in Brussels and Spain. Returning
to Ireland he took up a teaching post at his former
school, and later worked in community development
centres across Belfast. He then went on to take an MA
in Anglo-Irish literature and an adult education course.
It was after taking up a position at Beirut University that
Keenan was taken hostage in 1985.

'The equal of *Darkness at Noon* – Koestler's account of his imprisonment during the Spanish Civil War. It is the vividly-drawn, sometimes funny, sometimes harrowing story of the author's four years in captivity in Beirut. Keenan comes across as an extraordinary man in an extraordinary situation'

Books of the Year
Alan Rusbridger, *Guardian*

'My non-fiction nominee is Brian Keenan's vivid account of his Lebanese kidnap, *An Evil Cradling*, plunging far deeper into a mind stripped to its essentials than one had a right to expect'

Books of the Year
James Saynor, *Observer*

'Could I bear to read this? Could I bear not to, having tortured myself with thoughts of the horror the hostages were enduring while they were still held captive? So I read it. The surprise is to find that, even though the cruelty and terror experienced are all in this amazingly fluent book, reading it is not a matter of recoiling. Brian Keenan wants to concentrate not on what was done to him but on what he made of what was done to him. In the process he gives us the most eloquent, moving and illuminating testimony to how man can triumph over senseless suffering. Not since I read Primo Levi's *If This is a Man* have I been so humbled and yet uplifted by the bravery of one man's spirit'

Books of the Year
Margaret Forster, *Spectator*

'There may have been more important books than Brian Keenan's *An Evil Cradling*, but its thoughtfulness and delicacy of feeling are unforgettable. Four years of savage captivity in Lebanon have been transmuted into understanding, not bitterness: a remarkable achievement'

Books of the Year
John Simpson, *Daily Telegraph*

'His book is colossal. Although it is painful, at times almost unbearable to read, it brilliantly relates the static conditions of his captivity and the awful odyssey of his mind. It manages this by a near-perfect balance of narrative and reflection… One of the remarkable things about this book is that while Keenan's experiences are, mercifully, unusual, and while his responses over the years take him into areas of self-knowledge that most people will never need to visit, the processes of his mind are entirely comprehensible. He is thus able to take the reader with him through unfamiliar levels of despair and self-discovery… Keenan has nothing extenuated nor set down aught in malice: the scope and grandeur of his reflections is supported by the concrete detail of his narrative. It is a moving and remarkable triumph'

Sebastian Faulks,
Independent on Sunday

'This is one of the most harrowing books I have ever read. It is the chronicle of Brian Keenan's suffering at the cruel hands, fists, feet and minds of his captors in Lebanon. The scale of torture to which he was subjected is terrible. The man had to face every humiliation imaginable. He endured violation of his body and of his mind calculated to drive him insane. This is more than the record of a season in hell. This is year after year after year in hell. And the tale is told unflinchingly, sparing no detail. Yet from this horror has come something wonderful. *An Evil Cradling* is a great book… it has been created from harsh reality, and it has been created by a true writer. Keenan's prose alternates between intense speculations on his fate and lyrical remembrance of times good and bad. His compassion can be tempered by sharp stabs of judgment, especially against himself. There is burning rage throughout the book, but it is controlled by a detachment born from the urgency to tell what happened, and to forget nothing… This is a mighty achievement by a magnificent writer'

Frank McGuinnes,
Irish Times

Brian Keenan

AN EVIL CRADLING

V

VINTAGE

VINTAGE
20 Vauxhall Bridge Road, London SW1V 2SA

London Melbourne Sydney Auckland Johannesburg
and agencies throughout the world

First published by Hutchinson, 1992

Vintage edition 1993

2 4 6 8 10 9 7 5 3 1

© Brian Keenan 1992

The right of Brian Keenan to be identified as the author
of this work has been asserted by him in accordance
with the Copyright, Designs and Patents Act, 1988

This book is sold subject to the condition that it shall
not by way of trade or otherwise, be lent, resold, hired
out, or otherwise circulated without the publisher's
prior consent in any form of binding or cover other than
that in which it is published and without a similar condition including this condition being imposed on the
subsquent purchaser

Printed and bound in Great Britain by
Cox & Wyman, Reading, Berkshire

ISBN 0 09 999030 X

Contents

Contents

Acknowledgements

Regina McCormack, who was locked up with this book for longer than I was. Without her patience and concerned skill this book would still be a work in progress. Thank you again Reg. Now give your fingers a long holiday.

Neil Belton, my editor, a fellow Irishman whose 'tender chastisement', advice and friendship pushed me over the 'humps' and gave real form to the book.

Matt and Geraldine Molloy, whose sensitive and caring friendship was more supportive than they knew.

A special and most grateful thanks to all the Corcoran family and staff at Castlecourt Hotel. Their giving hand was never withheld. To Ann, especially, a guardian angel, who proved more truths about the joy of life than I could ever write. Without her coaxing and cajoling, I would still be fumbling to find a finish.

Seamus and Ann Geraghty, my first 'minders' and now my constant friends.

Father McGreal, who lent me his cottage in the hills beneath Croagh Patrick, where healing first began.

Frank and Mary from Dublin, who did so much to help me in my return home and to write this.

To John Lydon, who showed me some of the beauties of Mayo and provided a house overlooking the sea in which to work.

Mike and Shelagh, eternal friends, who have been forever helpful. Many, many thanks.

Gerry and Dorothea Dawe and their daughter, Olwyn, who gave me my first shelter: 'Memory's the Great Minder'.

To all the people of Westport whose quiet and unobtrusive embrace was a balm beyond measure.

To Johnny Furse, who helped wipe the scales from my eyes and held my hand while my vision cleared.

Finally to my family, who understood my need of space and time.

'They also serve who only stand and wait' was never more true.

My abject apologies to the many people I have missed. There is a sea of faces and names before me. Forgive me.

To my close friends from Belfast, thanks for understanding and not asking.

Finally I am extremely grateful to the following for their kind permission to reproduce their poems: Leland Bardwell for *The Colour Orange*, Luis Veiga Leitào for *A Bicycle Designed in the Cell*, Trevor Magee for *Exile*, Conor S Carson for *The Hostages* and Frank McGuinness for *The Corn Crake*.

I feel like a cross between Humpty Dumpty and Rip Van Winkle – I have fallen off the wall and suddenly awake I find all the pieces of me, before me.
There are more parts than I began with.
All the King's horses, and all the King's men, cannot put Humpty together again.

Brian Keenan
Dutch Embassy,
Damascus,
24th Aug 1990

Preface

I think it was D. H. Lawrence, speaking about the act of writing, who said that writers throw up their sickness in books. So it is with this work. It is the process of abreaction in art form, both a therapy and an exploration. I once wrote in an article about the process of re-adjustment that we are our own self-healers. The writing of this book has been part of that healing.

The book will not be the usual conventional chronology of events, people and places. This kind of neat patchwork does not capture or represent the significance or the depth of experience in that quarter-life, enclosed in a very heightened and very different reality – a strange reality far removed from normal human experience, yet one in which, paradoxically, so much more of what we are as human beings was revealed. Such intimate and profound exposure of mind and body was a kind of branding and unholy stigmata, an affirmation of the richness, perhaps even enchantment of humanity. A zealous poet might describe the experience as a deification of one's humanity. In the most intense moments of despair and suffering, something of this was truly present. The book will be an attempt to reveal men 'in extremis'.

I wish to reveal the richness of that phrase 'in extremis'. It is a kind of pun or play on words. There were many types of extremes. The extremes of language, for example: its savagely humorous crudity; the contrived and concocted language that McCarthy and I invented almost instinctively and spontaneously with intimate understanding. A strange and wonderful contrivance considering our very different backgrounds: an Irish, working-class socialist from Belfast; an English ex-public schoolboy and inter-national journalist. It was a language that one might associate with the private world of children, created out of fantasy and need, which others cannot enter, a language impervious to holy warriors filled with righteous rage: all God-tormented and screaming Allah-u-Akbar.

In this linguistic haven we established a refuge for ourselves and at the same time made a world richly meaningful for us.

There was also humour 'in extremis': that vast playhouse of situations, resources and creative impulses that repulsed again and again the crucifying despair that drove some men to less than animal condition, to a state of inanimateness – day-long, unmoving silence when the body became to all intents and purposes a corpse, where normal bodily functions shut down and where the mind found its own place outside the mind. Here was the real terror, and the desperately anguished clawing back to some semblance of reality or half reality was the real pain. The real hurt was psychic and terrible and made the bruises, beating and torture insignificant, a mere passing inconvenience. Freud described insanity as 'a flight from a traumatic reality into another world of madness'. I saw it, I travelled it, I left men trapped in it, not wanting to return. I want now to imprison it on paper.

I hope to illustrate this humour, that special quality which acted as a shield and also to show this humour as a counterpart to the depravity. In terms of the book's structure it serves to reinforce and highlight the cruelty, involving the reader in the emotional highs and lows of hostage existence. Further, this story seeks to evoke the extremes of human communication. How, in those conditions, discussion turned into debate and debate degenerated into poisonous argument. How men misdirected their anger and aggression onto one another, and mutual support turned into mutual dislike and seething silence. Yet why did John McCarthy and I, who had more reason for mutual antipathy, find a deep, enduring bond of friendship and support that eventually became a prop for others? Most assuredly, all of us changed, and deeply. For some it was a re-humanization and affirmation of something lost or forgotten. For others it was loss – a turning away from oneself in awe, in horror and in fear.

There will be, I am sure, a desire to know of the torture and brutality. I will not spare the reader but neither will I feed the voyeuristic vulture. I will reveal the moments of physical abuse but with extreme care and sensitivity so that what might be vicarious and even terrifying may be underscored with sympathy. I, who grew up in Belfast, perhaps knew the terrorist mind better than any other hostage. Knowledge was my sword. I could cut through our captors' aggression, their perversion, their constant humiliation. I could see the man, a man not defined by Islam or by ethnic background, perhaps a man more confused than the man in chains; a man more hurt and anguished than the man he had just beaten.

The book is also an exploration of the mind and personalities of hostage and captor, and their shifting and changing roles. For example, it was the psychological and emotional shock of the beatings, rather than the pain, that struck each man. The beatings were not merely a bodily encounter. The mind engaged itself with another kind of intensity quite unrelated to the event; it fused with something previously unknown. For such experiences one developed strategies of mind to hold oneself together.

Writing this book was most certainly self-exploratory and therapeutic. Its content is based on fact and experience. However, in piecing together memories to get the right mix of colour, texture and insight, the reader will find a book that is more reflective and meditative – a kind of reflective symphony of incidents, feelings, words, thoughts.

I try to illustrate not only what happens to the mind during prolonged periods in tiny cells without light or any other form of stimulation, but also, when a man seeks desperately to unite vision and will by whatever power is within him, how adversity is overcome. The process is long and awful.

I hope this preface, at least in part, reveals the implicit paradox that will be the principal subject matter of the book – how in the most inhuman of circumstances men grow and deepen in humanity. In the face of death but not because of it, they explode with passionate life, conquering despair with insane humour. There are other paradoxes, such as the degree to which, in a sense, the captors became our prisoners, perversely depending on us. And, that most awful paradox of all, how men under such extremes, knowing that they must do everything to support one another, can still fall into a kind of frenzy of rage and despair more soul-destroying to watch than all the brutality.

As I have said, the act of writing the book was part of a long process of healing which in truth commenced under the most extreme conditions of deprivation and abuse. During my captivity I, like my fellow hostages, was forced to confront the man I thought I was and to discover that I was many people. I had to befriend these many people, discover their origins, introduce them to each other and find a communality between themselves and myself. These 'people' included those which perhaps set me particularly apart from my fellow hostages.

Unlike them I did not come from the professional middle class. I was brought up in that harsh, divided landscape of the Northern Irish working class and I came into captivity with all its attendant baggage, good and bad. John McCarthy, from the utterly different background of the English upper class, discovered his own 'people' and baggage. In the circumstances in which we found ourselves physically chained together we both realized an extraordinary capacity to unchain ourselves from what we had known and been – and to set free those trapped people and parts of ourselves. We came to understand that these trapped people included our own captors and we were able to incorporate them in our healing process. All these people that John and I discovered and shared in the deepest intimacy of our confinement spoke, I believe, of a world familiar to us all – a world laden with social, cultural, political and philosophical divisions which manifest themselves in their most extreme and confused forms on the streets of Belfast and Beirut.

The extraordinary bond that developed between John and myself was a bonding not just of two separate human beings caught up in a mortal whirlwind. It was also the bonding of our own innermost selves or 'people' in a manner which all of us perhaps deep down aspire to. This act of transformation and transcendence could be seen as a metaphor for the times we live in, an age that has seen the massive transformations in Eastern Europe and the Arab world and the West's own sea-changes.

John and I discovered not only a love for each other which transcended our divisions and backgrounds. We also discovered a renewed love for the world and its possibilities which, whilst nascent in us as children, had become buried by the accretions of the conscious worlds we had been brought up in. In a way the book is a 'love story' in the fullest sense, a story which speaks beyond the confines of what happened to us physically and addresses many of our unrealised and unarticulated feelings and aspirations.

Perhaps all art is created out of malformity. If it is so then this book is only a beginning; a first phase of re-entry into life. Ultimately, not everything can be told. Each man experienced his imprisonment in his own way. Each man selected and chose his own truths. This work is only a selection of moments in search of a truth that is certainly meaningful to me.

Whether I have achieved my purpose I cannot know. All our

lives are but a story, and this is only another. Stories should be a mirror held up to life. Sometimes those mirrors are cracked or opaque. Only those who look into it can truly know; you the reader will decide.

The Beginning

It is always difficult to find a beginning. All good stories have one, no matter how inconclusive or unexpected their end may be. The end of this story has not yet come, so it is particularly difficult to know where to begin. Were I older and had I lived fully the greater part of what life has been given me, then perhaps as in any good autobiography it would be easy to find a starting point, a rationale or a structure for my life: a place from where memory might begin to unfold the full and meaningful pattern of my time and how I have lived it.

But here is a different kind of search for a beginning. I do not wish to tell of a whole life, but only of an incident: an episode in time, a short sequence, yet one that seems dreadfully long and meaningful to me.

I think of the opening lines of the Bible: 'In the beginning was the Word, and the Word was with God.' Somehow those lines kept ringing back to me in the long captive silences, with a head full of words, a confusion of images, a mind not sane enough to find a rational perspective from which I could understand what was happening to me. Again I recall that ancient prologue to try to convey to you something of that imprisoned time and hopefully to explain something of what it meant and how it continues to have meaning; sometimes good, sometimes bad, and sometimes I don't know. Those easy definitions of good and bad, right and wrong seem inadequate to my purpose: the same inadequacy that overcomes so many things that we as human beings are forced to deal with and to understand.

So now I try to find a starting point from which I can share with you part of the self that I knew, and to find the self that I may have become as a result of my strange sojourn in the Lebanon. Because 'myself' could never again be an easily defined and well-summed thing. I have been asked so many times 'Why did you go? What took you to that place?' In answering, I can at last find my beginning.

All of us are beings of our age and time. All of us are a consequence of the depth or limitation of our understanding of the world about us, sometimes faulted in our development by the kind of commitment we make to that world, the people who share it with us and the historical events that touch our lives. I am a product of my city and of this awful period in its history. Before I left Belfast, I had been torn with a desperate kind of love and distaste for my place and my people and even after coming back these scars of anger and of desire still mark me.

A love that cannot find an outlet turns inward, and not being able to reach out and touch the thing it loves, be it a place or the people in that place, turns to anger and becomes confused. I have lived through a terrible time, but seen something of the loveliness that is in a people and a country, and have known people who struggle, who insist on trying to rise above the forces that threaten them. But we all become tired, like a man struggling with a great load: Sisyphus pushing his awful stone only to feel it roll back and topple him down to the bottom of that hill from which again he must begin his upward heave.

When I think of my choice to leave Ireland, I constantly ask myself was it a wearisome walking away? Was it time to find another set of values, breathe another kind of air? One in which I would have to recharge myself with new ideas, new thoughts, new relationships, new feelings? I remember talking to a friend before I made my decision to go. I said to him 'There comes a time when you get so utterly empty that you've got to move somewhere else to satisfy an inner hunger.'

So I sought change, not knowing fully what form that change would take. I suppose it was a kind of inner compulsion that I had not then articulated or understood. As we sat, my friend and I, over a few pints in a local pub, we talked of ageing. We had been friends from school days – one of those few constant friendships that a man or woman has in their lives. I remember remarking how I suddenly felt myself becoming afraid of never going anywhere, afraid of the challenge that life itself presents.

My departure was a way of taking up that challenge. All my friends and professional colleagues in teaching and from community work in Belfast had married, bought homes, started families; settled into a cosy domesticity which I had avoided and had perhaps feared. Lines from W. B. Yeats's poem 'The Choice' had imprinted themselves on and directed my understanding of life's trajectory:

> The intellect of man is forced to choose
> Perfection of the life, or of the work,

And if it take the second must refuse
A heavenly mansion, raging in the dark.

That 'heavenly mansion,' domesticity, love, marriage, eluded me for so many reasons, and I was fearful that I was going to be swallowed up in the emptiness that was encroaching upon me. I was gripped by the irresolution of life that seems to drive us to take decisions.

Unlike many of my contemporaries, I was not tempted to take up the cudgels of full-time politics. Politics can only be a small part of what we are. It's a *way* of seeing, it's not all-seeing in itself, and people like me, who were fortunate enough to be born and educated before the start of the tragedy that has engulfed the North of Ireland, found the panacea of politics to be a bitter cul-de-sac. What was happening around us had moved beyond meaningful reality. So it was for me a time to move, to find out if I could remould myself. The energizing effect of politics had dissipated, the vibrant radicalism of our generation had become ghettoized and subterranean; the rival slogans of 'Ourselves Alone' and 'Who Shall Separate Us' marked political backwaters, stagnating and debilitating. At worst they were full of perverse arrogance, vindictive and malign. At best they were a sheltering place from the long war of attrition: bursting full of community and fellowship, they were a loud testimony to people's determination not to be subdued.

I think of that decision to move as one which many men must face. I speak of men because I am one and because I understand as a man. I think something happens to us; people looking for a colourful expression call it the male menopause. We come to an age when choice is forced upon us. Some of us choose to change our job, knowing that in our late thirties it will be the last and final change we might comfortably make. Therefore we make it with some urgency, perhaps with fear, certainly with anxiety. Alternatively we decide on a change of house. It will be the last house we will ever be able to buy for we will never be able to increase our income. Some seek out the companionship of a younger partner, a kind of emotional assurance that we can still achieve, that we are still valued.

During my period of incarceration I felt that perhaps this urge to change is not unlike a woman's in her late thirties or early forties when she decides to have her first or final child. Maybe something in the male psyche wants a child and since we cannot have it we redirect our inner compulsion towards something that vaguely declares itself as a renewing of love, a revitalizing of what is creative in us.

In the grey back streets of Belfast, aware of people's unresolved desire and need and sensing myself becoming rooted and dead, burdened with a feeling that I had ceased to choose life, I forced myself to change, and consequently to go.

I had a half-formed notion about the effects of change on the personality. We seem to undergo a reactive process before any transition. A person's initial reaction to change is one of immobilization. We feel overwhelmed, and the more unfamiliar the change, the greater our paralysis. With the growing negative expectations resulting from this paralysis we feel ourselves frozen up. Such was my experience. I felt the debilitating cold of ice-floes gathering about me. I knew that I must find some free water, an open channel through which I might escape before I was trapped. How was I to know that I was to confront the same entrapment in another place? Literally as well as metaphorically, it seemed that islands of ice followed and gathered about me: dry ice, so cold that it burned the skin, melted into it. My resolution to action, as it turned out, simply drove me further into blinding snowfields of the mind.

My personal history is quite ordinary. I grew up in a working-class family in Protestant East Belfast, the only male child, the middle of the family. Being the son, I was given advantages over my two sisters. When I sought out books and education, my family facilitated me. With scholarships and reasonably good exam results under my belt I was able to continue my education.

But first I left school at fifteen. I was an academically bright lad, who was cajoled by some of his teachers not to leave, but I wanted out, to see life and not to reach beyond the expectations of the mates who left school with me. I worked for a year in a laundry, as a van-boy delivering dry cleaning.

On turning sixteen and feeling destined for an apprenticeship, I applied, and eventually began working my trade as a heating engineer with a medium-sized company in East Belfast. I still remember my first pair of overalls. They were strange, after the black blazer and grey flannels of secondary school. I can't remember if they made me feel any older or more of a man. I just remember that the bloody things were so baggy. I walked to work every morning and walked home again in the evening, with my 'piece-box' snug under my arm.

As with most apprenticeships, those first months were boring. The work was not demanding but I found the environment of a factory tiresome. I remember my first week. I left the factory to meet up with a friend in a pub next door – the usual Friday evening occupation for all workers in Belfast. I realized after having my first drink that I had forgotten to collect my wages. My friend thought I was an idiot.

After many months working in the factory, I was sent off to the 'Tech', as it was called, to study for my City & Guilds in Heating Engineering. This different kind of classroom routine became oppressive. I remember feeling a sense of limitation. Five years of this, to end up a glorified plumber and continue with that for the foreseeable future, was not an enthralling prospect to me.

Although I had left school against the advice of my teachers I had, without telling anyone, tried to continue my studies in literature at night school. It was a tedious walk from one end of the city to the other every Tuesday night, and to sit amongst adults studying for 'O' levels was confusing. I was the youngest in the class, so the companionship that I knew at school was absent here. I stuck it for a short period. It was too long a walk on cold winter's nights, and then to try to concentrate on Shakespeare with wet shoes and soaking trousers, wondering how I was going to get home when the buses stopped. So I persisted in reading books at home, and compensated for the boredom of the days in the factory and the hours studying for my City & Guilds by going away every weekend.

From the age of fourteen I would catch a train or a bus every weekend to somewhere outside Belfast, and as I got older I would go off youth-hostelling. It was a need simply to go somewhere, anywhere, with a sleeping bag and stay wherever luck would take me for as long as I could. The seeds of the need to travel and to be free of immediate pressures – the home, the family, the streets that I grew up in – sprang up early. Something always nags, especially in the young. I wanted more.

By freak of circumstance, for which I am not sure I am entirely grateful, I won some prizes and literary awards in national competitions. A young woman from the BBC came to the Tech one day. She told me in the quiet of the corridor that I had won a national poetry award. I stared at her in astonishment and disbelief. She wanted to film a small piece, to which I said: 'No, I couldn't do that.' Not that I had any real excuse. I was just frightened. She eventually persuaded me that I should do it the following day, and it was her good looks, her charm and my sudden rise in the estimation of my friends that made me grudgingly agree.

Off I went to Shaws Bridge, on the outskirts of Belfast. They made a short film piece of me reading one of my poems and I was thence and forever condemned, I think, to a fascination with words. I wondered what I should do after this, and decided some weeks later that I could not bear to weld pipes for the rest of my days in broken-down factories. So coming home one evening from work, I fumblingly told my parents that I wanted to return to school. They were shocked, and I think a little afraid. But they never tried to dissuade me. They wanted to know if I was sure; if I knew what it meant; and whether I was aware that if I left my apprenticeship it would be very difficult to get a good job – to get a trade. But nothing would deflect me, and they pursued the matter no further.

I returned to education and the following year received another national award. My commitment to language was doubly stamped. And thus alone among my friends in East Belfast I went to university and I suppose to another world, another way of understanding, which set me at a remove from all those things that were familiar to me. This was my first real leave-taking.

Leave-taking

The decision to go to university came about because, apart from further study, I couldn't think of anything else that I wanted to do. I had toyed for some time with the idea that I might join the merchant navy: always that travel instinct, that need to be going somewhere niggling in the back of my head. However, it was difficult to join the merchant service, unless you had a father or some other relative already in the ships.

Ultimately university seemed a greater prize and I chose to go to Coleraine. When I think back on it, the reason for that choice was the area surrounding the college itself. The university was built only a few miles from the great, majestic coastline of North Antrim. Near the university in the small villages where the students lived, we always had access to that turbulent North Atlantic, those huge stretches of desolate beach and those small provincial pubs. Coleraine also offered the best course in literature, particularly in the contemporary field. I specialized, over my three years, in nineteenth- and twentieth-century British and American literature and of course in the literature of Ireland known then as 'Anglo-Irish'.

I was not an outstanding student – just about average, but after my first year I became increasingly convinced that teaching literature is an impossibility. To go into a lecture room and listen for an hour to a capable lecturer delivering his assessment of some writer and then to go off and talk about the lecturer's ideas in a small tutorial group didn't provide the kind of stimulus I was looking for. I became more and more in the last two years of my university career a communicant of the library, choosing to follow the course on my own, instead of being a passive recipient of the understandings of my lecturers. Still, university provided me with a new set of interests, and more importantly a new set of friendships with people I could never have met had I remained in Belfast working at my apprenticeship.

I have maintained most of these friendships to a greater or lesser degree and each of them I am grateful for. But beyond this, two events during the three years spent on that northern coast stick out in my memory. I suppose they remain so vivid because they weren't directly related to my studies in that place. They are memorable now because during my first period of incarceration they came back to me so sharply.

I lived in Portstewart, one of the small villages on the coast. I rented a small room at the top of an old dank two-storey Victorian terrace house. The house was the last one in the terrace and from its window I could look out on the grey, ever-restless ocean. I can still remember the view from the window and the constant changes in the sea. The weather in that part of the North of Ireland was never the kindest, though when the summer came the landscape around us, the easy access to Donegal and to the remoter parts of the North gave the area its own particular delight.

An old retired couple who owned the house lived in two rooms on the ground floor. Mr Paul was in his eighties and I remember him going for his nightly walk accompanied by his walking stick and a small mongrel dog. His bent figure would brave even Portstewart's weather as he walked along the sea front. I never saw the old man at any other time apart from these walks. I heard him occasionally in his own room. His wife, his second, would sit quietly in the kitchen beside the old range constantly knitting and offering us cups of tea as we came in from the pub or back from studying. She never bothered us much, was always friendly and enjoyed a cup of tea with those of us who would sit and chat with her.

Mr Paul became ill very suddenly. We were not surprised, aware even then that age can be cruel. But what moved me most was his rapid decline, the fact that I never again saw him walking bent double against the wind, and the sight of his walking stick always lying in the hall. It became a strange kind of symbol. Late into the night I could hear him coughing and throwing up. The fact that we were only aware of this old man's illness through his rasping cough and his wife's ministrations lent the house a kind of ominous gloom.

One evening I came in from the cold and straight to the kitchen to heat myself at the range. Mrs Paul sat alone. There was a silence I couldn't understand. I recall now that her knitting needles were for once not in evidence. There was no steam coming out of the old kettle normally kept simmering on the hot plate. Her face was very still. It took her some time to look up, to acknowledge me coming into the room. 'Would you like a cup of tea?' I asked. She looked up slowly and I remember her old, lined but still quite beautiful face as she said calmly and without emotion: 'My husband is dead.'

Although I was in my twenties, it was my first confrontation with death. And with the immediacy of its presence I hurriedly made some tea, and began my naive questioning . . . 'When did it happen? . . . Have you told anyone?' He had died in the past half-hour, she was sure, and no-one knew. So it was left to me to be the bearer of grim news to the sons and daughters and the grandchildren of this old man, whom I knew only as someone walking against the wind and the rain in the dark evenings of Portstewart.

This incident is one of two from my student days that came back to me in my solitude while I was in Lebanon: a situation in which there was a dead man lying in his room and me trying to cope with my own loneliness and fear. I remember striving to recall some poetry I had written back then. This attempt to remember became for me a mental exercise to overcome my own pathetic and frightening condition, reaching back to what I had originally written as a memorial to this old stranger and to my first confrontation with death.

The second event that so affected me was a moment in our history that many Irish people, particularly in the North, cannot forget or come to terms with. 'Bloody Sunday', the carnage in Derry city when paratroopers shot dead thirteen unarmed demonstrators, has become a fixed symbol of horror in most Irish minds. I remember the news of the killings suddenly being broadcast on television. The news-flashes seemed to cause a kind of seizure of the whole of the university campus, among students and teaching staff alike.

There was much urgent activity. The student body met with teachers and administration staff to discuss the traumatic news. Among the student radicals, there was much talk of protest and of organization. Everyone was angry and everyone felt they must do something. But I sat with the kind of stunned amazement that I had recognized in Mrs Paul as she told me her husband was dead. Here I was at this second confrontation with death, feeling something of what I assume she must have felt with years still in front of her without her husband. What could I do. . . ? How could I understand this. . . ? And why was there such mass frenzy amongst the students. . . ? Some of them I felt were too young, too naive or perhaps too enthusiastic to believe the sentiments I heard at that mass meeting.

A decision was taken to stop work: a strike by the lecturing staff and the students united in one voice of protest against the massacre. I remember leaving the university that day long before lunchtime, and going home to my room which had become my eyrie up above the waves that beat outside my window. I sat hoping that some friend would call. No one did. So many people were engaged in demonstrating or had gone to the pub to pick over the highlights of that incandescent mass meeting. The following day, the first day of the strike and of the protest, I found myself – not quite believing what I was doing – packing a bag, putting on my coat and heading into university. I had never broken a strike in my life.

My politics were always of that working-class kind which believed in the necessity of trade unions and of such actions as unions can take. And here I was breaking faith with everything that I had so long supported. I remember entering the main door of the university, which was picketed by three of my closest friends. They were amazed and embarrassed to see me going into the building against all the recommendations of the students' union, a stand supported by ninety per cent of the students and teaching faculty. I heard the voice of a friend, who stared me coldly in the eye, and asked without emotion or anger: 'You are going to break the strike, Brian. . . ?', and some pent up anger in me, something resilient, something that did not want to be broken by this event returned his cold stare and said 'Yes, I am. Get out of my way.'

As I thought back on that moment, from confinement in Beirut, I wondered was my action another kind of leave-taking, and how much was it a kind of self-sustaining arrogance, and how much was it that inner compulsion to do *something*. I entered the university, and keeping clear of the strikers as much as I could, I went to the library. I did no work for my course but sat down with the few other students who for whatever reasons had decided to break the strike, and tried very hard to understand what I was feeling, and how I could understand an event like Bloody Sunday. These lines from a poem that I wrote soon after the event give some insight into what I was trying to cope with:

> Conflict is elemental
> A challenge of opposing minds

Identities shift, man-fish, fish-man
Primal passion takes its form
Patience, pause then . . .
Strike!
And play.
The line takes life
Taking life away.

A matter of matching bait and play
Like causation and effect
Coupling ideas with certain minds.
The net is cast
The fish are caught
Only the gutting remains.

I relate these moments of my personal history and quote this youthful poem in all its morbid immaturity because it gives some sort of colour or shape to the young man I then was, and because those two incidents came hammering back at me in Lebanon. In that lonely place I suppose I was trying to exercise my mind out of that same morbidity and edge myself away from that precipice of insanity which was a constant threat, and to which time after time so many of us who lived that experience were drawn so terribly near.

I spoke earlier about the inner compulsion to change, to remould or remake myself in some other situation as part of the explanation for my going to Lebanon in the first place.

This critical sense of stagnation took me there, and into captivity and another kind of frozen state. The ice of indecision and the ice of captivity met and fused. The breaking down of that icy immobility that afflicts the hostage, deprived of any but the most degraded human contact, that feeling of total constriction in which the normal faculty of reason seems stunted, demands of us some kind of survival strategy. We must look within to find it. For there is nothing in four concrete walls that can supply the needs we have as human beings. We turn back on memory. Or rather our memory comes to us, to give the mind some sort of positive means of egress out of that immobility. And so it was with me, over and over again throughout that long period of captivity. These memories, and many like them, were part of my strategy for breaking free.

Beirut Remembered

Dawn is cruel in Lebanon.
Rocket holes have gutted this place
As would a blunt and rusted blade
In the flesh of a fish.
An unkempt forest of rushes sprouts
Amid minefields
Fed on sewage, watered by years
Of unstaunched pipes
The ghosts of the night have no place
In Lebanon.
Here they are masters of the light
Made substantial in the sun.

Today,
L'Orient le Jour has a headline
'Decouverte Macabre'.
A record of bodies discovered the previous day
Spills out,
Like the innards of a disemboweled animal.

One dawn, perhaps
Such secrets may not be
The burdensome fruit
Of Lebanese earth.

Brian Keenan

It's like sitting in the petals of a poisonous
flower. It's beautiful, but it kills you.

Jonathan Broder
Chicago Tribune

Arrival

I arranged my flights from Belfast via London to Beirut, hoping to arrive on the fourth of December. I wanted my first Christmas abroad to mark this new life that I was heading into half unconsciously, yet sure that it was something I needed to do. In the days before catching the flight I spent some time traipsing around the old haunts of Belfast, talking with friends about my plans and what the future might hold for me. But most of those last few days I spent alone.

I suppose I had to take a parting look at the place I was leaving. I remember driving or walking around the back streets of the areas in which I had worked with different community groups. I particularly remember those stark murals, colourful and grotesque, which have come to be part of Belfast, and part of the historic expression of the people and their city. A great lumbering white horse and small rider painted obscurely on a gable wall of some tiny side street: this Dutch king in a foreign land, taking different form and shape from the hands of the naive painters. And always there was that Viking bloody red hand, the symbol of Protestant Ulster.

In the Catholic areas the murals reversed out of a black background. I remember somewhere a crude copy of Michelangelo's *Pietá*, painted against a backdrop of men with Armalites: raised, defiant, clenched fists which declared more rage against God and man, I thought, than any conformity with the politics of nationalism.

Lines from James Joyce came to me as I looked at the murals, those images imprinting something vague, political and half-believed in the minds of the people: 'Oh Ireland my one and only love where Christ and Caesar are hand in glove . . .' But the images had become more than just paintings on a wall, more than just a statement of belief. They seemed to have taken on the form of icons, but not icons venerating different gods, more like a loud discordant orchestra of crude images clashing and jarring in the dark; our history, our past and our violent present twisting and kinking out of proportion and out of harmony.

There was no interlacing relationship between these images: what people thought they meant and what relationship they bore to each other was lost in garbled clichés of tribalism. These were the icons thrown up in the collective mind in a kind of epileptic turmoil. And they reflected my own turmoil about the place.

Those nightmare images that so possess us in our sleep had moved out of mind and into time. They had become our reality. On every corner the impress on the mind was reinforced. Underneath the skin of the city there was contagion. A kind of malevolence festered and spread uncontrollably and unseen. Out of a sense of frustration, of fear, of a raging thirst for identity and purpose, it seemed that people were drinking in this poison: some unconsciously, and some by choice until they became intoxicated with rage and despair and helplessness. Walking through the town looking again at these images and places was for me an expunging, taking a last look so that I could put it all behind me, and go on to whatever Lebanon and the future years held for me.

For years I would not let the dark gods of politics and religion possess me. Unlike many of my age and background, I had made that mythic leap and crossed the Jordan. My Protestant working-class background and all its shibboleths would not contain me. I chose to ask questions and not accept ready made answers. We discover our own answers if we have the will to do so; and if we are not afraid of the confrontation with ourselves that such a journey might entail.

I am grateful for my particular background. I will not call it Protestant or Loyalist or British, for they are terms barely adequate to explain my understanding or perspective. The oft-quoted adage comes to mind: 'power concedes nothing without a struggle.' There are those who 'cross the Jordan' and seek out truth through a different experience from the one they are born to, and theirs is the greatest struggle. To move from one cultural ethos into another, as I did, and emerge embracing them both demands more of a man than any armed struggle. For here is the real conflict by which we move into manhood and maturity. For unless we know how to embrace the other we are not men and our nationhood is wilful and adolescent. Those who struggle through turbulent Jordan waters have gone beyond the glib definitions of politics or religion. The rest remain standing on either bank firing guns at one another. I had had enough of gun-fire, the rhetoric of hate and redundant ideologies.

My last hours in Belfast I spent in my local, The Crown Bar, well-known in the city and a pub that made a mockery of those passionate certainties that move people so much. For here in this city-centre pub everyone socialized peaceably, keeping their beliefs to themselves and enjoying the company of strangers as of friends. It was a convivial place and I always enjoyed the companionship there. However, because these were my last few hours in Belfast, I was there early, just before lunch, and I was the only customer in the bar.

It was quiet. Its elaborate Victoriana, all shiny polished mahogany and glinting brass, seemed to speak out loud. I remember that embossed ceiling, full of reds, browns, blues and gold, heavy and intricate above my head and the gleam of the polished copper accoutrements. And those fabulous cut-glass mirrors and richly coloured Italian glass windows, full of frills and fancies of ivy leaves and bunches of grapes and pineapples. Apart from being grossly elaborate, they were very Mediterranean in their richness. The whole impression I had that day and remember still is of being in a holy place. Perhaps the silence and the rich ornateness give it the feel of church.

I had a few words with Billy the barman, and told him I was heading off to Beirut. He looked at me in silence and said 'I'll give you a pint of the devil's buttermilk on the house.' I smiled. The devil's buttermilk: I wondered how long it would be before I would have another pint of Guinness.

Finishing that last pint, I caught a bus to the airport. Strangely, just as it had been in the Crown, I was the only person on the bus. This lonely trip to the airport was, in retrospect, a kind of figuration in advance of the existential journey I was starting. We exchanged the usual pleasantries, the driver and I. He didn't know where Beirut was but wished me luck anyway.

Sitting at the airport awaiting my flight to London I met, as one always does at airports, a friend I had not seen for years. He was waiting for his wife. We shared a cup of coffee and a chat. When I told him where I was going he looked at me querulously and said 'Mmm, Beirut.' Then, he went off into raptures about the joys of being an expatriate and how he thought he would enjoy such a life. As he continued good-humouredly painting a picture of expatriate pleasures, I listened quietly but certainly not calmly. He continued rhapsodizing and I felt frustration rising into a slow, quiet anger. Whether it was those last few days spent walking through the town looking at and experiencing that violent intensity, it all came to a head at this, my moment of departure – frustration and anger and loneliness all feeding off one another while I smiled at my friend's odd picture of living abroad.

It was necessary for me to spend a night in London before catching my connecting flight to Beirut. I had arranged with two friends to stay at their home. I had not seen them for twelve years since working in Brussels with them. It was odd to be seeing them again after so many years, knowing that I would only be spending a few hours with them. One of my friends, Shelagh, had relations living near the area where I would be staying. We chatted about Beirut. She remembered being there as a young girl. I went for a drink with her husband Mike while Shelagh prepared dinner. 'A last supper', we called it. We returned to the meal and exchanged stories of our lives, telling jokes and drinking wine. Shelagh passed me some houmus, a Lebanese speciality, saying 'You better get used to it, you're going to be getting plenty of that where you're going.' I still laugh at that now and think how true it was.

Early next morning Mike and I exchanged shirts. I don't know to this day why we did that. Shelagh drove me to the airport. It was early in the morning. Shelagh parked her car, helped me out with my bags, and gave me a parting hug, telling me to enjoy myself. I said I would do my best. She also gave me a warning. 'Be careful, Brian.' I answered 'Shelagh, I come from Belfast, I know how to be careful.' She looked at me again and said 'I didn't mean that.' I asked her what she meant exactly. She said simply 'The Lebanese women are more liberated than you think they may be, Brian, so be careful.' I smiled, quite happy with that knowledge, pleased that, at least, I was not walking into a kind of Middle Eastern backwater where I would not be able to make friends and associate with the people with whom I would be working.

In Terminal Four I went to the check-in desk. A young Lebanese girl took my ticket and baggage and with some surprise asked me was I intending to stay in Lebanon long. I said 'Yes, for a year or two.' She seemed even more surprised and told me that not many people were travelling to Beirut any more. I nodded. She asked me was I perhaps a journalist, so I told her I would be teaching there. She smiled, and told me how much I would enjoy Beirut and that Lebanon was 'a very nice place'. I was somehow encouraged, thanked her and went back to await my flight call.

All around me were Indians, Africans, Pakistanis: a whole tapestry of humanity parading itself in its different costumes with its different habits and its jumble of baggage. Children of different nationalities were sitting close to their mothers. Others, excited by the airport, and perhaps frightened, seemed to be crying louder than I could bear to listen to. I remember feeling strange as I looked around at all these people so differently garbed, talking in so many different languages, each with their own preoccupations. My own Irishness, whatever that was, seemed to be quickly submerged and lost in this mass of humanity.

I had brought some books with me to read on the flight but I was too fascinated by what was going on around me. I occupied myself by trying to recall some of what my friends had told me about Beirut, about places to see, where to live and how to spend my holiday time, visiting places such as the temple of Baal at Baalbek – under which I was to reside for some time with my fellow hostages. But I was seeing too many sights now. My eye was caught by the features of an old Indian gentleman sitting quietly, remote from all the traffic about him. Where was he going? Was he glad to be leaving what was obviously not his home? Suddenly I found myself feeling the kind of inner loneliness that I'm sure so many people experience, passing through that way-station.

I boarded a Middle East Airlines flight and we took off. I remembered the airline clerk's remark that not many people now travelled to Beirut. The plane was more than half empty. I took some newspapers from the stewardess out of habit, and to pass the time. Airline flights are always boring for me. I only really enjoy that first moment when the plane travels along the tarmac at speed and then is suddenly airborne. But I remember some of the articles I read.

Flicking through the pages, my eyes homed in on reports from the Middle East. I particularly remember one, because I kept the newspaper and later used the article in my teaching seminars. It was a report on ritual slaughter methods in England. The small piece caught my imagination:

'Leaders of Jewish and Muslim communities said yesterday that their followers would become vegetarians rather than accept a ban on ritual methods of slaughter.'

The article went on to describe how the religious leaders of both the Jewish and Muslim communities in London had been meeting in conference to formulate some protest against the banning of ritual slaughter. I remember thinking how I had watched the TV a few days before and seen these people killing one another in Lebanon; now here they were in London sitting together at a table sharing ideas about the merits of ritual slaughter. I loved the incongruity of it, especially since another column in that day's paper spoke of how the South Lebanese Army, backed by Israeli military advisors, had made several armed raids into south Lebanese villages, killing five men and taking several more prisoners.

There were other prophetic pieces that I would also remember. They were articles about the film *Rambo*, which was very popular at the time. One small column spoke about how the BBC was postponing the showing of the film, saying that it was unsuitable for family viewing. And another much larger article, entitled 'Revisionist Rambo', spoke of how the film had been making huge sales in the Middle East and how it had been dubbed and redubbed to be made suitable and more acceptable to Middle Eastern audiences. The article spoke about how Rambo's anti-communist antics would not go down well in such places as Syria, which still had close associations with the USSR.

I recalled these articles because later this man, this image of Rambo, was to haunt me for a long time. But the article I most remember and quote at length was about the Lebanese economy by Robert Fisk, one of the best writers on the Middle East, if not the very best.

New notes a hollow boost to ill economy

A few weeks ago, one of the Middle East Airlines' ponderous old Boeing 707s flew into Beirut national airport on a scheduled flight from London with a six ton cargo of cash. De La Rue's printing works had just produced the latest financial drip-feed for Lebanon's collapsing economy; and there, next to Runway 1–8, the Lebanese army was waiting to collect it.

Stashed in boxes, the brand new bank notes were loaded into armoured personnel carriers. The Army's Sixth Brigade had brought along heavy machine-guns, rocket launchers and even a couple of Saladins to guard the cash on its four mile journey to Central Bank in Hamra Street.

However, it was not until the powerful little convoy actually left the airport runway that the real protectors of the national treasury revealed themselves; four scruffy youths in combat jackets holding AK47 rifles, waiting to climb on board one of the vehicles. They travelled into Beirut perched atop an armoured personnel carrier with the government troops sitting meekly beside them. Nor was anyone surprised: if Lebanon's economy has to be defended by the Army, the Army has to be defended by the local militias.

It is not just a question of erosion of power. The legitimate state authorities in Lebanon long ago forsook even the basic governmental duty of raising taxes. So many illegal ports have now been built by the Christian and Muslim militias that the Finance Ministry believes the private armies are now collecting taxes worth more than £175 million sterling that should rightfully have gone to central government funds. Every militia in the country – Christian Phalangist, Shia Muslim 'Amal', Druze, Palestinian, pro-Syrian and pro-Israeli – now levies its own taxes on shopkeepers and businessmen.

If corruption and smuggling permeate Lebanon's financial affairs to an unprecedented degree, however, the civil war militias have ironically become a mainstay of the economy. Many of the leftist Muslim groups are paid in dollars by other Arab states while Mr Yassir Arafat channels millions of US dollars – funds given him by the Saudis – into Lebanon to buy the continued loyalty of his PLO guerrillas. The Syrian Army, whose troops are spread across more than a quarter of the country, generates its own economy. Militias have meanwhile initiated their own housing projects, hotels and businesses which in turn replenish Lebanon's depleted financial resources.

In one sense, therefore, an end to Lebanese conflict would bring almost as many financial problems as it would solve. Yet as long as hostilities continue, so Lebanon's economy is going to decline.

I read this article and reread it. I got a contrasting insight into the country I was travelling to from the one that my friends Mike and Shelagh had given me, though their memory was a much older one, of the place long before the civil war began in 1976. But I found it funny in its own way. Here I was entering a kind of Rambo-land, an Arabic John Wayne country where everybody was toting a gun and everybody was part of some paramilitary machine. So was I really travelling from the frying pan into the fire, from one kind of political and social turmoil to another? I suppose I was, but it didn't worry me too much.

I keep the article and still reread it, and still find the humour in it, particularly that passage where Fisk talks about '. . . four scruffy youths in combat jackets holding AK47 rifles'. I felt old bells ringing, echoing out of the place I had just come from, where local militias had become the defenders of a half-understood political aspiration and had taken upon themselves a brief not drawn up by the people they claimed to defend.

They say that an aircraft arriving in Beirut has to make a careful approach and a difficult landing. The nearness of the city to the airport and the proximity of the sea and hills add immeasurably to the pilot's difficulty; no-one lands by computer card in Beirut. Entering at dusk I couldn't see the landscape below me. Only the jostle of the Lebanese emigrants we had picked up in Frankfurt indicated that our journey's end was at hand. The fume of cigar smoke and the reek of whiskey began to disappear as the travellers made ready their baggage and said goodbye to their workmates.

The darkness as I emerged from the aircraft seemed to intensify the night heat. A short walk took me to the airport proper. It was small and decrepit, far removed from what I had left in Heathrow. But it was packed with people. Strangely there were no women. The night, the heat and the strangeness of the place gave it an eerie quality. I felt myself, along with two other Irish teachers who had been on the flight being watched, stared at. It was disconcerting, I felt very much at sea. I was an alien here and I felt it from the moment of my arrival. It was difficult to distinguish simple curiosity from mindless animosity or worse still a kind of festering hatred that seemed to lurk behind some of the faces.

A small, fat man shambled quickly forward, holding up a piece of paper with my name and the letters A.U.B. written alongside. I hurriedly moved to shake his hand, hoping that some confident human contact with him might dispel the oppressive atmosphere. Beside him, grining from ear to ear, stood a burly sergeant of police. They were an odd couple. The thought of a comic double act crossed my mind and perhaps made my greeting more honest and relaxed. The policeman's exuberant handshake, complete with hand at his heart contrasted with the smaller man's obvious anxiety about getting us quickly through the customs and the tedious bureaucracy of officialdom. A surly customs man asked me if I was English without bothering to look at my passport. I answered, pointing at the passport 'No, Irish'. He was puzzled for a moment, brightened and embraced me warmly: 'You are welcome to Lebanon,' he said with some enthusiasm. I felt myself becoming less apprehensive, though still anxious to be gone.

As we crossed the car park with this strange twosome I noted that we were being accompanied by ten or twelve men in full uniform, all of them armed. The whole airport was stiff with them, sitting or standing on the tops of cars. Each of them had a gun and they watched our amoeba-like movement, encumbered with luggage, the way predatory birds might watch the last living movements of their intended prey. I thought of the articles I had read on the aircraft and asked 'Why the soldiers?' The burly policeman opening his hands, shrugged, smiled at my foolishness and answered 'They are for you, they are your bodyguards.' I looked at the huge green cadillac, in which our bags were being loaded, then at the 'military escort' and the sea of staring faces around us, and thought that such precautions were more likely to highlight us as potential targets. I sank low in the rear of the vehicle and wished I could take a deep breath and disappear. Such reception committees I could have done without.

The journey through the southern suburbs did not make me any less uncomfortable. Here was a night time landscape of such desolation and destruction that it made me seriously question why the hell I had come here. That drive through a night of squalor reinforced the sense of intimidation that seemed to surround me at the airport. To break the nervous silence in the car, I asked the driver his name. 'Omar Sharif' he answered. I was dumbfounded and could only find an outlet for my nervous tension in laughter. The edge of hysteria in the laughter barely concealed my apprehension. Omar laughed also, but he assured me he was not joking.

We arrived, eventually and uneventfully at The Mayflower Hotel in the Hamra area of Beirut. There was a curius comfort in this. Apart from the reassurance of light and convivial surroundings, the name itself was welcoming. My home in Belfast was in Mayflower St. 'Home from home?' I thought and then again: 'Frying pan to fire? Another Belfast?'

A few drinks with some members of the teaching faculty who were there to welcome us helped dispel some of the feelings my first impression of Beirut had left lingering. A momentary thought that these new friends were as desperately happy to see us as we were them I put from me as the product of an over-excited and over-anxious imagination. We chatted politely, exchanging backgrounds and work experiences for some hours and finally I retired. Someone said, 'Don't mind the call to prayer at dawn, you'll get used to it!' . . . And how right they were!

Morning came. I had not heard the 'call'. My mind, more tired than my body, had dragged me into a deep sleep. The day was so dazzlingly bright it took me some minutes for my eyes to adjust and focus. One of the new friends from the previous night called and showed me

around the neighbourhood and the University. The next week I spent
wandering the streets getting to know my bearings; finding the
location of the Irish Embassy, the Library and walking around the
University campus. Most of all I remember the noise. The
deafening racket of the street life. Street sellers calling out their wares,
people arguing and shouting conversations. The continual stream of
traffic blaring horns insistently. People talking with their hands,
sometimes in wild excitement, sometimes with slow deliberation.
When hands are engaged in driving, the car horn becomes a
compensation for this restriction on expressiveness. On more than
one occasion the horn proved inadequate and someone would let loose
a few rounds from his hand gun to make his point more clearly.

Kidnapped

The weeks before my disappearance were filled with apprehension, particularly for us foreigners living in Beirut. We were quite obviously targets. Everyone knew by our appearance that we were not Lebanese and probably knew where each of us lived and the routes home that each of us took from the University. Leigh Douglas's disappearance, along with his friend Philip Padfield*, had only exacerbated this anxiety.

Those of us who lived outside the University campus felt ourselves even more threatened. The teachers who lived on campus had the security of the University perimeter, with its Lebanese army and police guards. Though life was pleasant enough in the wooded and landscaped grounds of the University, the sense of being contained there, of it being the only sanctuary made it its own kind of prison and it was not for me. I had come from a city where such anxieties were rife, where people were contained within their own ghettos and lived out their lives in a small area of perhaps only a quarter-mile radius which they were fearful to go beyond. I felt that I must have a life separate from the University and not be a prisoner inside it.

My friends and I had agreed that since we lived off campus we should maintain contact with one another. We should regularly ring each other just to say 'Hello' and let one another know that we were at home, that we were safe. It was necessary, if we were going out for dinner or visiting friends, that we should ring our homes to let the people we lived with know where we were and what time we would be returning. If we did not return at a given time they would know immediately that something was wrong. I had been doing this with the people with whom I shared my Turkish villa for some weeks. I could not abide the containment of the villa, the forced necessity of

* Leigh Douglas, a lecturer at the American University of Beirut and Philip Padfield, a teacher at Deirut's Internation College, were kidnapped about ten days before me and later executed by their captors – probably about a month after they were taken.

finishing the teaching day, going straight home and locking myself in until the next morning.

The night before I was taken, I had been out to dinner with a friend and had rung home to tell my house-mates that I would be home around ten o'clock in the evening. I duly showed up. I went through the garden gates, up to the patio of the villa, unlocked the gates and entered my barred sanctuary. I had coffee with one of my colleagues. We discussed some of the events of the day at the University, and then he told me that the teachers who lived in the apartment above our villa had suggested that we should henceforth all leave together for the University. I thought it was a good idea. But as I lay in bed that night I thought to myself 'I don't know how this is going to be really helpful. After all if they want you they will get you, and it may be just as easy for them to take two or three people as it would to take one walking alone to school.' I put the thing from my mind, remembering that I had an eight o'clock class in the morning and no one else was teaching until nine or ten o'clock. So I had to go on my own in any case. I went to sleep.

The nights were becoming warm. The summer was approaching very quickly and sleep was difficult. I tossed and turned, throwing off sheets. The next morning was bright and clear. There was a noticeable lack of street noise. This was always the best time, before that hustle and din of noise and voices: people arguing, people talking, motor cars blaring horns, which I always found oppressive. I had to condition myself to turn my mind off so as not to hear this constant racket. I had a quick shower, packed my briefcase and dressed.

I left at twenty minutes past seven. It only took ten minutes at the most to walk from my villa to the University. In a hurry I could easily make it in five. I left the villa, walking through the long garden that fronted it and separated it from the street.

I stopped as I always did to look at three or four carp which swam in the fish pond with its fountain, which is so much a part of a traditional Turkish villa. I was never sure exactly how many carp there were in that dark murky pond. I could never see them all at once. The garden was about to break out in flower, giving its first hint of the colours that would fill it as the summer approached. I went to look at some of the creeping plants that were already beginning to spread with some vigour along the wall, wondering just what colour would emerge from them. I had previously planted some bulbs and seeds in the very sandy soil, not sure whether they would take and break through or whether it was just wishful thinking on my part.

I had come to understand the importance of the garden in Arab culture as a source of peace, of rest, a place for meditation, a kind of sanctuary, and this garden had become the same for me. I remember the day that one corner of the garden seemed to have come alive with butterflies. It was not unusual if one woke at the right time to look out and see the garden filled with a blizzard of butterflies. It was like looking through a child's kaleidoscope. Before leaving the house I had carefully watered the indoor plants and hanging baskets which I had been buying, feeling that today would be oppressively hot and that the plants would be glad of a drink before the sun got up and its ferocity began to dry them out.

I went out through the gate, locking it behind me, and began to walk off in the direction of the University. I had taken, I suppose, no more than twelve steps. I was barely away from the gate and the fence which enclosed the garden when an old Mercedes, hand-painted dark green with a cream roof, pulled up alongside me. The driver's door opened, preventing me from passing on the narrow street.

Out jumped four men, the driver with a hand pistol and three other young men in their mid-twenties, each with a Kalashnikov in his hand and a hand gun in his belt. I stood and we exchanged silent glances. How long this took I do not know. But I remember looking at them, them looking at me. Then I was quickly pushed into the back seat with two of the Kalashnikov-toting gunmen.

The doors slammed and the car moved off quickly. I remember smiling to myself, looking at these men. The driver was watching me in the mirror, and his friend on the passenger seat turned full face towards me, half-smiling. The two men in the back seat beside me were silent, grim and I think somewhat fearful. The car gathered speed and I was ordered down on the floor. I could not, would not go down on the floor amongst their feet. I simply bowed my head, resting it on one of the men's knees. This seemed to cause much confusion. The driver was angry, he wanted me on the floor. His friend in the passenger seat was smiling and laughing. The guard on whose knee I rested my head seemed perplexed.

Only the man in the passenger seat seemed to speak some English, not particularly well. The questions began. 'You know where you go?' Of course I told them I didn't know where I was going. It seemed a lunatic question. 'You English?' At this point I sat up quite determined: 'No . . . I am not English, I am Irish . . . Irlandais.' They looked shocked and puzzled. The passenger in the front seat said something quickly to the driver. The driver looked at me, looked at his compatriot and there was a moment's silence again. 'You like Thatcher?' was the next question. I could quite honestly say with a smile on my face 'No, I don't like Thatcher. I'm Irish,' foolishly thinking that these men might understand how impossible it was for any Irish person with an ounce of imagination to even consider liking Thatcher. The questioning at this stage was pleasant enough, though answering such questions half squatting, half lying in the back seat of a car with a hand gun in your ribs and a Kalashnikov lying across the back of your neck was not only difficult, but ludicrous.

The car travelled for some distance. I tried to look up but all I could see were the tops of buildings, and the occasional tower of a mosque. I had no idea where I was. We travelled for some fifteen minutes. The car then entered darkness, and after some minutes stopped. I was aware of some argument going on between the driver and the man who spoke English. He seemed angry and kept looking at my shoes. I knew this was an ominous sign. They had already begun to reckon up and divide the spoils, my clothes and my possessions, amongst themselves. There was very little I could do about it. Not that I was carrying much, but to be present when men talk about sharing you out is disconcerting.

The kidnappers all climbed out of the car and I was told 'Get out, get out.' We seemed to be in a kind of subway. I remember it was strewn with litter. It must have been difficult for a car to make any headway through the mass of garbage that had been dumped there. I was told to walk to the back of the car. When I did so I was stopped. Immediately off to the right of where I stood at the boot of the car there was a tiny alleyway, perhaps an exit from the subway we were in. I thought to myself, 'Oh no not here, not here of all places.' My first thought was that I was going to be taken up this little narrow tunnel and executed.

I don't recall feeling any sense of panic or fear. I can still remember thinking that this was such an awful God-forsaken place in which to die. My next thought was that I was wearing my father's shirt and how unkind it was to him that I should die wearing his shirt, even though he himself had died some years previously. This preoccupied me to the exclusion of everything else, regardless of the fact that within seconds I might be shot. I said nothing. The men looked about, talked rapidly with one another. The boot was opened and I was told 'Get in . . . get in'; I crawled in, their hands pushing and squeezing me. The panic was more on their side than on mine. I lay crumpled and curled in the boot. The kidnapper who spoke English said to me viciously 'No noise, no noise', the boot slammed and the darkness was complete.

The car doors shut, the engine started up and we moved off. I could not tell when we exited from that underground passage, but faint glimmerings of light and the noise of the street, which was now a roar in my ears, told me that we were in the daylight and moving through a congested area. There were people all around, going about their business and their lives, oblivious to the fact that a man was at this moment disappearing out of life, lying quietly in the boot of this dilapidated Mercedes.

The car stopped once; two doors slammed; there was loud talk. I assumed that we were at some check point belonging to one of the various paramilitary groups, though which one I shall never know. A couple of minutes' brief exchange, then the slamming doors again and movement to God knows where. The car drove briskly. I could hear the crunch of the gears and then an almost screeching sudden halt. Again the doors opening. Again the lid of the boot being unlocked. I was not blinded by daylight but was in what I thought might be the enclosed car-parking area of some building. I was quickly hauled out of the boot. This time only French was spoken: 'Vite, vite, vite' was hissed at me, but not angrily. These men were simply urgent to finish what they were doing.

I was run some twenty or thirty feet to a doorway on my right and quickly pushed through it. All the gunmen entered after me. I noticed two of them breathing very fast. These men were not exhausted by any expenditure of physical energy, but by fear. That erratic breathing was a deadly give-away, something I was to hear time and time again during my long period in these mens' charge.

We moved down a short corridor and a door was opened to my left. I stopped and looked in and was nudged gently into the room. It contained only a folding camp bed and I was told to sit on it. Then an odd question was put to me by the smiling guard with the poor English: 'You are fine, yes?', to which I could only say 'Yes.' He went off, and the door was locked. I remember sitting on the bed and thinking, 'So this is it.' This small fearful room. How could anyone survive a stay in a place so small. I felt some sort of relief that at least I had a bed. I had heard stories of the conditions that hostages were kept in and none of their descriptions included a bed. I sat and tried to order my thoughts. Again without panic, just slowly putting piece upon piece together to work out what exactly had happened, how long I had been travelling, and where I was likely to be. Something to keep the mind calm.

The door opened. The English-speaking guard came in and told me to take off my shirt. I remembered again my thoughts in that tunnel. It was my father's shirt. I slowly unbuttoned the shirt, looking at this man, half smiling with my own puzzlement as I tried to contain my growing confusion. What could these men want with my father's shirt? With slow deliberation I removed the shirt and handed it at a full arm's length to this man, looking always into his eyes, and smiling at him. As I remember it, it was a kind of sardonic smile; what he understood by it I will never know but I believe to this day that that sardonic smile, and my staring him full in the face restrained him from whatever violence he was prepared to offer.

I was told to sit again. The shirt was folded in a band and my first blindfold was my father's shirt, tied tightly about my head. With two men on each side of me, holding my arms, I was walked out of that small room. There was a descent down three flights of roughly concreted stairs and bare concrete walls. I could feel them scrape against my skin as I stumbled. I wondered how far underground I would be going. At the bottom of those three flights, the ground levelled off. I seemed to be walking slowly in a straight line.

I could hear noise in front of me, not loud, but the sounds of people talking and moving about. I sensed some light as I tried to peer underneath the blindfold down along the line of my body to my feet. My captors restrained me as I tried to walk on and simply said 'Stop'. I stood wondering 'What next?' My blindfold was removed. I saw two other faces, of men who had not been in the party that kidnapped me. One looked at me, the other spoke to the men who had brought me in. It seemed they had no English.

The passenger in the car, who had begun his questioning about my nationality and about Margaret Thatcher, asked me if I would like a shower. I said quite politely 'No thank you, I had one this morning before leaving.' It seemed like a natural response, but in retrospect it was a ridiculous one. My captor spoke then to this man who was in effect in charge of this underground prison. In halting English, the prison officer said that there was no hot water, speaking almost apologetically, again adding to my confusion and increasing the breadth of the smile on my mouth. I said 'It's OK, don't worry.' I was then taken by four men to a small cell. It was no bigger than the last one and it had no bed. A mattress was laid out on the ground. The room was probably smaller than a bathroom in an average suburban semi-detached.

I was left for some minutes; then the door opened again. The English-speaking guard came in with my briefcase. He sat it on the ground, squatting in front of me. 'You want to eat?' If this was four-star service, I thought, it was extremely pushy. I had just arrived, they offer me a shower but apologize for not having hot water, now they ask me if I want something to eat. I was in no mood for eating and told him so. He asked again 'You want anything?' I said 'No' and then thought again and said 'Yes . . . I want some newspapers.' He grunted, nodded and left, taking my briefcase with him. The door closed again. Like so many doors that were to close. I sat on the mattress waiting and wondering how long, that awful anguished question that I was so frequently to ask.

Psychologists tell us that one of the first and instinctual reactions of the personality when faced with a traumatic transition is to attempt to trivialize or to minimize the event and the consequences it may have. Our denial stimulates a euphoric state. Obviously the extremes to which denial can be taken are dependent on the qualities and strengths of character the person has acquired over the years. But it is important to distinguish this process of minimizing danger from the idea of flight; of running away in horror, in fear, in confusion, which is another and different road. Denial is often a necessary phase in the process of adjustment, a normal and necessary human reaction to a crisis which is too immediately overwhelming to face head on. Denial gives time for a temporary retreat from reality, time for our internal forces to regroup and to regain strength, to begin to deal with the loss that has been forced upon us.

For most people the effects of change and the resulting stresses begin to become apparent. We exhaust the strategies of denial. Reality slowly but surely overcomes our attempts to hold it at bay. As we become aware of the new realities we begin to experience depression. Depression can be a kind of extreme mania: the highs and lows of a movement between awful despair and a giddy euphoria coming wave upon wave, day after day attempting to erode whatever degree of resilience and resistance one has in one's self. With this depression there is associated an awful frustration. It is difficult to know how best to deal with the new requirements, the new relationships that have to be established.

As we move further into awareness of our new reality, the new conditions about us have the effect of reconditioning us. We move into a process of acceptance, but this acceptance should not be seen as a defeat of our powers of resistance and of maintaining the integrity of the self. It is simply that in a situation of total confinement one has to learn to unhook from the past in order to live for the present.

My first hours, then days and then weeks I found myself constantly having to deal with the slow hallucination into which I had been dropped. I had been removed from a known reality. The four concrete walls of my shoe-box-sized cell formed my only vista. Beyond these I could see nothing, only my imagination gave me images, some beautiful, some disturbing and unendurably ever-present. The vast landscape of the mind unfolds on its own. At times I felt the compensations of this gift and at other times cursed my imagination that it could bring me sensations so contorted, so strange and so incoherent that I screamed; not out of fear but out of the rage and frustration of having to deal with these flashing pictures of which I could make little or no sense.

Exaggerating this distorted sensitivity were the voices of my captors in a disembodied language which I didn't understand but could hear being spoken, being whispered, being shouted beyond the walls of my cell. There were the cries, too, of the other prisoners, all in Arabic as I recall, some of them weeping and in the long hours of darkness some of that weeping becoming screaming. At other times the shouts came from a street vendor selling fruit or fish, reminding me starkly that there was something outside, but that I was buried away from normal life and could only hear its echo. So many thoughts, so many ideas, so many feelings came hurtling into my mind in those first days; too many to take hold of and deal with in an ordered and coherent way. You simply had to sit in lethargy, letting them wash over you and holding on to some point of resistance that would only let them wash over but not sweep you away. The dangers of that were too great and too apparent. There was nowhere to run to.

I chose, as all men in those circumstances would, to disbelieve that I would be held for very long. I immediately set a date in my head and I look back now with some amusement on it. I decided within those first few hours that I would be kept no longer than a few weeks. My nationality was worthless to them. It would be pointless to hold an Irishman: they could trade me for little or nothing. It was while thinking this through that I fixed my mind on the only option open to me: somehow to convince these men of the fruitlessness of keeping me as a hostage against some political demand. While I was forcing this belief on myself so as to hold back all the vast confusion and fear, the cell door opened for the third time on the first day.

I was given a bottle of Coke and two sandwiches wrapped in Arabic bread. I was told by the guard 'Soon, my boss he come.' I shrugged my shoulders, confident and nonchalant. The door closed again but it was not locked. I could dimly see the guards moving past. There seemed to be several of them. They hovered about my door trying to look in, me looking out, convinced that it was only in this eye contact that I could maintain a distance from them. In those first weeks when confronted by them I would not take my eyes from their faces. In the few times that I did see a face, all the faces were as one to me, each blending in to one another, and I could hardly distinguish their separate features.

The door opened again, four men in their mid-twenties, some with hand guns, peered in at me. They stood in silence. Two of them just inside the door, two of them standing in the hallway beyond, looking intently at me as I looked back at them. I felt like a fish in an aquarium. They were silent and staring and I stared back. There was something between us. Maybe it was the fear in the air.

The long minutes of gazing down at me as I sat on the floor were oppressive. Then suddenly there was movement. The men parted, and an older man in a brown suit, with grey wavy hair and a full grey beard was standing in the doorway, studying me. He was obviously a man of some rank. The other men stood back in fearful respect. He looked at me, and I looked back at him. I was unmoved and did not blink. He asked me 'Are you English?' I noted that his English was an educated one. He spoke it well and I answered him. 'No, I am not English . . . I am Irish.'

He looked at me again in silence, with long pauses between his questions: 'Where do you come from?' I answered with the same nonchalance, perhaps this time filled with the native stubbornness of my city: 'I'm from Belfast . . . Do you know it?' There was a touch of anger and aggression in my voice. He noted it, nodded, yes he knew it. He asked me how long I had been in Lebanon. I was uncomfortable that I had to sit on the floor while I was being questioned. It put me at a disadvantage. I wanted to stand up to him face to face, but something told me that that would be foolish, perhaps dangerous.

He muttered something to the guards, and there was an exchange between them. He looked back at me and asked calmly did I have an Irish passport. I told him of course I had an Irish passport. He asked 'Where is it?' I saw that it was time for a joke. 'Well if you'd like to take me back to my apartment I'll get it for you.' I smiled. He did not return the smile, but turned again to the men with the guns and said something in Arabic. There seemed to be some confusion. It was hard to tell with these excitable men. He turned and quietly told me that if I co-operated I would not be harmed. He told me he would return, and the door banged shut again. The padlock rattled, accompanied by the babble of this fearfully incomprehensible language.

Jailhouse Rock

I was pleased with my first interrogation. I sensed that my interrogator was confused about my nationality. I was equally pleased that I had made him feel I was not afraid of him, though secretly I was. I had simply not allowed myself to think of what could have happened, only what I could prevent happening. The Arab mind is often dominated by its cult of masculinity. It admires what it conceives to be courage, a show of power, of fearlessness. I tried to maintain these defensive self-images in my head, and wondered how long I could continue if things got much worse and if they began to play games – psychological torture games – or resorted to some more brutal violence.

Yet I told myself constantly that I was of no value to them. What did I know? What did they think I knew that might make them turn to more severe methods?

I looked at my two sandwiches and Coca-Cola still sitting untouched in the corner. I was not hungry, but I began to wonder what a first prison meal tasted like, and out of curiosity and boredom I began to eat. The food was tasteless. Though it was like much Arabic food, heavily spiced and flavoured with vinegar and pickles, its acidity didn't affect me and I could taste nothing. I took only a mouthful out of each sandwich, hoping to jar one taste against another. But there was just a blandness in my mouth. I thought that the shock of what had happened was finally ebbing slowly into me, dulling the faculties of taste and perception with tension and an unacknowledged fear.

The day progressed but I didn't feel the drag of it. I lay on the mattress or paced up and down the six-foot length of my cell wondering how long it would take until they realized how useless I was to them. Strangely, another part of me wanted to be held for at least some time to make the whole thing worthwhile. I felt a curiosity growing in me, at first minimal, yet I was constantly asking myself with interest rather than apprehension what my two weeks' captivity would mean to me. I was convincing myself that it would be two weeks, and only two weeks. And after that time perhaps I might have something interesting to say about my experience in Lebanon.

They had taken my watch, my ring, a necklace that a friend had given me, and what little cash I had on me, leaving me only what I stood up in: my father's shirt, a pair of grey trousers, socks and a pair of shoes that I had bought just a few days previously from a street vendor in the Hamra area. I thought of the shoes constantly in those first few days, remembering how when they picked me up there had seemed to be some dispute about them. The driver, the most aggressive and oldest of my captors, seemed to want them for himself. I dreaded the loss of those shoes more than the jewellery and the watch and the money. Perhaps as long as I had my shoes I had some dignity.

A friend told me when we were having dinner one evening on the road to Sidon that on the beaches outside Beirut which were normally the haunts only of local people, I should not be seen exposing the soles of my feet. There was some religious connotation in this, and I still don't know whether it's true. But I know a fanatic's mind is fed by such superstition, which removes him from the reality around him and in some strange way permits him to be aggressive and abusive to others because his own world is controlled by authoritative denial – all is forbidden to him.

I don't know when I decided it was time to sleep. I remember hearing loud bullish snoring from one of the Arab inmates and I thought it must be evening. The time had gone quickly, quicker than I imagined. The prison had been empty of its guards for several hours. I remember thinking as I heard the snoring that if it's night perhaps the inmates here will begin to speak to one another, unafraid of being heard. But there was no talking. I found this hard to believe; that men could sit all day in a tiny cell and when given the opportunity, not even try to communicate with their fellows. I think I slept contentedly enough, that first night, having convinced myself that the first interview had gone well. I was not in any immediate danger. I had not been threatened or abused, and I refused to let myself believe that that would happen before I was set free.

In the early hours of the morning, I woke and thought about that moment in the underground pass, when they had taken me from the car and I thought I was about to be shot. Recalling that incident from only the day before was abhorrent to me. Not the thought of death itself, but the cruelty and anonymity of it. Death should have some meaning even for the justly condemned. Those who know they are about to die should have the time and the opportunity to receive death without fear, without hatred or bitterness. To be driven to some filthy hole in the ground and executed without justification was beyond my comprehension. In those early morning hours when my mind was only half awake I imagined myself lying there, my father's shirt blood-stained and filthy. Why it was my mind stuck so tenaciously onto this image I cannot tell; perhaps it was the gross indignity of it, a kind of insult to him. I spent hours wondering what this second day would hold.

Doors banged in the distance. Voices shouting. The guards were returning. I quickly got myself up, tried to dress. Strange how we preserve some kind of minimal vanity even when there is nothing to be vain about. I heard the other prisoners' cells opening, heard them shuffling past my own, and water running in the distance. It was obvious they were being taken to a shower or to a sink to wash. I waited my turn, eager to be out if only to see what the shower room was like. But my turn did not come. All the prisoners were taken back, but no one came for me.

My cell door opened, only a few inches. I saw the face of an old man looking in at me. His hair was askew, several days' growth on his face. I looked at him. He kept staring and then the door opened wider. I stood up thinking I was going to be taken to wash, to use the bathroom but he gently put his hand out as if to tell me no, and I sat down. I was given bread, some cheese and a cup of tea without milk. A small glass of hot, and very sweet black tea, and the door was locked. I looked at my second breakfast, without desire and without hunger.

After some minutes the door opened again and in came my captor; the one who spoke English and sat in the passenger seat of the car. It seemed I was to have him with me frequently, perhaps because he had some English and the others had none, only very poor French. He squatted beside me. 'How are you today?' I answered that I was fine, what other answer was there? 'Do you want anything?' I shook my head wanting to say: yes, I want to get the hell out of this place; but I didn't. I simply nodded, remembering always to look him in the face and not to flinch. He offered me more tea. I refused trying to explain to him it was too hot and too sweet, but I don't think he understood. Instead I asked for some water and it was quickly brought.

He watched me as I drank slowly, then came the second interrogation, if that is the proper definition. A lot of questions: Why did I come to Lebanon? What Lebanese people did I know? Did I know any Lebanese people *before* I came to Lebanon? Who were the political advisors to the foreign teachers in the American University of Beirut? Though I tried to answer these questions as uncomplicatedly as possible, I think that he was unused to asking questions and getting answers. He was simply a messenger boy, a gunman or a warrior given an order to go and collect someone. Anything beyond that he would have been incapable of dealing with. But nevertheless he asked the questions again, trying to fix one word in his head so that he could report back. I explained again how I came to be in Lebanon, and that I knew no Lebanese before coming and had only met a few since arriving; that I knew of no political advisors to the foreign teaching staff. I think he understood the nos and the yeses and that was enough for him. He rose to leave and said he would be back. I asked him when. He simply said 'Soon, soon' and went.

I spent some time wondering about the significance of these questions. My answers hardly gave any information and couldn't be of any use to them, so I waited to see what would be the outcome of his report to his superiors. I was soon to find out. Within an hour he returned, this time accompanied by the much older, more literate and intelligent interrogator of the day before. It was a repeat of the previous day's confrontation. He stood in the doorway and I sat on the floor on my mattress. We stared fixedly at one another and held the silence, each contemplating the other. He asked me how I was, as his younger friend had done previously, and I gave the same innocuous answer. 'I am fine.'

He then gave me back my briefcase which had been withheld from me since the day I was taken. I thanked him, still staring at him. Abruptly he said 'I want the names and addresses of fifteen English teachers.' Something in his expression had changed. He was now giving me an order. I looked back at him and said 'I have not been here long enough to know fifteen English teachers.' He was silent and I repeated that I had not been in Lebanon long enough to know so many English teachers, and then emphasizing my Belfast accent and retreating into a stubbornness that has always been part of what I am when I feel myself cornered or under attack, I told him 'I am Irish, I am from Belfast . . . Why do you think I would have made friends with English teachers . . . I do not know where these English people live.'

He insisted that I must know their addresses, I insisted that I did not. Those few foreign teachers that I had got to know all lived on campus and I told him surely he must know this. As he knew where I lived and where to come and get me, he must also know that many of the foreign teachers lived within the University for their own security. He took from his pocket a piece of paper folded neatly, passed it to me, and I opened it. On it were written the names of two English members of the teaching faculty, who had arrived some weeks after my own appointment. One of them I knew reasonably well, the other was a much older man and I had only a nodding acquaintance with him. I said that I did not know their addresses, only that one of them lived on campus and the other near one of the Embassies.

He talked to me in some detail about one of these men. He knew that he had been in some of the shops in Beirut that sell hi-fi equipment and flashy transistor radios and TVs, enquiring about the possibility of ordering a piece of computer equipment. I could tell him only that I knew him on campus and that I knew nothing about his interest in computers. Whether or not he was satisfied with this information, I cannot tell. He left the paper on which the two names were written with me and insisted that I add the names of other teachers and their addresses. I reiterated that I knew some of their names but did not know their addresses, beyond the fact that they lived on the campus, and that had I had more sense, I would have done the same. I tried to make this sound funny, but he was unresponsive. He said something to the guard who was with him and they left.

The guard came back within a few moments. He asked this time whether I had registered with the Irish Embassy. I told him that I had, and he replied 'We do not think so.' I gave him the address and the precise location of the Irish Embassy and the name of the first secretary to the Irish Ambassador, with whom I had had dinner and occasional drinks. It seemed to make little impact. I doubt if he understood much of what I was saying. He rose, said 'Goodbye' and left.

Again I was alone. I passed the rest of the day listening to the noises of the people in the street, aware of the smells of the men in the next cells, and also an obnoxious and throat-choking smell of some kind of paint percolating into our prison from outside. I remembered once having driven through Beirut and noticing a number of small car repair shops. Beirut is a great place for having your car stolen and seeing it the next day, driven by someone you might know. It would definitely be your car, but it would be a different colour and there would be no number plates on it. There was little you could do to prove it was yours, and it was dangerous to try and claim it back.

As yet the different emotions of resignation, rebellion, of religious abandon, fear, despair, anger, frustration had not fully taken hold of me. I was to know them in their fullest and most profound sense much later. At the moment I was still riding that high wave, convinced that my time would not be long. It would be a matter, I supposed, of them authenticating my Irish identity, realizing that there was little they could obtain from me and then setting up some mechanism for releasing me without endangering themselves.

Sunday came and went. I buoyed myself up thinking of cracks and jokes that my friends in Belfast would make when I returned. I thought also with some degree of anger that I had come to Lebanon to work for a couple of years, had been kidnapped as a British subject, locked up as a British subject, and questioned as a British subject. I had run away to this country to escape the consequences of British policy in Ireland and here I was about to be sent back for all the wrong reasons after only four months. It angered me and the anger kept away those dark moments which were yet to possess me. I was not discontented with my imprisonment so much as with what my release would mean: the loss of a job, a feeling that whatever was to be my future had been chosen for me.

On Monday, after the usual ablutions, my kidnapper and aspiring confidant came back. A social visit this time, not to interrogate me but to give me some news. He seemed excited, telling me that the Irish Government had placed a large advertisement in the local Arabic newspaper with my photograph and a copy of my passport, appealing to my kidnappers for my release. He laughed. He found it funny. I laughed too, but I laughed out of relief that finally something was confirming my own insistence that I was Irish, and that it was pointless to keep me for it would surely only complicate matters for themselves. However my increasingly acute discontent was not to be relieved by this good news.

One day during those first weeks of my captivity, I was brought a towel and a toothbrush, having asked for them on several occasions. My mind reeled on receiving them, trying to understand what this meant. Did they want to keep me in good shape for my imminent release, or had they resolved to hold me for some time and keep me in condition to endure my imprisonment? I was soon to learn the significance of the towel. It was not only for cleaning myself but it was also to become my shroud. It was a drape which I had always to put on my head and face so that I might not see them nor see anything around me when they were present. So began the real monotony of my imprisonment.

Each day became another day, unmarked by any difference from the day that preceded it or the day that would come after. Always it began with a door banging and the guards crying out to one another in Arabic; the sounds of the preparation of food, boxes or tins being opened; and then the opening and closing of doors and the shuffling footsteps of the men who occupied the cells next to mine fumbling their way to the bathroom. It was always an old man in filthy ragged pyjamas and broken and torn bedroom slippers who came to my cell. Henceforth I was forbidden to look at him but saw only the door opening, the broken shoes, the legs of the pyjamas and heard his soft, feeble voice saying something to me in Arabic. I came to call him the 'Shuffling Acolyte'. There was only this old man and perhaps one or two other guards. One of them was in charge, and gave the orders, more shouting than ordering. I always recognized the sliding gait of my old man. As if to hold the shoes upon his feet, he would slide himself forward, his feet in constant contact with the ground. Sometimes he would hurry me and at other times he was content to smoke as long as I was content to wash or do whatever else I could find to do in the toilet. But I always knew when he was coming for me, that telltale shuffling slide outside my door. The other, much younger guard who seemed to be in charge, I called 'The Grim Reaper'. These were the only two human beings with whom I had the barest contact.

The Grim Reaper was given his name because of his occasional outbursts of violence and his frequent beatings of some of the younger Arab prisoners. It was not unusual to hear him shouting abuse at one of the passing prisoners and continuing the scolding until he had worked himself into enough of a frenzy to make his abuse more physical. Either outside my cell door or in the cell of one of the Arab prisoners he would kick and beat and scream at some unfortunate. It seemed as the days passed that he had one favourite, a pet he enjoyed tormenting. I would hear this pathetic creature trying to run past The Grim Reaper on his way to and from the toilet, and then there would be the familiar flurry of abuse followed by the beating and the screaming.

The toilet was no more than a hole in the ground, and beside it a water tap, where I could fill a plastic jar to flush away whatever needed to be flushed away. It was a filthy place. I doubt if anyone had bothered to wash it in years and indeed, as I came to learn, no-one would want to wash it. We were prisoners, unwanted, unworthy and according to our jailors' convictions, unclean. They would not enter a place which we had used to wash or relieve ourselves. But it was what lived in there amongst the rubbish and the filth that made those minutes in the toilet so disgusting. The place was alive with cockroaches, large and shiny. Their hard body armour and their claw-like legs made loud scratching noises as they moved. They scurried rather than crawled. Their speed and the hardness of their shell made it impossible to crush or kill them. The toilet was their nesting place. It was necessary on each visit to poke through the filth and chase these monsters out of our privy. I remember once trying to drown them in the water of the toilet hole and to my horror watching them climb unscathed from this pit of excrement and dart glistening around my feet again. Using the toilet was, because of this insect menagerie, a painful experience. I sat half squatting above the receiving hole while nervously watching every dark corner.

The toilet was screened off from the cell block by a crude and tattered curtain. I would sit at times and watch the daily procession of bodies, their faces draped with filthy towels, move in slow silence to and from this place. It was like some unholy ritual at which I was a secret observer. One day during that first week, I can't remember precisely when, they took me for my first shower. The shower space was like the toilet, a cubicle of filth. It was fitted with a brace of pipes and an ancient shower head. The walls were of crude block construction, about shoulder-high. I noted that some of the blocks had fallen away and revealed a dark space beyond; through it I could hear more clearly the noises from the street, voices of children and occasionally what I took to be their mothers calling to them. What was immediately beyond the shower room I could not clearly see, nor could I risk looking. But it was possibly a way out. I took my time showering, wanting to establish in the minds of my guards that when I was brought again I could be left there for some ten or fifteen minutes, enough I thought to climb the piping and slither like one of those cockroaches through the opening. But it would have to wait. I was also still trying to convince myself that I would soon be released. There was no point in pre-empting that freedom by making a failed escape attempt.

Showered and refreshed, and my head filled with plots and hopes, I was returned to my cell. I think now how much like one of those hateful cockroaches I had become. Crawling every day, fearful and half-blind, to the toilet hole and back to my corner. My food awaited me. It was the same as before and would be the same for many days to come: a round of Arab bread, a piece of cheese, a spoonful of jam, a boiled egg. The bread was my plate, the floor my table and my fingers became my fork. This was my morning and my only meal. The guards came only to wash us and to feed us, much as one does with animals, the terminally ill or the deeply insane.

During those days as I sat complementing hopes for release with plans for escape, I had occasional visits from my kidnapping friend. He was always amicable. He seemed intrigued that I was relaxed, that I seemed unafraid and that I was able to laugh. He told me of his time in London and how his English teacher, who was of Scots origin, had called him a 'Sassenach'. He didn't understand what this word meant. I tried to explain it to him. He became even more confused while I thought quietly to myself, I have another name for you, my friend. On one of his last visits I recall him telling me that if any of the guards should beat or punch me I was to tell him. Instead I told him, filled with cocky self-confidence, that if anyone punched me I would most assuredly punch them back. He heard this I am sure not knowing exactly what my words meant, but feeling the confident force of them. He only looked at me for a moment and perhaps then the thought crossed his mind that maybe he should beat and frighten me to avoid such happenings. The moment passed, and nothing happened.

He had taken to wearing my new sunglasses. I boiled with anger, but concealed it. He seemed oblivious to the fact and I wondered what had become of my ring and my watch. Insignificant and inexpensive things had now become so vitally important to me. Parts of me had become parts of someone else. I wondered, as they walked about and looked at my watch, did they ask where it had come from and what had happened to its owner? Was there one split second of thought about me, as they twisted my ring or wound my watch?

Sometimes my kidnapper would ask me to give him English lessons, which I agreed to do, more out of boredom than any desire. I remember looking through the textbooks that he had brought with him for an appropriate lesson, and somehow I found the right one. One of the passages was based on the well-worn cliché that 'one man's

An Evil Cradling

terrorist is another man's freedom fighter'. I gave him the passage and listened to him read. His reading was not good and though he could repeat the words as he saw them I was convinced that he had little knowledge of their meaning.

I tried explaining what I thought were some of the more difficult words and then tried to discuss the set phrase with him. I quickly became aware of something that I was to become convinced of during my time with these men – that their capacity for conceptual thought was severely underdeveloped. He became bored and I was relieved. For to try to teach any language, which is overwhelmingly about meaning, to someone who does not have any kind of analytical capacity is extremely wearying.

My relationship with this particular guard yielded one fortunate result during this early period. On one of his visits he chatted and then on preparing to leave he asked me the usual question, 'Do you want anything?' I said 'I need exercise, I have not done any exercise for many days.' He looked at me for a moment and then said, without any further consideration 'OK is fine.' He told me I must cover my eyes and I was taken from the cell with a towel draped over my head and walked along the cell block corridor, turning and starting slowly and carefully to climb the stairs which I had been brought down many days before. But this time I was only taken up two flights, guided and turned towards a door which was opened for me and locked behind me. The guard whispered through the door 'I knock when I come, you cover your eyes.' I said 'OK.'

The room was empty and had not been lived in for years. It was dirty but it was not the same sort of squalor found in the toilets or in the shower area. It was about twice the size of a double room in a good hotel. At the far end of the room was a door which was locked, but by lying on the floor and looking underneath it I could see piles of mattresses like the one I had been lying on, and stacks of chairs. This was a building that had some communal purpose. I was later to learn that many of the buildings under which we were held were Islamic community centres. I walked around the four bare walls of the room slowly. On one wall someone had written the word 'Amal' but I assumed it was a member of that organization who had been held there as a prisoner. There were two large holes in the wall facing the entrance door for some kind of air vent. They were blocked by an old pair of workman's overalls. I walked past them many times, considering what could be behind them. If I should pull out those old overalls, would I be able to see into another room? Would there be someone there? In the end curiosity caught hold of me and I carefully pulled the clothing out of the air vent. I stared into blackness; I could see nothing. Perhaps there wasn't a room on the other side; certainly I could hear nothing.

I searched in the pockets of the overalls and to my surprise I found a bank book belonging to a Frenchman. I laughed to myself thinking how careful we are with our money and I imagined this man being taken hostage and furtively hiding away his bank book for fear that his kidnappers might get his money. There was nothing more in the room to hold my attention and I decided to use the opportunity as it had been given me. I tried some push-ups and I barely managed five, my heart pounding, my head thumping. I began to worry. I paced around the room trying to think out different forms of exercise that I could do here. After some twenty minutes there was a knock on the door. I donned my towel and waited for my captor. These short exercise outings continued for some days.

On one of those long evenings I heard the outside doors opening. This was most unusual; no guards ever came to our prison after we had been washed and fed. I wondered what was happening. A lot of Arab voices percolated down the corridor and into the cell. They were shouting. People were being beaten as they were being brought in. I heard the voices, the noise, and the shuffling as what seemed to be two Arab men were taken to cells down at the far end of the prison. It was early evening; I could hear from my own cell the new inmates being questioned and then their doors were closed and padlocked and the guards left us again in the silence – that silence which was to become increasingly oppressive and increasingly demanding in the days that lay ahead of me. After some hours the guards returned. This is an eventful day, I thought. They went to the cells of the two new occupants and one of them was brought out and taken past my own cell and up to a room somewhere above me. I could hear a noise and wondered whether it was from the room where I had in the last few days been exercising. Then my idle pondering was abruptly brought to a halt. I heard what I had never heard before. A man crying out loud, the type of cry that tells you a fierce blow has been laid upon him and then another and another cry. Then those cries of pain becoming screams of a kind of animal helplessness. These were not screams of fear but of pain. This was a man being tortured. But it seemed more awful for the cries sounded like those of a young man, the voice seemed so immature. I wonder still today how we can tell the age of a man from the way he expresses his fear and helplessness and pain. The beating and the torture continued.

And I felt my stubborn, self-confident self taking its own kind of battering. With each tortured cry I felt my own fear claw at and crawl over my flesh. There is a capacity in each of us and sometimes I think even a need to reach out to others in pain. Why that is I didn't know at the time but have since learnt a lot about it. The more we discover the different degrees and different aspects of our own unhappiness the greater our capacity to sympathize instinctively or to reach out to someone in distress. Maybe it's a hangover from those days when we practised a sympathetic magic: by reaching out and touching someone else's distress or suffering, we took a little of it on ourselves as a kind of protection against the fullness of such suffering taking hold of us. That night I slept fitfully, thinking of what I had heard and wondering how I myself would deal with this situation when I was forced to. But to dwell on things for too long hammers home a deep nail of fear that is hard to extract. Instead I forced my mind for the first time to think of those other men who were here, all Arabs as far as I could understand; for what reason had they been locked up? What crime had they committed? What kind of court had condemned them? How long would they be here?

The next day brought the usual routine: the Shuffling Acolyte guiding me to my morning wash, and bringing me back; breakfast on the floor, and then the visit from my kidnapper friend and back upstairs for my exercise. At first glance, the shabby emptiness seemed unchanged, and then I noticed the chair upturned as though it had been kicked over. The bed had a pillow on it which had not been there before. I wandered over and saw that the pillow was bloodstained, and saw the same brown stain on the floor and on a canvas stretch cover on the bed that had not been there yesterday.

Rather than look too long I started my slow pacing around the room. Having taken in three walls of the first circuit, I came to a stop and stared at what lay in front of me. It was a pair of pliers. As if mesmerized I stared, hoping the horror of what I thought had happened here would wash out of me, trying to tell myself 'Don't let your imagination run riot.' This had been the instrument of torture; its application could have taken many forms. I thought: there's no point in dwelling on this, but think what you can do with a pair of pliers. Or think at least what may be done to you with these pliers if you don't get rid of them. Out of sight, out of mind.

To keep some hold on my own freedom I had to have some kind of control over that of my guards, however limited that might be. I continued pacing around the room, stepping over or around the pliers, the way a superstitious person avoids cracks in the pavement or walking under ladders. Those pliers had become an unlucky black cat crossing my path. They hinted at no good fortune in the future. But I had to resolve something; to try to hide them in this bare room or to take them with me. Everything was worth the risk, I decided. I pushed them down the front of my trousers and practised walking with them. Would they fall out as I negotiated the blind descent back to my cell? This was my agonizing worry as I waited for the guard to return.

In the end all went well. I was returned without mishap or discovery. The padlock snapped in my cell door and I sat feeling a slow flush of exhilaration wash away the tension that held me.

Realizing there was even less hope of concealing the pliers in my small cell my exhilaration was short-lived. I scanned the cell in minute detail, but there was nowhere safe. I finally decided to put them in my brief case which had been returned to me, telling myself that if they found them I would say they had always been there and that I had intended using them to fix something in my tutorial room at the University. It was a ridiculous lie. They would know exactly where they came from. But I had to make myself believe something or fear would incapacitate me.

Day followed day in a monotonous rhythm. I kept telling myself I would be released and reinforced this hope by going over the details of the escape plans I had concocted in my head. Because eventually I attempted a few of them, I will describe them as they arise in this story.

The first plan, to get out of the shower room, ended like a piece of circus pantomime.

My unspoken wish to be left to my own devices in the shower was granted. I had established a pattern of going to the shower with my shirt on, and washing it as well as myself. The guards were content to allow me fifteen or twenty minutes to complete my ablutions and laundry. Should I get through the hole in the wall, I would at least be dressed: the prospect of fleeing through the streets of the southern suburbs of Beirut topless in broad daylight with a bunch of Arab terrorists screaming and firing guns at me was more appropriate to the Keystone Cops than the reality of my situation.

On the day I had decided to execute my plan, which I jokingly called 'Operation Clean Getaway', I was duly delivered to the shower cubicle. I waited some minutes for the guard to take himself back to the main cell-block. Slowly I turned on the water and rapidly put on my shirt. I remember stupidly rubbing my shoes against the calves of my legs to polish them. I must have thought I was going to 'Come Dancing'. First, I tested the pipes, and they seemed secure. I reached up and placed one hand into the hole through which I hoped to disappear. With the other I reached up and clasped one of the pipes. I next had to lift my foot onto the lower bend of the pipes, then heave and push myself hand over foot into the hole. Thus positioned I waited, steeling myself and trying to calm my nervous breathing by taking huge gulps of air. I chose the number eleven in my head and began to count slowly. On reaching eleven I was supposed to disappear, head first like a rabbit down a hole. ELEVEN!!! Up and Away!!!

With an arthritic creak and groan the pipes came away from the wall and the bend snapped under my foot. Water roared and poured everywhere. Whoever coined the phrase 'drowned rat' must have had a vision of my state of dripping idiocy. But the flying cold water did nothing for the sudden panic that came charging over me. I expected to be immediately hauled from the shower and beaten senseless. But by whatever stroke of luck or Grace of God, no-one came. I hurriedly removed my shirt and then, holding my handing over the jetting pipe, like the Dutch boy on the dyke, shouted for the guards. After some minutes they heard and shouted back to me to wait. They had been oblivious to my predicament. Anger at their stupidity overcame my panic. I cursed loudly at them.

Eventually the guards reacted. Whether because of my shouting or the rush of water into the passage I can't say. Sudden voices were raised and feet were running towards me. The Shuffling Acolyte pulled back the curtain and for a moment stood stunned at the sight of this naked man clinging to the broken pipe joints while water showered and sprayed him from every angle. He muttered something and threw himself into the cubicle.

In his striped pyjamas and broken slippers he grabbed at me and then the pipes. The water displaed itself to another point and from there jetted on to us more fiercely. Like two clownish ballet dancers in a comic pas-de-deux, our underwater jig was outrageous.

Defeated, drenched and in desperation my dancing partner thrust my shirt and towel into my arms and bundled me out of the shower. His pyjamas hung from him like thick coats of dripping paint. My towel was thrown over my face, and I was quickly marched back to my cell, a dripping twosome leaving a wet trail behind them.

I sat, soaking into my mattress. My senses were like those jets of water, coming at me from every angle. Confusion, fear, frustration, laughter and panic all showered over me. A thought flashed through my head, a line from a hymn I recalled from my childhood: 'I have tried the broken cisterns, Lord.'

Surprisingly, nothing was said to me and nothing done to me. All those fearful expectations amounted to nothing. And I got more angry with them because my escape had failed and they were too stupid to punish me for it. I think back on those spasms of anger and how they were helpful in crushing back the panic that was always waiting to take possession of me.

My next attempt was made a few days later. I had become increasingly anxious about those pliers stashed in my briefcase. Sooner or later I was convinced they would find them. I thought I had better attempt to use them before this happened. My cell door was sheet metal welded on to a frame of angle iron. Above the door there was a small grille, some two and a half feet wide and perhaps a foot or fifteen inches high. To look out through this grille it was necessary to pull oneself up. It was above head height and it looked out on to the long corridor. I had on several occasions in the evening climbed up so that I could look out, but it was too narrow to see much. The cells were all on one side, so I could not communicate with anyone. A large section of this grille had been cut away to accommodate a piece of piping which occasionally blew air into the cell. It only worked infrequently and it also blew in the heat and dust of the streets; layers of dust had gathered in the piping over the years. When the pipe did blow, I quickly grabbed one of the bed sheets, which was an old curtain, and stuffed it into the pipe to avoid suffocating in the dust-laden heat. I had noticed that this piece of piping was held into the ceiling immediately outside the grille by one nail. My idea was to pull myself up as high as I could, lock my arm around the bars of the grille, and with the other hand reach out with the pliers, grasp the nail and wrench it from its anchor point. I would then be able to push this ventilation piping out and create a space large enough to climb through.

I was reasonably confident about this. It could be done at night, when there were never any guards. I was unsure where I would go once I got into the cell corridor, but there was always the large hole in the shower wall which I had previously failed to get into, or there was the possibility that there was a window or a door that would give me access to the street. At least, I thought, if I couldn't get out of the building I could climb back into the cell, reposition the piping and the guards would know nothing of what had occurred.

I had lost any idea of time, beyond knowing it was the morning when food arrived, at (I assumed) around nine o'clock. Now, since it had been quiet in the cell block for many hours, I reasoned that it was very late. It was a particularly hot and sweltering evening and I had been sitting through those quiet silent hours naked on the mattress. The cell was too warm to wear clothes. My body dripped with sweat and it was better to sit naked and use the towel to wipe off the rivulets of perspiration. In this condition I began to heave myself up the door jambs, locking my arm through the grille and around the bars and reaching out with my pliers to prise and pull out the single nail that was imprisoning me. Just one nail from freedom. 'Here is a nail for your coffin, boyo,' I kept saying to myself as I pulled myself up.

Once I had secured my arm-lock on the bars and reached out clawing with my pliers onto the nail, I was suddenly thrown back, falling on the gritty floor. I was perplexed. One minute I was hanging bare-arsed pulling out a nail and the next minute I was on that same backside on the floor of my cell. I stood up shaking, but this time not with nerves. I looked up, studying the surround of the grille where it met the wall. Finally I saw what had happened. There were two exposed wires, one obviously live, attached to the outer face of the grille, whether deliberately or by accident I was not sure. But I knew that every time I wrapped myself around those bars I would be instantaneously repelled from them by the current. Such was my rude awakening to the fact that this shoe-box of a cell was not going to yield easily to my efforts to get out of it.

My two attempts at escape had ended in abject failure, and were even comic and ludicrous; but as failure bore down on me and removed my hopes from me, I began to feel the seriousness of my plight.

Days now passed in an excruciating boredom in which the mind ran hither and thither looking for a place, an idea, a memory of the past in which to hide and absent itself from this tiny cell. The anger that I had found so beneficial in overcoming despair at my helplessness was slowly becoming a mindless rage; a kind of madness which was more punishing, more hurtful than any beatings would have been, beatings which I had expected and continued always to expect.

Occasionally this grey monotony would be broken by an apple being thrown through the bars above my head, or perhaps half a banana. The way a zoo-keeper throws food to the animals. I would never eat this food. I felt the humiliation of it and the humiliation made me angry. This precise anger I held onto, rather than let it slide into that unfocused rage.

Another memory comes to me now as I write, and I think of it as a kind of metaphor for the madness of that place. One afternoon, sitting in the corner, twiddling with an old piece of elastic, not knowing where my mind was at the time, I heard the door open and I quickly covered my eyes with the flat of my hand, for the towel was out of reach. It was not wise to grab for it in case the guard thought that I was lunging at him. The door opened slowly. I squinted through my fingers, expecting to see the usual pair of bare feet in plastic sandals. Instead a figure was squatting and a hand was outstretched to me. I pretended not to see the hand for I could not reach out to take what was there or surely the guard would know that I was looking through my fingers. The outstretched hand touched me on my forearm and a voice said 'Take.' I reached out as a blind man would, pretending to search for the outstretched hand and at the same time raising my head a little to see the face. To my amazement, what squatted in front of me with its hand outstretched was the film creature ET. I was frozen between laughter and confusion. The guard was wearing a false face, a replica of the gentle alien. After so many days and hours of silence, rage, despair and hope climbing out of despair, and falling back again from the tension of my escape attempts, now here suddenly, with an outstretched hand filled with peanuts, was ET quietly staring at me. I fumblingly took the nuts, and thanked ET, wishing to Christ he would please go home and leave me alone.

On another day in the late afternoon I heard the sound of the outside door opening, the one that led into the corridor of the prison. There were many voices, each of them subdued but excitedly exchanging words which I did not understand. The voices and the noise drew nearer to my cell. Then, as they were passing the door I heard one voice say in that broken English of theirs 'You English?' In the quick precise diction that one associates with an English aristocrat or perhaps a well-bred newscaster, a voice said 'Yes, I'm English', then the question, again, 'Your name?' to which the precise and impeccable voice answered 'My name is John.' I crawled quickly to the door, sticking my ear against it to hear more, for this was the first English I had heard for many days and it most certainly did not come from the mouth of an uneducated Arab terrorist. But I heard no more. The person who had arrived and who was clearly another captive was quickly rushed out of hearing into another cell.

I sat down again on my filthy greasy mattress to think of all the Johns that I had known who were teaching at the University and which of them it could possibly be. It was the accent, the manner of speech that confused me. No one that I had come to know while teaching there spoke with such polite and refined diction. The next day's visit to the toilet and shower told me something. I could see as I left the cell a large black case just outside my door. It was obviously a TV camera, or large portable camera of some other description. On the ledge opposite my cell door, on which the food for the inmates was normally laid out before being delivered, there was a luggage bag which had not previously been there. It gave me only a hint at what this John might do, but nothing as to his identity.

I tried as usual to watch the procession of prisoners being taken to the toilet as I squatted behind the curtain. It was no good, for everyone as usual had their faces covered by filthy towels. Then a new person. I hesitate to use the word person, because these faceless men by virtue of their facelessness ceased to be individuals. But here was a new and different form, slowly walking his way to the toilet. He did not have a towel covering him, but he was wearing a T-shirt, and the front of it was pulled up and over his head. I had not seen him before, but his white skin told me clearly that he was not an Arab.

The next few days I spent thinking, working out who it might be. I did not know anyone in Beirut who was a cameraman or who worked for the press. After a couple of days I decided to try and communicate with the new prisoner. Since I had been made shockingly aware of the wires attached to the grille, I was careful in climbing up the two side jambs of the door. Ludicrously I put on my shoes, those same shoes which I had bought a few days before they took me. I had, since I arrived, kept these shoes carefully hidden from the guards' sight when they brought food and I wore them always when going to the toilet or to exercise, which I had not been permitted to do for the last few days. I carefully squeezed myself up between the door jambs and held myself hand and foot on each wall like a coiled spring squeezed tight into the door but careful not to touch the grille. I shouted out in the long quiet of the evening at the top of my voice 'Is there anybody here speaks fucking English?'; and waited. I held myself in that coiled-spring position, out of breath with tension, all my muscles aching for release, but no-one answered. Minutes later I shouted again as loud as the energy in me would allow 'Is there anybody here speaks fucking English?'; again the silence. I fell back onto the bed exhausted, and after catching my breath called out 'Well good fucking night then . . . sleep fucking tight and mind out, the buggers will most certainly bite!'

Two further incidents that occurred in this prison may give a clearer picture of what each of us who was held there had to deal with. I have mentioned before how the guard in charge of the prison, The Grim Reaper, would frequently pick on one of the prisoners and beat him on his way to the toilet and in his cell when he had returned. On one occasion while squatting in the toilet, careful of those monstrous cockroaches but also watching through the tattered and worn curtain, I saw one of the cell doors being opened. On it had been chalk-marked a very poor representation of a skull and cross-bones. Whoever was occupying it awaited something that the mind didn't want to imagine. I forced myself to believe it was not the English man.

A few days after my discovery of this peculiarly marked cell the entrance door to the prison opened in the late afternoon and many men came in. They moved with swift deliberation along the corridor to a cell below mine. I thought perhaps they had brought a new prisoner. The cell where these men gathered was unlocked. I could hear shouted questions in Arabic. I could not hear the answers, only the loud questions, then occasional blows accompanied by groans. I thought at first it was the young Arab boy again, but the quality of the groaning and the depth of the voice suggested that it might be someone older. The questioning continued and the blows became more frequent. I had the impression that the prisoner was being beaten by more than one of the guards. There was much noise. Then silence. The babbling voices quit, an order was barked and I heard feet shuffling quietly past my door, and subdued voices whispering. Then, suddenly, the silence was broken deafeningly by a pistol shot. The close confinement of the prison and the cells seemed to prolong the noise of the gun's explosion. Feet walked past my cell door.

I sat quiet in my corner, calmly as I think back on it now. There was silence again. I thought the guards had left the building but some time later, I can't recall how long, the feet returned. Again there was no voice, but I thought I heard fumbling. Something was happening there in that silence.

The next morning's routine was a little different from usual. I returned from washing and back at my cell found my usual breakfast. I entered and sat down and awaited the closing of the door. The door was duly closed, but not padlocked. I lifted the food, putting it in a corner, covering it with a plastic bag to keep it fresh. I always ate after the guards left. But to my surprise another fresh portion of food, the same as the first, was brought in and set down on the floor by my old friend who had danced with me in the shower. He looked at me and left, locking the door.

I thought to myself, how strange; was this an act of kindness? Had he just forgotten? I lifted the food and quickly put it in the corner, hidden from sight with the first portion. I was not hungry and simply thought for a moment that I had won a small victory by stealing this extra portion. Later, as all the inmates were fed and washed and returned and locked in the small cells I again heard something that I had not heard before. Instead of leaving the prison, the guards lingered about at the kitchen and near the washing area. Then I heard what confirmed my worst fear. Someone went down to that cell and began scrubbing and washing it out. I could hear the splash of water, the brush scraping on the rough concrete floor and walls. Never before and never after that time were our cells washed out by the guards. If you wanted to clean your cell, you had to ask for the equipment to do it. Never would a guard clean the cell of someone who, deep in his unconscious, he considered unclean. The cell was simply being washed of the bloody debris of the shooting, and being made ready for its next occupant.

The prison was, after the first few weeks, a place where there were no incidents to stimulate the mind or the imagination; there was no colour, no character, nothing on which the mind and the personality might feed and nurture itself into meaning.

I was becoming increasingly distraught. The two weeks that I had allowed myself for this thing to be resolved were nearing their conclusion. I could not believe that it would take longer than this for someone, presumably from the Irish Embassy, to effect my release. I suppose my clownish attempts at escape ceased to be humorous after they had closed off and sealed up permanently two doors of possibility as effectively as the real door that held me. I decided that I must again be forceful in my demands; that I must obtain some information as to why I was being held. My strategy was one which I had turned over in my mind as a third possibility or a third door: a door which was always to remain with each hostage, and which we alone could open and go through.

Hunger-strike is a powerful weapon in the Irish psyche. It overcomes fear in its deepest sense. It removes and makes negligible the threat of punishment. It powerfully commits back into the hunger striker's own hands the full sanction of his own life and of his own will. I was desperate for information. I needed to know something, anything, even a lie, something on which the mind could fix and, like a life belt, cling to for survival. I simply stopped eating. I recall now that in those first few weeks I had eaten very little and felt little need to. Hunger never seemed to affect me. Perhaps the mind, constantly shifting and readjusting and falling back, grew so preoccupied that it never turned its attention to the needs of the body. But because of this I felt supremely confident about what I would do. So each morning as breakfast arrived, I would simply consign it to a corner and forget about it. It was not an effort. The food accumulated in my plastic bag. I considered it to be a wise move not to inform the guards of my intention but to go it alone until I could use the threat of my own death to obtain the information for which my mind was ravenous. I thought I would leave it for some days until I was fully launched on this course and fully committed to it, until I was so fixed on it that they could take no action to break me from it.

Day after day, the food piled in the corner, forgotten, untasted and unconsidered. I thought that this rotten food might infest the cell with all the horrors of the toilet. In the mornings I concealed what I could of the food in my shirt, carried it with me to the toilet and got rid of it there. I thought also to keep enough sitting in the room so that when I revealed my intentions to them, they would see I was serious. After seven or eight days, I thought it was time to make a move. I had felt myself growing dizzy as I stood up in the mornings to walk to the toilet: that short walk of some thirty feet exhausted me. To let this thing run too long and not to pressurize them when I was sufficiently alert and strong would put them under little enough compulsion to respond. I took from my briefcase a stub of pencil which the guards had not found and scribbled on the cover of one of the textbooks a note to the chief, declaring what I was doing and why I was doing it.

When I had been given my food and before the guard had left, I called him back. The Grim Reaper arrived, and squatted in front of me; I simply handed him the note and told him to take it to his boss. He was puzzled. His English was very poor, so with some pidgin English, mixed with pidgin French, I was able to communicate the purpose of my note. He understood the word 'Boss' and looked at the note. He did not understand what I had said, but pointed to my name at the bottom and then with his finger pointed at me. I nodded 'Yes'. He explained falteringly that he would take this note to his 'deck boss'. I understood that term to mean some junior lieutenant. He left and locked the door.

One way or the other I was committed to confrontation. But the days of hunger, or rather of indifference to hunger, had steeled my purpose. I remember as I refused to eat each meal feeling myself grow stronger. A fierce kind of pride met a fierce determination of will as the food heaped in the corner. My resolve was banked equally high and my purpose became more strongly fixed. Within the hour, the door of my cell was opened and in came the kidnapper who had been in the car when I was taken. He read the note quietly to himself, pointed to some words he was unsure of and I explained them at length. He looked around the cell. I lifted the plastic and pointed to the food. He appeared very anxious and upset by this. There was no anger. His voice was pleading when he asked 'Why you don't eat?' Again I told him that I would not eat until someone came here and told me why I had been taken; how long I was going to be held; what was being done and whether they had had any communication with representatives of the Irish Government. I was amazingly calm. I had not lost that defiant self-confidence but for some reason, whether it was the effect of a long period without food or the mind fixing itself so definitively on its purpose, I felt no need for anger or aggression. My stubbornness had interiorized itself. The guard left, telling me he would return with his chief.

The next morning, after I had been brought back from washing, my kidnapper and a man I presumed to be his boss came to my cell. The chief stood just inside the door while the kidnapper squatted beside me and talked to me. His chief would say something to him in Arabic. He would translate it for me. I would answer but he never translated the answer. I was sure that his chief spoke English and knew exactly what

I was saying, but for some reason, and this was to happen again and again, the chiefs when they came would not let their voices be heard speaking English. I repeated again what I had earlier told him, so that this boss might hear my reasons and my purposes. I spoke slowly and calmly. I recall that this seemed to cause them some concern. They were probably worried that I was already becoming ill. They explained that they had no doctor. I answered that I did not want a doctor. If they brought one I would refuse to see or speak with him. I was made to stand, then to sit, then to walk in the passage. I assumed my light-headedness and my weakness were obvious to them, for they quickly brought me back to the cell and told me to eat. I refused. They said that I would die. I simply shrugged. I was then told that they did not care if I died, there were many hungry people in Lebanon. I said 'Feed them with this food, for I shall not eat it.' Words were exchanged between the chief and the young kidnapper and they left, saying simply 'OK, you die.' I smiled.

The next day, they were back, the young kidnapper and the prison chief and The Grim Reaper. They checked that my day's ration of food was untouched. Again the question 'Why you don't eat?' I answered, 'I will not eat until you tell me *why*?' They talked outside my cell. For a moment I thought that they would try to punish me, but I was beyond caring. The young guard came back and told me that he did not know, it was simply his job to do such things. I told him that I still wanted to know and would not eat until I was told. He left, and as the door closed I heard him speak outside the cell. I knew that his chief was standing there, listening and saying nothing.

For the next few days nothing happened and I ate nothing. I was confident, I was strong-willed and almost ecstatic as I pushed each meal from me. Occasionally one of the guards would come and tempt me with an apple. But I was beyond desire. Things would come flying through the grille. A piece of cheese, and different pieces of food. I remember carrots were occasionally flung at me. I laughed and laughed. Here was a game I was winning; I was in control and control could not be taken from me.

My hunger strike ended the day the cell door opened and in came my young kidnapper. He had with him copies of *Time* and *Newsweek*. There were dramatic headlines on the front cover of each magazine about the attack on Libya by the US Airforce, the death of some of the family of Colonel Gadaffi, and the bombing of Tripoli. My kidnapper told me 'My boss he say this why you here.' I was amazed, half-laughing and half angry but holding both in check I said 'What the hell has this got to do with me? . . . I am not American. I am not British. I am Irish.' The young guard talked excitedly about the events in Libya. I could only follow part of what he was saying, but he concluded: 'Now we give you what you ask . . . now you eat?' I simply answered, my mind reeling with what had happened and my sudden involvement in it, 'I cannot eat.' The shock waves of what I had become associated with made it doubly impossible for me, at that moment, to consider food. Exasperated, he walked out and left these magazines with me. I had become a tiny, insignificant pawn in a global game over which I had no control.

The Colour Orange
For Brian Keenan

The man with the skin
The man within
The man in the bright light, silent
The Atlantic beyond the window
The face behind the window
The face at an angle
The man remembers the colour orange
The colour of the orange
The ribbed texture
Of the orange skin
The man within the skin
The skin's the man's cage
The Atlantic beyond
The memory of no light
And no colour orange.

                                        Leland Bardwell

Water, because it gives life; The Quran the mirror, because it is as the eye; and
a bit of greenery – these are the first things to be brought into a new house.

                                        Old Arabic Saying

Into the Dark

I had, of course, like all of us, seen prison cells. We have all seen films about prisoners, or read books about prison life. Some of the great stories of escape and imprisonment are part of our history. It seems much of our culture is laden with these stories. But when I think back to that cell, I know that nothing that I had seen before could compare with that most dismal of places. I will describe it briefly to you, that you may see it for yourself.

It was built very shoddily of rough-cut concrete blocks haphazardly put together and joined by crude slapdash cement-work. Inside, and only on the inside, the walls were plastered over with that same dull grey cement. There was no paint. There was no colour, just the constant monotony of rough grey concrete. The cell was six feet long and four feet wide. I could stand up and touch those walls with my outstretched hands and walk those six feet in no more than four paces. On the floor was a foam mattress. With the mattress laid out I had a pacing stage of little more than a foot's width.

In one corner there was a bottle of water which I replenished daily when I went to the toilet, and in another corner was a bottle for urine, which I took with me to empty. There was also a plastic cup in which I kept a much abused and broken toothbrush. On the mattress was an old, ragged, filthy cover. It had originally been a curtain. There was one blanket which I never used, due to the heat, the filth and the heavy smell, stale and almost putrid, of the last person who had slept here. The cell had no windows. A sheet steel door was padlocked every day, sounding like a thump on the head to remind me where I was. At the head of the mattress I kept my briefcase with my school text books. Behind the briefcase I hid my shoes. I was forever afraid that I would lose those shoes. If I did, I felt it would be a sure sign that I would never leave that cell. I was insistent that they should not have them. They had taken everything else by now, but the shoes I guarded with jealous and vicious determination. The foolish things one clings to. A pair of

cheap shoes off a street trader's stall! Since the day they had given me
Time and *Newsweek* I also treasured these magazines. Initially to read,
reread and look at the pictures and read again. But later they served a
more needy purpose.

Come now into the cell with me and stay here and feel if you can and if
you will that time, whatever time it was, for however long, for time
means nothing in this cell. Come, come in.

I am back from my daily ablutions. I hear the padlock slam behind
me and I lift the towel which has draped my head from my face. I look
at the food on the floor. The round of Arab bread, a boiled egg, the
jam I will not eat, the slice or two of processed cheese and perhaps
some houmus. Every day I look to see if it will change, if there will be
some new morsel of food that will make this day different from all the
other days, but there is no change. This day is the same as all the days
in the past and as all the days to come. It will always be the same food
sitting on the floor in the same place.

I set down my plastic bottle of drinking water and the other empty
bottle. From bottle to bottle, through me, this fluid will daily run. I set
the urine bottle at the far corner away from the food. This I put in a
plastic bag to keep it fresh. In this heat the bread rapidly turns stale and
hard. It is like eating cardboard. I pace my four paces backwards and
forwards, slowly feeling my mind empty, wondering where it will go
today. Will I go with it or will I try to hold it back, like a father and an
unruly child? There is a greasy patch on the wall where I lay my head.
Like a dog I sniff it.

I begin as I have always begun these days to think of something,
anything upon which I can concentrate. Something I can think about and
so try to push away the crushing emptiness of this tiny, tiny cell and the
day's long silence. I try with desperation to recall the dream of the night
before or perhaps to push away the horror of it. The nights are filled with
dreaming. The cinema of the mind, the reels flashing and flashing by and
suddenly stopping at some point when with strange contortions it
throws up some absurd drama that I cannot understand. I try to block it
out. Strange how in the daytime the dreams that we do not wish to
remember come flickering back into the conscious mind. Those dreams
that we desperately want to have with us in the daylight will not come to
us but have gone and cannot be enticed back. It is as if we are running
down a long empty tunnel looking for something that we left behind but
cannot see in the blackness.

The guards are gone. I have not heard a noise for several hours now. It must be time to eat. I tear off a quarter of the unleavened bread and begin to peel the shell from the egg. The word 'albumen' intrigues me for a while and I wonder where the name came from. How someone decided once to call that part of the egg 'albumen'. The shape of an egg has lost its fascination for me. I have exhausted thinking about the form of an egg. A boiled egg with dry bread is doubly tasteless. I make this meaningless remark to myself every day and don't know why.

I must ration my drinking water for I am always fearful that I might finish it and then wake in the middle of the night with a raging thirst that I cannot satiate. I think of rabies and the raging thirst of mad dogs and I know how easy it would be to go mad from thirst. Now I know the full meaning of the expression so frequently used in our daily lives: 'He was mad with thirst.' If I were to knock over this water-bottle there would be nothing I could do because there is no-one here. Until tomorrow there will be silence in this tomb of a place so far down under the ground.

Then it begins, I feel it coming from out of nowhere. I recognize it now, and I shrink into the corner to await its pleasure. What will it be today? That slow down-dragging slide and pull into hopeless depression and weariness. The waters of the sea of despair are heavy and thick and I think I cannot swim through them. But today is a day of euphoria. A day in which I will not walk my four paces but in which I will glide, my feet hardly touching the ground. Up snakes and down ladders my mind is manically playing games with me and I cannot escape. Today it is teasing me, threatening me, so far without the full blast of its fury. I squat and rock backwards and forwards reciting a half-remembered nursery rhyme like a religious mantra. I am determined I will make myself more mad than my mind.

Blackness, the light has gone. There will be none for ten hours. They have given me candles. Small, stubby candles. I will not light them. I fear the dark so I save the candles. It's stupid, it's ridiculous. There are a dozen or so hidden under my bed. I will not light them, yet I hate the dark and cannot abide its thick palpable blackness. I can feel it against my skin.

I am going crazier by the day. In the the thick sticky darkness I lie naked on the mattress. The blanket reeks, full of filth. It is pointless to try to shield myself from the mosquitoes drooling and humming, their constant buzz, buzz, buzz everywhere, as if it is inside my ears and inside my head. In the thick black invisibility it is foolishness to hope to kill what you cannot see but only feel when it is too late, upon your flesh.

Always in the morning I see the marks of the night's battle. Red lumps like chicken pox, all raging to be itched and scratched. I sit trying to prevent myself from scratching. The more I try to resist, the more difficult it becomes and the more demanding is my body for the exquisite pain of my nails tearing my own flesh. For some reason I do not understand, the feet and the backs of my fingers suffer the most from these insistent fleas. The pain of the bites on these tender areas can be excruciating. At times I exchange one pain for another. Deciding feverishly to tear and scratch the skin from my feet, and with it the pain of the bite, knowing that in the morning my feet will be a bloody mess and I will be unable to walk on this filthy floor. It's all so purposeless. I am naked in the dark and I try to wipe the perspiration from my skin. The night noise of these insects is insidious. I cannot bear much more. I thrust my body back upon the mattress and pull the filthy curtain over it to keep these things from feeding on my flesh. I cannot bear the heat and smell of this rag over my body like a shroud. I must content myself, let the mosquitoes feed and hope that having had a fill of me they will leave me alone to find some sleep.

Another day, no threat of manic torment here. I calmly think my way through old movies that I have hated. I remake them, rewrite them and make them better than they ever could be. This fills a few hours and I wonder how many more hours; how many more old films are there in my head that I can rescript into pristine epics? I never knew I had seen so many movies, and I never knew I remembered so many films which I had considered not worth watching in the first place, but here all the movies I despised are back with me. But now they are all mixing one with the other. The world's gone mad. El Cid is riding across some Western plain. Images from World War Two films are there, and other scenes are equally historically mismatched. It's a piece of lunacy at which I force myself to laugh. I am tired of this. I have done it all before. Anger overcomes imagination and boredom begins to set in.

Then another leap. My mind jumps over a huge crevasse and I am taken to somewhere else. I am panicking. Panic is a seizure like a fit. It clamps onto me iron-hard, and will not let me go. I have been impotent for weeks. I am reduced to this animal thing, to this failure of my genitals to come alive in me. What have they done to me, this final insult and indignity. That most primitive and animal part of me has been ripped from me. Panic becomes rage and rage reinforces panic and then fear takes them by the neck and hangs them up. I am possessed by fear, by what it means not to be potent any more. I have tried for weeks to tease myself into life but it will not happen. I have tried to force into my imagination memories of old love affairs, even reliving those love affairs that were drastic failures. I try to force an instinctual life back into me but still it will not come. Hours and hours, or is it only minutes, of full, voluptuous eroticism. Fantasies half dreamt, half imagined, half forced, half crawling up from God knows where. Where did I get these things that come into my head, but will not make my body leap to life.

And back I drift into a more mundane fear. I might never be a father, might never hold a child, things I never before thought about having for I never wished for them. I am bereft, riven with self-pity and grief. There might never be a part of me living after I have gone. I might never teach a child of my own to be and do all the things that I thought to be and do. These things trouble me and with each day they are driven deeper into me. I cannot let them go.

Now I am hurtling down the back streets of my youth and into childhood. All comes flooding back. So many unremembered things that panic me, surprise me, delight me, grieve me. All these emotions rising and falling, they are pistons driving and beating into my head. I have neither time nor energy to put them into focus. I am driven to distraction; this is the beginning of madness. All order has gone from my world, I am invaded at random by unwanted and unknown images. In this place where there is nothing, full-fed fantasy and craziness are my frequent tormenting visitors. I try in desperation to bring some order to this carnival of lunacy which memory has become. I am dragged and pushed and torn with every emotion known to me and some previously unexperienced. I try and try to find words somewhere to bring logic into my head. Here I quote some of the words that I remember having etched on the wall with the charcoal stalks of matchsticks, as if in that chunk of verbal madness I might put a screen between me and that emotional onslaught, so that those images from the deep might not possess me.

> *Python*
> Shape without form
> Not shape, nor form.

A blot,
A burden
A life's time dismembered

Nor logic swelled with imagination
Can control
The image
That haunts my brain

One serpent arm
Pythonic at my throat
Suffocating.
You are sickness in me

That makes the body
Despise the mind
Crushing metaphors
As they rise to ensnare
To create you there
Mythical beast

Then,
Remove the tendril arm
Amputate the detonator
Threatening
Implosion in my mind.

Collar you in my consciousness
Lead you to some dark and
Primal place
Unseen
A vision in a shroud.

I take up one of the magazines, *Time* or *Newsweek*, and tear one page from it. I set it on the floor beside my bed and squat down over it. I defecate on it. I defecate on the reason why I am being held in this asylum of a place and then I carefully wrap my excrement in a parcel and push it into the corner, knowing that if it is found I will suffer. Tomorrow I will lift this piece of myself and carry it with me in my pocket and cast it into that cockroach-filled hole in the ground. I cannot relieve myself at a fixed and set time. I am reduced to sleeping in the smell of my own filth. Excrement, sweat, the perspiration of a body and a mind passing through waves of desperation. All of everything is in this room. I am breaking out of myself, urges, ideas, emotions in turmoil are wrenched up and out from me; as with a sickness when nothing can be held down. I tell myself again and over again that this will pass. I convince myself at each day's down-plunging into an abyss of crushing despair that there will be an up day. I have forced myself to believe these doldrums will be followed by a few hours of euphoria in which the mind, tired of its own torment, drifts off to walk in some sun-lit field. I feel the soft pleasure of it, as a child must feel when its mother or father gently cradles it and rubs its tummy. Ups and downs, the tidal wave and undertow of days and hours of unending manic shifts.

Swaddled briefly in this soft loveliness, I am careless of my cell. The world that has forgotten me has no meaning for me. In a half-blissful state, my mind caresses and delights me and I am content with all that is about me and I do not want to leave it. I am reaching out and feeling an ecstatic embrace enfold me. Now I am thrust suddenly into agonizing torrents of tears. I am weeping, not knowing from where the tears come or for what reason, but I am weeping and weeping is all that I am. I cannot think or feel, this thing has possessed me. I weep with a great rage, with a slow deliberation, these tears seem to tear the skin from me. I cannot stop it, though I crush myself against the wall to assure myself that I have a body, I cannot quell the grief. It comes, with no premonition, no warning. I exhaust myself.

How long have I wept for? I drift into exhaustion and into melancholic sobs. For many days now I have tried to scream, but nothing will come out of me. No sound, no noise, nothing. Yet I try to force this scream. Why can I not scream? But no noise comes from me. Not even a faint echo of a cry. I am full with nothing. My prayers rebound on me as if all those words that I sent up were poured back upon me like an avalanche tumbling around me. I am bereft even of God. My own words becoming bricks and stones that bruise me. I have been lifted up and emptied out. I am a bag of flesh and scrape, a heap of offal tossed unwanted in the corner of this filthy room. Even the filth here has more life, more significance than I have.

I have been and seen the nightmare exploding in the darkness. I am in the charnel house of history, I am ash upon the wind, a screaming moment of agony and rapture. I have ceased being. I have ceased becoming. Even banging my body against the wall does not retrieve me to myself.

I am alone, naked in a desert. Its vast expanse of nothingness surrounds me. I am where no other thing is or can be. Only the desert wind howling and echoing. There is no warming light. I am the moment between extremes. I feel scorching heat upon my skin and feel the freeze of night cut me to the bone, yet I also feel empty and insensible.

Many times I think of death, pray for it, look for it, chase after its rapturous kiss. But I have come to a point of such nothingness that even death cannot be. I have no more weeping. All the host of emotions that make a man are no longer part of me. They have gone from me. But something moves in this empty place. A profound sense of longing, not loneliness, simply longing.

In my corner I sit enclosed in the womb of light from my candle-flame. I lift my eyes and see a dead insect held in a cocoon made by a spider and I know that I too am cocooned here. Nothing can touch me nor harm me. I am in a cocoon which enfolds me like a mother cradling a child.

Another day. The Shuffling Acolyte and I take part in our daily ritual, that long short walk to the toilet. That same walk back and I am home again. I don't look any more at the food, knowing its monotony will not change, not even its place on my filthy floor. The door closes, the padlock rattling, and it's over again for another day. With calm, disinterested deliberation I pull from my head the filthy towel that blinds me, and slowly turn to go like a dog well-trained to its corner, to sit again, and wait and wait, forever waiting. I look at this food I know to be the same as it always has been.

But wait. My eyes are almost burned by what I see. There's a bowl in front of me that wasn't there before. A brown button bowl and in it some apricots, some small oranges, some nuts, cherries, a banana. The fruits, the colours, mesmerize me in a quiet rapture that spins through my head. I am entranced by colour. I lift an orange into the flat filthy palm of my hand and feel and smell and lick it. The colour orange, the colour, the colour, my God the colour orange. Before me is a feast of colour. I feel myself begin to dance, slowly, I am intoxicated by colour. I feel the colour in a quiet somnambulant rage. Such wonder, such absolute wonder in such an insignificant fruit.

I cannot, I will not eat this fruit. I sit in quiet joy, so complete, beyond the meaning of joy. My soul finds its own completeness in that bowl of colour. The forms of each fruit. The shape and curl and bend all so rich, so perfect. I want to bow before it, loving that blazing, roaring, orange colour . . . Everything meeting in a moment of colour and of form, my rapture no longer an abstract euphoria. It is there in that tiny bowl, the world recreated in that broken bowl. I feel the smell of each fruit leaping into me and lifting me and carrying me away. I am drunk with something that I understand but cannot explain. I am filled with a sense of love. I am filled and satiated by it. What I have waited and longed for has without my knowing come to me, and taken all of me.

For days I sit in a kind of dreamy lethargy, in part contemplation and in part worship. The walls seem to be singing. I focus all of my attention on that bowl of fruit. At times I lift and fondle the fruits, at times I rearrange them, but I cannot eat them. I cannot hold the ecstasy of the moment and its passionate intensity. It seems to drift slowly from me as the place in which I am being held comes back to remind me of where I am and of my condition. But my containment does not oppress me. I sit and look at the walls but now this room seems so expansive, it seems I can push the walls away from me. I can reach out and touch them from where I sit and yet they are so far from me.

The moment dwindles and dims like a dying fire. I begin again to plot and plan and try to find a direction for my thinking. There are strange occasions when I find myself thinking of two different and completely unrelated things simultaneously. I can grasp and understand the difference and the conceptual depth in each. They neither cross over nor blur into each other. They do not confuse me. I can ask and answer questions on each of these very different subjects at one and the same moment. My mind now moves into strange abstractions. The idea, the concept of time enthrals me. I build a complicated and involved structure which redefines what time is. Time is different now. Its flux and pattern is new, seeming so clear, so precise, so deeply understood yet inexplicable. I am calm and quiet. The manic alternations between despair and euphoria seem to have less potency. When I feel them coming I can set them aside and prevent their theft of my understanding. They can no longer master me, nor drive me where they will. Now I know them and can go with them and hold them in my control.

Today I am returned to my cell and as the door closes I sit in my corner and wait for the guard to go. But today the door is opened again. I sit, my face draped in my towel. The Grim Reaper squats before me and with his faulty English asks 'Why you don't eat?' I look down to see his hand hold the bowl of fruit under the towel. 'Why you don't eat?' he asks again. I feel the hopelessness of trying to explain to him. He doesn't have enough English to understand. How can I, in any case, explain to him what is only understood in my senses and not in my mind? I shrug, I say I do not want to eat. There is silence. Then I feel him rise and move as if to leave my cell and take the bowl with him.

I reach out, grab his hand by the wrist and say anxiously, angrily 'No.' He stops and stands looking down at me. There is silence and I try hand gestures, pointing to my eyes blinded by the towel, and pointing again to the fruit saying 'I want to see, I want to see.' Again the silence and I know he is confused. He cannot understand that I will not eat but that I do not want this fruit taken from me. It is now rapidly softening and becoming over-ripe in the heat. I tell him again 'Leave' and gesture the fruit onto the floor in front of me. I feel slow panic rising. What if he should take this from me. This thing that I have become obsessed with, dependent upon. I try to hold my anger and my rage.

He sets the bowl in front of me and the door bangs and the padlock is rattled into the lock. The force of the bang, the loudness of the key in the padlock tell me he is angry and I quietly think at that moment we have shared something of the same feelings of anger and confusion about this bowl of fruit: he for his reasons, unable to understand mine, and I barely able to explain them to myself.

Prepressed

Ready as I'll ever be,
With some support.
Face them.
Stern, authoritarian;
Clutching the tools of their importance
To twitching, twelve-year-old egos.
Eager to fill their daily tasks.
T'is their life.

Facing them.
So many.
As the blur of so many others
In coming to this place.
Blink back nervous swallows.

Steady now.

Clutching tight
The deep-etched pages of my mind.
These hallowed pages, do I mind
Turning them over to blind
Insensitive appetites-for-more?

Doubting now.

These precious distillations from the deep,
Oh deep, deep, unspeakable, unspoken
Places will I keep?
Jealously?
And not feed like offal
To this sheep
–like, mart-like arena of the world
Press upon me?

Ready now.

Anonymous.

Music

My days now seemed to a pass in a slow, gentle delirium; like the comfort and reassurance that a child must feel as its mother rocks and sings it a lullaby. I found myself sitting on the floor and gently rocking myself back and forth, for how many minutes and how many hours I cannot tell. I looked wildly at the dead insect hanging in its cocoon. I felt a strange contentment. I derived reassurance from it. A new quality of strength pervaded me. I imagined I was moving inside that cocoon and I liked it. I was suspended in space. Minute and insignificant things in my cell intrigued me. I sat staring at them with fascination. A small mark on the wall. The flickering flame of my stub of candle which I occasionally lit, not that I might eat by it, but just so that I could sit and look at it, entranced and captivated. I felt no desire to leave this place. I found myself thinking with the shadows of panic rising in me that I was not ready to leave, that I did not want to leave.

I began to dread my freedom, if it should come. But then as if the coin of panic and fear had been flipped over I began to dread my growing attachment to this tiny cell. Something in me sensed danger and I told myself that I should not surrender to this temptation. I found an enemy within, powerful and insidious. I felt him caressing me and growing stronger, seeking to possess me. I had to find a way to take control, master my own mind, reasserting myself. I returned to an old strategy of thinking through the books that I read as a child, and which I remembered so clearly now. And began again to recall films and make them different or simply use them as a stepping stone to direct the mind away from this desire to remain captive.

I particularly remember many hours spent thinking about the story of Robinson Crusoe. Even to this day I will always watch a film of it or listen on the radio to this story being retold. I made my own version, finding the original too simple and already having exhausted the story so many times. I thought of the story that the native called Friday would tell. How he found this white man so strange, so unpredictable, and I tried to tell this story from Friday's perspective: how this white man's world and white man's thought seemed part lunatic, part comical. I wrote the story of Friday and Crusoe's return to London: a London and an England that Friday found to be a fantasy that his mind could not comprehend or contain. I told myself the story of Crusoe's return to his island many years later, to seek out his friend Friday and how they would meet and what they would say; all the turmoil and impressions that Robinson might experience, having known freedom and then returning to the island. I was able through the eyes and the mind of Friday to blast the inconsistencies of the European society that confronted the 'natives'. It was a kind of pastoral romance. But it protected me from that dangerous friend who seemed to creep up and want to take me off with him somewhere.

I sat upon that foam mattress and it became for a me a raft in a vast sea. All around me was nothing but moving water. No land, and without land, no hope. I was stranded on this tiny piece of floating rubber and subject to its mercy. I dreamt of dolphins riding along beside the raft. They would roll out of the water and look at me with their mystic eye, and roll under its surface. And I wanted to reach out and touch them and know their comfort. There were other creatures that came to look at me and I wanted to fall into the sea and roll with them into its depths. And then alone without food, without water I would rage at the sea and rage at my thirst and hunger and helplessness.

I dreamt one day a bird came and landed on my raft from out of nowhere, suddenly this other living thing was, sharing this floating raft with me. He stood and looked at me and I was filled with fear of him and then with hunger so filling me I thought to take him in my hands, to break his neck and rip his flesh so that he might feed me. In my dream I found that I could not do it, for as I took the bird in my hands and held him I could not crush him in spite of my hunger. His flesh I could not eat nor think to eat. I sat alone again floating, and moving but never moving anywhere, always about me the same grey expanse which seemed to emphasize my hopelessness.

As I think back on that dreaming raft and myself afloat and the bird that came to me, I remember other birds that came to that cell when my mind had taken flight in hallucinatory fantasy, yet not as in a dream for I remember being conscious of the place I was in. It was momentarily filled with birds flying erratically and crashing into the walls, to fall broken and bloodied at my feet and then they would gather themselves up again in furious flight, flinging themselves again into the wall. The cell seemed to be littered with feathers and the dying and broken bodies of birds. Their frightened flight seemed endless. These birds flew backwards, flew upside down, with broken wings they would seem to walk the walls and I would try to brush them away from my head knowing that there was nothing there to brush away. I remember one of those backward-flying birds flying upside down into a fire. I saw its feathers flash and watched it decompose as if melting in the flame. I found myself hissing 'Enough, enough' as I tried to flail my way out of that insane aviary.

I needed anger to pull me back from these moments of madness. I spent many days in those morning hours while we had some light hunting the night's mosquitoes and squashing them against the wall. I watched the blot of blood that their crushed bodies would make and cursed them and wondered that such a tiny insect could hold such volumes of my blood. My nails grew long and filthy, my beard unkempt. And I wondered would I ever be able to cut them.

It took many days to explain but eventually The Grim Reaper came with a pair of nail clippers. He would not let me cut my own nails, for fear that I might attempt to injure myself with the clippers. He held my hands and cut my nails and I sat in silence wondering what thoughts were running through his head and half convincing myself that there were probably none. Occasionally I would hear voices shouting from the street and I would spend the time imagining that they were voices from my own streets in Belfast. I would imagine what they were saying, what they were arguing about. It was as if I could hear the voices of my friends. By effort of imagination I simply translated those voices into the voices of my own people, and created a safer world outside, than I knew it to be in reality.

The long hours of darkness with the mosquitoes droning and buzzing now seemed less savage and more endurable. I told myself that perhaps I had been bitten so much that they had given up feeding on my flesh, or perhaps it was just that I became more resistant to them. The pain and the itching and the bloody feet were something that I was becoming accustomed to and able to forget. I still dreaded those huge cockroaches that lived in the toilet space and in the dark nights I would often take my father's shirt and stuff it along the bottom of the cell door hoping that it would prevent them from crawling into my cell while I slept. In the dark I could hear the scrape of their armoured bodies and claws but I could not see them.

I was running out of magazine paper on which I could excrete. The insult of having to sit all day and then sleep all night beside one's own excrement was less offensive to me. The long hours of blackness were filled with my singing to drown out the noise and the annoyance of the mosquitoes, to create a sound that I could listen to, for there were no other sounds. To this day I wonder why none of the other prisoners would shout or cry out to one another. Sometimes I sang to try to stifle the hysterical weeping of the Arab prisoners. Some of them would cry and bang the door, their cries filled with fear of the dark. I would simply sit and say 'Shut up' and then sing. What kind of man is it, I wondered, that spends his whole day in those tiny cells and cannot find energy in himself to confirm his existence by crying out to another human being, regardless of whether he can speak his language or not? It was as if they had ceased to be human.

My thoughts were frequently occupied by the loss of my humanity. What had I become? What had I descended to as I sat here in my corner? I walked the floor day after day, losing all sense of the man I had been, in half-trances recognizing nothing of myself. Was I a kind of kafkaesque character transformed out of human form into some animal, something to be shunned and locked away from the world?

In my creature-condition, for hours I would question myself about the differences between the wild and the tame. A wild animal lives in a constant state of awareness and readiness. It must decide for itself. A domestic creature makes no decisions. I thought it must be like this with the soul. It is always ready for life, choosing and deciding and instinctively creating life. The wild are more fearless than courageous. Their instinct is to be constantly mobile, in a state of readiness to face the unexpected. The untamed soul is exclusively interested in simply being. It has no desire to sit in quiet contemplation of the world. I thought of animals in the zoo, with their desperate patience or spirit beguiled into some neurotic state pacing to and fro, their minds empty.

I began to understand why it is that so many creatures in captivity will not mate. And with it I began to understand my own rage at my impotence, at the powerlessness of my flesh. Perhaps the power of love is only meaningful in freedom. Such thoughts were frequently interrupted by panic. Time was taken from me. How long, how long would I be here? Would my period here, however long it was, erode from me that capacity to indulge and to be fully engaged in life? I would think back on those moments of insanity, all those strange and fantastical places to which the mind took me, running after it or being dragged behind it. And I began to see the awful limitation of one lifetime.

Death held no fear for me. The contemplation of a mind gone part-mad had convinced me that there was no death, that its moment would come, when it came, as a door opening. It would be an adventure, free from all contagion of fear. I would try to calm myself out of this panic about lost time. I would not suffer to be forever pacing this cell. I was trying to build around me some sort of barrier to shield me from addiction to this place, a contentment with being captive. As I sat remembering the past, trying to put some sort of coherent order on it, I thought of my first days in Beirut and suddenly there came the image of the entrance to the American University of Beirut. Carved in stone above the gate were the words of Homer: 'To strive, to seek, to find, and not to yield'. It came with such blazing clarity that I felt myself knocked back as if someone had landed a heavy blow on me. I repeated it over and over, quietly fascinated, hugely enriched, and knew that this was a meaning, a motto that I must permanently stamp on my being for however long a time I would be here.

The most difficult thing to deal with was that the harder I struggled to find a way out of those moments of lethargic contentment, the more confusing was the ensuing war inside my mind. At times losing the battle, I flung myself down while my mind went reeling off.

I remember one day I was fiddling with a spoon which I had been given. Without thinking I played and twisted the spoon through my hands, the way a child would do with a play-thing in a pram. I looked for a moment at my reflection in the convex curve of the spoon and was frozen with shock. I didn't recognize the reflection staring back at me. I had become someone else. My imagination was stunned. How could I have become this thing that I saw? Even though I understood that that curve on the back of the spoon would, like the mirrors in a circus, distort and malform my features, still I could not recognize my face. I turned the spoon over and looked into the concave bowl of the spoon and again the face had changed. It was as if some Janus reflection of myself was looking at me. I set the spoon down and laughed and picked it up and half giggling, half fearful, turned and twisted from one face to the next and back again. Staring unbelievingly at my image. Black pools under my eyes, my hair long and askew like a wet mop that had been left to dry in the sun. My beard was longer than I had known it ever to be. My body from the neck down seemed so frail in that curvature, like the body of someone with serious malnutrition. I looked tiny and bony and my face sat huge upon my shoulders, out of proportion, not part of this body.

As I think back on it now, I think of how important that spider's cocoon and my image in that tiny metal bowl became for me. I know that those two things more than any others drove me to find the solution to the delirium in my mind.

I decided to become my own self-observer, caring little for what I did or said, letting madness take me where it would as long as I stood outside it and watched it. I would be the voyeur of myself. This strategy I employed for the rest of my time in captivity. I allowed myself to do and be and say and think and feel all the things that were in me, but at the same time could stand outside observing and attempting to understand. I no longer tried to bruise myself by attempting to fight off the day's delirium or tedium. I would let myself go and watch myself, full of laughter, become the thing that my mind was forcing me to be.

I knew they had a motor-generator to light the prison at night whilst bringing in new prisoners. On one occasion the generator was running, though there was no light, and the ventilation pipe was blowing in dusty hot air as usual. I could not see the dust falling. I wasn't bothered by it. But I remember listening to the noise of the machine and the air as it passed through this long vent of piping. My mind seemed to be pulled into the noise until the noise became music. And I listened entranced in the dark to the music that was coming from this pipe. I knew that there was no music and yet I heard it. And flowing out melodiously was all the music that I had ever loved or half remembered. All at once, all simultaneously playing especially for me. It seemed I sat alone in a great concert hall in which this music was being played for me alone. I heard the ethnic music of Africa. The rhythmic music of bone on skin. I heard the swirl and squeal of bagpipes. I heard voices chanting in a tribal chant; great orchestras of violins; and flutes filling the air like bird flight, while quiet voices sang some ancient Gregorian chant. All the music of the world was there, playing incessantly into my cell. I lay at first smiling and listening and enjoying this aural feast. I kept telling myself 'There is no music Brian, it's in your head.' But still I heard it and the music played on and on ever-changing, ever-colourful. I heard the uileann pipes' lilting drone.

I heard fingers strum and pluck a classical flamenco. I heard ancient musics of ancient civilizations coming all at once to fill my cell and from simply smiling and laughing I fell into a musical delirium and began to tap and dance and beat softly upon the walls the different rhythms offered to me.

For how long I did this, I cannot tell, but then suddenly I was fearful. This music that was not there but that I heard had taken hold of me and would not let me go. I could not silence it. It was carrying me away. I called for it to stop. I pressed my hands over my ears foolishly trying to block out a music that was already thumping in my head and it would not go away. I could not end this or silence it. The more I tried the louder it swirled about me, the more it filled the room. And in its loudness I was gripped with a fear that was new to me. I did not know how to contain myself or how to end this thing. My fight against it was defeating me. It was crushing out every part of me and filling me with itself. I could not bear it.

I fumbled under my mattress to find the stubs of candles that I had squirrelled away. I took out one candle and lit it in the hope that light would dispel the music that filled the room, but it did not. With my mind only half conscious, I lit another and another candle until I had filled the cell with candlelight, bright, dazzling, soft, alluring light. But still the music played around me. Everywhere the bright burning of the small candles and me waiting and hoping that this imagined music would stop. And then I remembered again you do not overcome by fighting, you only concede the victory to the madness within. You overcome by going beyond it.

Like a somnambulist, I got up from my mattress and in that tiny cell, naked and wet with sweat, I began to dance. Slowly, slowly at first then going with the music, faster I danced and faster until I went beyond, and beyond the music's hold on me. I danced every dance I knew and dances unknown to me. I danced and danced until the music had to keep up with me, I was a dancing dervish. I was the master of this music and I danced and danced. The sweat rolled off me and I bathed myself in the luxury of it. I felt myself alive and unfearful. I was the pied piper who was calling the tune. A tiny cell, a dozen candle stubs and a madman dancing naked. I was laughing. The laughter was part of the music around me. Not the laugh of hysteria, but the laugh of self-possession, the laugh that comes with the moment of victory. Every part of me, every limb, every muscle energized in this dance. For how long I danced or how long I laughed I cannot tell. But it seemed that I would be dancing forever.

Finally exhausted, but content, the sweat rolling from me, my body sticky with myself, I sank into my corner and smiled as the music faded and left me not in silence but with a sense of contentment and of peace. And so my strategy again had come to my rescue. I had looked upon myself enraptured in this primal dance. I had seen myself go with this moment of ecstatic madness and had come back from it, unmarked. As I sat glowing in candlelight, I thought to myself it was not enough simply to react to these moments that came to captivate me but I must record them and harness them to my will.

It seems absurd to me now as I think of it but I had had with me all along in my briefcase a tiny stub of a pencil and some pieces of paper. I had refused to use them. I remember days before when I first thought that I would write or draw or do something that would liberate my mind, I had convinced myself that to do so would make me completely dependent on the resource of paper and pencil. I was also afraid that they would be found and confiscated, but now I didn't care. It was more important for me to repossess myself. For the next weeks I recorded the minutiae of my existence. Everything that happened, every moment of madness, every thought I recorded in a writing so tiny and cryptic that had anyone found it they would not have been able to understand it. If they did they would most assuredly have condemned me as completely insane.

I began to scratch away at the cement surface on the blocks that formed my cell. After days of scraping I had created a tiny, tiny crack between the blocks and I could see out. I would stand there behind my wall, no more than two feet from my captors and watch their every move. Watch them prepare the food in the morning. Watch them take each man to wash and bring him back. I would record all that I saw and heard. I would record the half-heard words in my head. I would record my feelings, never trying to work them into a structured language or comprehensible form, simply recording everything as it happened, how it happened. I would not edit or rearrange anything. At intervals of three or four days I would read over what I had written and then deal with what confronted me: a rigmarole of confusing ideas, of abstract thinking, of religious mania, of longing, of grief for my family, so much of it incomprehensible to me but there in front of me, a witness to myself; I had thought this, believed this, written this. How could I make sense of it? In all its confusion this surreal manuscript had become my magnum opus. How little a person knows what is in himself. To see all the fissures and fractures, to throw light into the dark cavities, to see the landscape of a mind and recognize no part of it but know that it is yours is a fearful and disturbing thing. Yet it was so, and I could not deny what my diary revealed to me.

At first I could see no meaning in this jumble of words, of images, thoughts, prayers, observations and emotions. At times I thought I should tear it up and throw away my two-inch stub of pencil. But I couldn't do it, and as the pages filled up more and more, and I recorded more and more of this unexplored landscape, I felt myself become helplessly lost in it. But I could not stop, for to see what has previously been invisible is powerfully captivating. Eventually it came to me that here in these pages there was something I could only dimly perceive, some threads running through and holding it together like the veins that carry blood to the living heart. Here in all this confusion some veins of life held everything together. I don't fully know what it was, yet remember feeling that in these strange pages was a whole human being.

Fear of discovery, of what would happen if they found this diary was a constant worry. They would surely not be able to read it. But they could surely make me read it to them. I had written what I had seen. I had written what I had felt and these things are only for contemplative perusal. I decided that I could not stop nor tear up this chaotic memoir but that I must find some means of continuing it. I resolved to write in the code of poetry which only I would understand. If it was found I could simply say 'Well I am a teacher, I teach literature, so I write poems' and hope that they would not pursue the matter.

Over the next few weeks I wrote about thirty poems. I can only remember that when I sat one evening in the candlelight trying to reread them I discovered with shock and amazement that the madness of my diary was multiplied tenfold. For here was a body of poetry, some of it quite well crafted, other parts of it at least illuminating. A body of work which I could not believe was any part of me. It was as if I had seen my face again in the spoon and had failed to recognize it. This poetry, it seemed, was written by someone other than myself. It delighted me, yet I could hardly bear to see, not so much the words themselves, but the man who had put them there: Mad Sweeny hiding in his tree of words.

A Bicycle Designed in the Cell

In this wall which dresses me
From head to foot, entirely
Blessed you, companion
For the journeys which you gave me

Here
Where the day is badly born,
Never tired me
The course followed
By the prohibited pencil

Blessed is the hand which creates you!

Eyes on your saddle
I have pedalled
I have crossed
I have journied
Beyond myself

Luis Veiga Leitào

On the Move

Each morning I awoke to find again the reserves of imagination and reflection to buoy me up from the murk in which memory's hot pin-points scalded me. At times I would feel overwhelmed by shame or guilt. It was always necessary to face such feelings and question why such emotional turmoil accompanied my memories. The habit I had formed of observing myself allowed me to distance myself from these emotional assaults.

My father, who had died a few years before, was frequently in my thoughts. At first there were simple incidents from the family history. Certain moments seemed to become more complete and more filled with meaning. I seemed to understand more about each incident in the history than I did when the event occurred. These memories became less and less a recording of the past. My father became not just simply a memory but more a real presence; a presence I could feel more than see, a comforting reassurance that eased the hurt into a deeply filled sadness, yet that same sadness as it became reflective, lifted me. I began to understand the hurt that was in me. We are all creatures in need of love. My pity moved beyond myself. I wanted to reach out and embrace life. I thought of how those who have gone from us come back to us, as a source of strength that fills us with warmth.

The days chased each other and the future stood before me grey as my walls and as invincible. I sought out this memory of humanity. I was outside this narrow world of negation. I was no longer afraid of my guards' violence, nor did I seek to judge them. Many moments came to calm me, but I could not retain them. I was always called back to my cell.

I had attempted to create imaginary pictures to decorate the walls. Each day I would collect these mental images and try to project them onto the wall, to hold them there framed and contained within my understanding. Like a painter at his canvas I sought to comprehend their strangeness. But their monotony exhausted me. I needed to be active. I had for weeks been keeping the dead ends of the matchsticks which they gave me with my daily supply of five cigarettes. I would burn them down until they were charcoal stalks. For hours I would sit and stare at the lines and water marks in the cement. I would trace out their form with my improvised charcoal. Where the corner of the walls met at right angles I could discern what I had drawn. A perfect life-sized half of a crucified figure. The meeting point of the walls had dissected, like a huge scissor-cut, the image that I had been tracing. I stood face to face with the half-man hanging there. Around the other walls I wrote half-remembered sayings or lines of poetry. Daily I tried to understand what relationship all these had to each other. I was a vessel in which these thoughts and words mixed and became meaningful. As with any work of imagination, I discovered new meanings every day in this strange tapestry.

On other days I was emptied of that contemplative understanding, but the theatre of the unconscious played on. Once I dreamed I saw a crowd of people, all gaily dressed. Some laughing, some dancing, all animated and engaged with one another. They moved across the surface of the palm of a huge hand. They seemed unmindful and uncaring of the direction in which they were walking. In their ignorance they toppled from the huge fingertips. I was there among them, moving slowly. Why could they not see? Why were they oblivious to where they were going? I looked up to my right and saw a prone figure reaching out its hand. It gestured to me to take hold. Slowly I moved towards it. I paused and tried to understand why everyone was unaware. I was drawn to them out of pity and concern and because I was unsure of this shadowy figure wanting to take hold of me and pull me up. In the end I had to go. Their oblivion was more helpless than the unknown hand that wanted to grasp me.

I experienced many moments like this which I have not recorded for to record them all is beyond me now. It would be difficult to build a coherent framework for them that would reveal something of what lay behind them.

For example, I tried to find sleep one afternoon, or the comfort of a daydream. But it would not come. I felt something building up inside me. What it was I could not understand, nor from where it came. With it I felt myself passing through every excruciating moment of birth. An anguished passage along a dark tunnel, and I was moving through it. Towards what end I couldn't tell. I was a creature without voice. In my half-consciousness I heard myself say 'Oh no not again, please no more.' But it was a journey that must be completed. I did not choose it. But I had to travel until it was done. I lay there wide-eyed, waiting for this thing to be over. But as it passed and I felt myself calm down and consciousness come back, I saw vaguely in my mind a new-born child. A voice inside my head spoke gently. 'This is how it is. It is over and I give it to you.' I thought of the lines scratched above my head from poems by W. B. Yeats: 'Things fall apart, the centre cannot hold. . . . A terrible beauty is born.'

Many days were filled with such experiences. Their assault upon me was less as my fascination with them grew. With that growth I gave myself to them. These moments now seemed pregnant with hopes of overcoming, welling up from the infinitesimal and drawing me back from the threshold of despair. I was living. Life was demanded from me.

On fishing boats there is a device called a fail-safe fixed on the anchor chain. In storms or in strange seas, when the anchor is let down to measure the fathoms, and it seems the anchor will not find a bedding place and the ship is beyond hope, the anchor chain locks at its 'Bitter End'. But it is not the end. It is simply a point of measure. It assures the crew that there is more. The bitter end is never the end. It is both warning and reassurance, from which we forge new hope and new determination.

Another day began, with the banging slam of the prison door and the voices of the guards. But this day was not to be like the others. Something in the atmosphere outside my prison door told me that this was different. The prison doors below me clanged open. I could hear pairs of feet moving swiftly past my cell, one, two, three. More guards than usual and everything was rushed. I rose to prepare myself for that walk to the toilet. When my own prison door swung open I couldn't reach the towel in time to cover my face. The guard looked at me and I at him. He seemed embarrassed by my nakedness and closed the door to allow me to dress. When the door was quickly opened again, the man I had christened The Grim Reaper told me 'Today you go.' The sudden shock of it made it meaningless. I was dazed and couldn't comprehend what he meant or where I might be going to. Two guards came in and a towel was tied around my eyes. I was walked out of the cell desperately clutching my old battered briefcase. In it the diary I had kept with such fear and trepidation, and those poems of silent witness which meant so much to me. It seemed so important to hold onto those remnants of my days in that deep and very small place.

I was walked carefully up those stairs I had descended many months before. Up three flights, carefully, holding the rough wall to steady myself and then at the top the sound of many voices. There was a brightness penetrating through the folds of my towel. I was sat upon a chair and told to wait. I could hear one or two men behind me so I asked them for a cigarette, desperately trying to crush out any anguished expectation, extinguish any thoughts of home or family. Holding back the will to believe that this was the day of liberation. Such thoughts I had already repressed in myself, allowing myself only to concentrate on getting through the day. There was too much pain in reflecting on people that I cared for.

A cigarette was given me and foolishly a cigarette lighter was flicked in front of my blinded eyes. I smiled, saying 'I can't see.' The guard's lighter was brought close to the cigarette and my hand placed upon his. Somehow I managed to light the cigarette. After a few puffs I asked in my incompetent French what day it was. I was told it was Wednesday. I asked the date. Either they could not understand or they did not know. The Muslim calendar is very different from our own. In any case I was not told. A hand gently patted my shoulder and I thought am I really going? Is it really over?

Two men came, lifted me from the chair, walked me out and helped me into some kind of van. The noise of the engine later told me it was a Volkswagen. I sat down along one side of the van. I sensed as I clambered in that other people were there, other prisoners. They were too silent to be guards. I squatted for some minutes, while doors banged. The guards made ready to drive us off. Waiting there, waiting to go to where I didn't know, I felt a hand touch my foot. This was not the hand of a guard. Some other prisoner had reached out and touched my foot. I took some reassurance from it and I am sure that the man who touched me was reassuring himself. I fumblingly put my hand upon his and patted it gently. It was a strange first human touch conveying such warmth and companionship in such desperate circumstances. I remember it still, that first mutual reaching out of concern.

The van drove off, its old engine roaring, the smell of petrol fumes mingling with the smell of sheep. Our first journey had begun, the first of what were to be many journeys. The man beside me sat still and unmoved. But there was panic in him. His fast and heavy breathing told me how fearful, how nervous and how uncontrolled he was. I sensed a contained trembling in him. We drove for some twenty minutes, the loud noise of the streets piercing through the steel of the van. In the silence I absorbed everything, half-dazed, confused, half hopeful and desperately shoving back that hope. There seemed to be four of us in the van. We drove on, away from the noise. Beirut seemed to be petering out. I had no idea where we were going. We seemed to be somewhere on the outskirts but not yet outside the town. With much tossing and turning the battered roads of Beirut's southern suburbs bruised us and we held our silence.

Finally the van came to a stop. The engine switched off. There were few street noises in the distance and the four of us waited in perfect silence. Only the panicked breathing of the man next to me filled the emptiness of the van. We waited for what seemed like an hour and a half in cramped silence, and as we waited the panic and the fear and the trembling of my neighbour seemed to grow. It disturbed and irritated the guards so much that they beat him about the head. His muffled cries suggested that he was a much older man than me. As the blows landed they made him cry out more in fear than pain. I recognized that tone from one of the prisoners who had been walked past my door and had attempted to speak Arabic with the guards. Certainly he was a Westerner and not an Arab, as I suspected that so many of the other prisoners in that dungeon had been. Several times this man trembling on the edge of hysteria was beaten as we sat there in that hot van. The idiocy, I thought to myself, of beating this old man who is so filled with fear he can not control even his breathing. The rest of us sat mute, cringing to ourselves as we felt the blows that only he received.

The street noises receded and the heat of the van seemed to have lessened. It must have been early evening, with the streets becoming deserted. It was time to move us indoors. Out of sight again. The heat baking the van like an oven and our four cramped figures sweating, uneasy, apprehensive, waiting: what was about to happen? The quiet in the streets seemed to intensify the tense silence inside the van. Only the continual nervous breathing of the old man beside me seemed to disturb it. Then suddenly the noise of excited voices outside. The door was swiftly slid back and the voices dwindled to a whisper, still hurried, still excited. There were some orders being given and the first man was taken out. Some minutes later the second was removed. So many things were now happening. That build-up of expectation mingling with our apprehension and then the third man was taken and

I was left waiting, wondering who these men were, and where they were going. I felt an overwhelming desire to be with them, to go wherever they had gone. Perhaps it was that touch of a hand upon my foot, perhaps it was suddenly feeling people near me who were sharing my own anguish and apprehension; that community of suffering which brings men together even without knowing one another. This sudden isolation was unbearable after that simple communication, the touch of a hand upon my foot and my hand upon that hand. Two hands lifted, and pulled me out of the van and walked me quickly along a rubble-strewn pathway where I tripped and stumbled in my blindfold, a hand on each arm holding me and hurrying me.

I entered a building. I could feel the coldness of the walls. That sudden feeling of compression again. There was less light filtering through the folds of my blindfold. I felt no dread. Suddenly the two hands let go of my arms. One man now behind me, shoving me violently. It was the first real aggression. I was being run into darkness. I tried to lean back and resist so that I could feel my footsteps. He hissed something in Arabic and pushed me harder, until I felt myself being flung across a room, falling against something that later turned out to be a small camp bed. I began to slowly lift myself. I had long promised myself not to lie down in front of these men, and where possible always to stand. I became confident that nothing serious was imminent and I stood cautiously.

Two men were in the room, talking slowly and quietly. I stood still looking into the nothingness of my blindfold and again waiting for something. One of them came to me, said something aggressively into my ear and pushed me back into a sitting position on the bed. There was silence. And I waited again, wondering. Then another voice spoke in my ear. Jerking the blindfold, saying something I did not understand, and then the door closed. This time a wooden door, not the clang of a prison cell door.

I sat still, then I stood up again, feeling along the edges of the bed to confirm what it was. I stood in silence trying to listen. Was there another person in the room? It was a habit with the guards to stand in silence behind you and wait until you tried to remove your blindfold, which would give them justification for beating or abuse. I stood desperately straining to hear if there was anyone else there. How long I stood I can't remember. Then telling myself that they had left, I slowly raised my hand to my face and very slowly, very cautiously lifted the end of the blindfold from my eye while lifting my head so that I could look from under it without removing it. Nothing happened, no-one struck me and as I peered out from beneath the blindfold I could see two feet. Raising my head slowly, I followed the line of the feet along the legs. Whoever was in this room with me was sitting on the floor. It could not possibly be a guard. They would not sit while I was standing. Fascinated, my eye followed along the bodyline. My head tilting ever so slowly backwards to allow myself to see more of this person. A smart blazer filled my gaze and as my eye travelled upwards I saw a man sitting on the floor doing exactly what I was doing. Slowly lifting the corner of his blindfold, taking in every inch of me as I stood looking down at him. Our eyes met from under the blindfolds, looking intensely at one another.

The confirmation that we were both prisoners was a relief to each of us. Both blindfolds were swiftly removed and for a split second we just gazed at one another. Who could this other person be? My companion sitting on the floor and staring up at me suddenly broke the silence and in most eloquent English he said 'Fuck me, it's Ben Gunn.' My mind raced, Ben Gunn, who is Ben Gunn? I didn't know anyone called Ben Gunn. I began to turn over all the names that I had known in Lebanon. Members of staff at the University, friends I had met, wondering: 'Who does he think I am?' He got up from the floor, walked towards me, shook my hand and said 'Hello, my name is John McCarthy, I am a journalist . . . You must be Brian Keenan.' It could almost have been that famous greeting of Dr Livingstone. I sat back on the bed. John stood looking around the room and then said 'I came here to make a film about you. It was the worst mistake I ever made in my life.' And I sat thinking desperately what film? What is this man talking about? John eagerly took in the room, walking around it. Reaching into his smart blazer, he took out a packet of Marlboro and lit his last cigarette, saying calmly 'Do you smoke?' to which I said 'Yes,' and thus we shared that one cigarette, a sharing that was to be repeated for many years to come.

John quickly filled me in about his work with World Wide Television News, how he had come to Beirut for a month and had just completed a news feature on my own kidnapping a few days before he himself, on his way to the airport, was taken by the men who now held us both. I was fascinated by this. My first concern was that whatever news had been reported by him or by anyone else should have established that I was Irish. I questioned him about this. He assured me that it was known I was Irish. John himself had interviewed a senior Irish embassy official I had known during my short teaching spell at the University. I drew great relief from this. We spoke quickly now, asking questions and exchanging information. I told John I had heard his arrival and had tried to contact him after some weeks by shouting through the bars of the grille in my cell door. He had not heard me, but he told me he heard me speak to the guards as he was being taken to the toilet. He said 'I was greatly relieved to know there was somebody else in the place who spoke English.'

Perhaps the suppressed joy of being able to speak to someone, to have a meaningful conversation, perhaps also the fact that the room was quite large and we could walk about in it, made us both very relaxed. The conversation was one that I could imagine having with a friend whom I had not seen for a long time. I asked 'Who is Ben Gunn anyway?' John looked at me puzzled. 'Ben Gunn, you know, *Treasure Island*,' and I tried to remember the book, wondering what this man was talking about. John reminded me of the shipwrecked sailor who had lived on the island for so long and had grown a huge beard with hair hanging in unkempt folds and drapes about his shoulders. I remembered the character, but couldn't think what Ben Gunn had to do with me. John said 'Have you seen yourself?' He came over and ruffled my hair and very heavy thick beard. I suddenly realized, as I had when I saw myself in the spoon, that I had not shaved nor combed my hair nor had access to scissors for some three months. I could see the association with the marooned and half-crazy sailor. And I began to laugh at the idea. Stevenson's book was one of the many I had reshaped, but this character had not entered into my rewriting of the story. I had forgotten him completely. And here I was, Ben Gunn, the forgotten man.

In comparison, John looked very chic, very well groomed. Taking up the joke I told him 'Well, poor Ben Gunn's got the bed this time, I don't know what you're going to do.' The size and the airiness of the room seemed to liberate our conversation. We talked without any meaningful reference to our situation and the danger of it. Then slowly we began to talk about the journey. We both agreed that there were two other prisoners in the van besides ourselves. John confirmed he was the person who had touched my foot and that he had also tried to touch the person beside him. But whoever that person was, he did not respond as I had done.

I remember in those first exchanges how calm we were with one another. Perhaps the presence of an absolute stranger, but one who listened and understood what I said was comforting in a very real and physical way. My whole body seemed relaxed, and the anxiety and tension melted away quickly and painlessly. I was reassured by this stranger whom I had instantly befriended and who had returned my friendship so warmly. We spoke about the conditions that we had experienced in our separate cells. The terror seemed, as we talked about it, to become less extreme. Much of that first conversation was disconnected. Perhaps coming together and talking in the way that we did, our minds had not yet structured themselves around this new experience. It was like little children swapping comics or playing excited make-believe games.

Our conversation was disturbed when we heard footsteps approaching and the key turning in the door lock. Calmly we pulled the blindfolds down from our foreheads. We waited in silence feeling our mood of relaxation quickly diminish. Two men entered, and stood in silence for a few minutes looking at us. They threw something on the floor and left. A key turning once more in the lock was somehow a signal of safety. We pushed the blindfolds up again and looked at what had been thrown into the room. It was a mattress.

'Well that solves the sleeping arrangements,' said John. 'Obviously we are going to be staying here for a bit.' To which I said 'Age before beauty, John, I'll take the bed.' He simply smiled. Even in those first few hours I quickly discovered what a curious creature John McCarthy was. For having scanned the room and having walked around it, he proceeded to examine its contents. A battered filing cabinet stood in one corner. The drawers were all open and it was empty. In another corner was a sort of chest for keeping documents and books, about the size of a small wardrobe. It too was empty. We agreed that the long hot wait in the van must have been occasioned by our captors hurriedly emptying what must have been some sort of store-room or poorly-equipped office. We were both sure that we were not far from the city itself. That was confirmed some hours later when we heard the roar of an aircraft. It was obvious that we were close to the airport.

While John was examining the room's contents, which seemed to me somewhat pointless, I turned to lie back on the bed and my eye fixed on something which made me suddenly very fearful and very angry. Beside the bed was a power point in the wall. From it hung a long wire with its ends exposed. I looked at the metal frame of the bed and looked at this wire and thought to myself 'I am not going to let this happen to me.' I held my silence, not saying to John what I thought it meant. I remembered that other bed and those screams from the room where I was given a few days' exercise in my first prison. I stared at the wires and wondered how we would deal with the situation if this bed was ever to become a torture rack. I carefully moved the bed some six inches to hide this potential instrument of torture, thinking absurdly to myself 'Out of sight, out of mind.' It was a case of hiding it not from myself or my companion, but from the guards who would frequently be in this room.

'It's so good to be able to walk about,' John said, not noticing that I had moved the bed. 'The rooms we were in were so God-awful small, I was only able to stand upright at one end of my cell. The other end, the ceiling sloped down to about waist height and made it impossible to walk.' He then began to laugh. 'Do you know they took one of the other prisoners and locked him in the broom cupboard? In that prison?' I was aghast. 'They did what?' 'Yes.' John's laughter grew more outrageous. 'They locked the poor bastard in a broom cupboard, pulled out all the brushes and bits and pieces and stuck him in it.' They had built a prison and it could not contain all the men they had imprisoned in it. I thought of this poor man, I presume an Arab, taken from a tiny cell and locked up in a broom cupboard. I chuckled in the shadow of John's laughter. It was the sheer comic lunacy of the idea, and something from a Walt Disney cartoon or early Charlie Chaplin film came flashing through my head as I was infected by John's laughter. I forgot the exposed electric wire and the metal frame of the bed.

The man in the broom cupboard remained for us throughout the years to come a pathetic image, but the thought of him always made us laugh uproariously. He became a metaphor for ourselves. We could imagine his utter despair, his madness, his hopelessness, all locked inside that tiny room and all of them crying to be released, and we in our way chose to release those things through laughter: sometimes on the edge of hysteria, but always life-saving.

Abed's Hotel

The warmth, the intimacy and companionship which came flooding to us both at that first meeting was always undermined by something deeper, which we did not care at first to share with one another. It was a curious wariness that each felt for the other person with whom he had to share his whole life.

Those first days were spent in a kind of frivolous skimming over the surface of deeper things that had risen in each of us during that long period of isolation. I remember spending many of those first nights as we tried to sleep speculating about what kind of man John was. The intensity of mind and heart that solitary confinement had wrought in me had filled me with questions. How much had I really changed? Was it possible to be open with this man and reach that type of brotherhood that is, I suppose, the hallmark of all those who have known suffering?

I felt a desperate need to be honest, always acknowledging to myself that whatever I had felt in isolation was excusable and everything should be understandable. We could only really know ourselves by being open about that experience and the meaning we had drawn from it. I lay in the darkness looking up at the high ceiling and remembering incidents in that small cell. I had dreaded ever being put in a cell with someone else, with whom I would have to live a kind of half-life, afraid of exposing myself, afraid of him seeing the hurt, the pain that had preoccupied me in isolation. I imagined that my new friend would be thinking the same things.

'All men are but teeth on a comb' is an old Arabic saying and so it was with us. Both of us had gone through experiences that opened up new definitions of what we were as humans. But to be truly humanized and to be truly whole again it would be necessary to expose that, to share it honestly with another person. Would this man be frightened of what I thought? We become our meaningful selves only if people receive meaning from us. I doubted suddenly if I could draw from those dark days in isolation a meaning that someone would receive and understand.

Now confronted with another human being who looked at me and observed me as I did him, I found myself wondering whether I was more frightened of my friend than I was of the men who held me and who might if they so desired end my life. As much as companionship filled me with a sense of joy it was an unresolved joy. I wanted to wash my conscience and my memory clean from the experience that had overpowered them and had in some way contaminated them. Dare I expose the scars of this outrage, and acknowledge my own ignominy? It might, I thought, be a kind of capitulation. So much of our experience had been dehumanizing. Would the confession of it make me permanently non-human? A part-formed creature?

Fear of self and fear of the other re-emerged as the constant undercurrent of our first days together. But if there was a gulf between us, our sense of mutual gratitude obscured it. Faced with the liberty we received from one another, we cast off our sense of loss, and of atrophy. The gregarious character which is part of what we are as humans slowly returned to us. We needed someone to share our beliefs, or even lack of them. This man, who might have been an ideological opponent forcing me to withdraw and become hostile and defensive, instead reached out to embrace as we all need and ultimately must do. But the breaking down of these fears, of these insecurities, of all this self-questioning was not an immediate thing. It takes a long time to come back to yourself. It needs a commitment to the courage of another person in order to approach them, be honest with them and know that you will not be shunned or rejected by them. That coming together over the long months and the years that lay ahead was the remaking of humanity and the re-creation of a meaningful future that seemed to have been stolen from us.

The routine of this new place was little different from the prison we had previously been held in. In the morning the guards would come. We would be walked perhaps fifteen yards to a toilet, and later returned to this airy room. We were now fed three times a day. As the days went by other changes became apparent. The change in location from a tiny squalid cell to a large airy storeroom was of major importance to us, of course. The more significant fact that the guards themselves had changed suggested to us that something outside had changed too. What it was we could not tell. We were never told who it was that was holding us, nor did we ask. As we tried to piece some logic into our move here, we decided that the only answer was that we had indeed changed hands from one group to another. We could not be sure but all the signs suggested it.

The guards would rotate in teams of two every two days. There were six of them and over the period of weeks in which we were held there we came to know them quite well. They enjoyed coming in to talk with us if they had sufficient English. Much to our surprise, they would attempt to tell jokes. One of them, a tall well-made young man of about twenty-six who called himself Abed, would signal his arrival by coming into the room and announcing light-heartedly 'Abed's Hotel is now open.' This Abed took great pleasure in cooking us different meals on each of the days he was there. I recall him once telling us that he enjoyed coming to 'care for us'; and we got to know a lot about him and his home and his family. We enjoyed his presence and the opening every two days of Abed's Hotel. Another guard spoke in the most polite English. He was extremely well-mannered and we always had the feeling that he was not entirely happy with his task. He was always deferential to us. John called him 'Jeeves'. Our introduction to the other guards was less pleasant.

During the first week in 'Abed's Hotel' things were very dis-organized. The meal-times were irregular and cigarettes were not forthcoming. When I had been thrown into this room my briefcase had been set outside the door. During my period in the other prison I had kept a hidden stock of cigarettes, as there were days when none would be given to us. So I had brought eighteen cigarettes in my briefcase and our need of them was now great. Desperation overcame apprehension and I walked to the door and knocked loudly, then slowly retreated to my bed and waited for someone to respond. No-one came. I repeated my knocking and again no-one came. I thought there was probably no point in this, and of how much my knocking might antagonize the guards, and I was fearful of repeating my demand. But the thought of eighteen cigarettes in a briefcase outside the door was too strong. I went back again and knocked and knocked and knocked, demanding some kind of an answer. At least if they refused the cigarettes we would not have to sit thinking about them, longing for them.

I retreated back to my bed and heard the key turn in the door. We waited, expecting someone to come in. A voice asked 'What you want?' We knew then that the man speaking to us was outside the door and had only opened it slightly, so we both squinted from under our blindfolds to see a man's forearm holding a gun, his hand trembling as he directed it about the room and hissed at us 'Pray to God, pray to God.' Fear and the desire to laugh at the stupidity of it gripped me. How could a man see what he was pointing at when his face was behind the door. I quickly asked for the cigarettes from my bag. The nervous voice behind the trembling forearm and wildly wavering gun kept hissing 'Pray to God, pray to God.' It was apparent that this guard was very frightened about coming into the room. The door closed and locked, and we still had no cigarettes.

We looked at one another. The menace and the fear in the voice of the guard and that gun seeking out a target began to strike home. We stared at one another in silence. I raised my eyebrows in amazement and John blew out a sigh of relief. It was our first real confrontation with what might be our eventual fate. The hissing chant of 'Pray to God' made it all the more ominous. We had long thought of death, of being executed during our long period in solitary confinement. But suddenly confronting a gun being pointed at us seemed to break up the ice barrier that had prevented us from talking to one another of our fear of death. We were in agreement about one thing, and perhaps it was a romantic notion, but we were both convinced that if it ever came to it, then we would ask to have one last look at the sun before the sentence was carried out. On reflection neither of us seemed frightened of the real possibility of this. So long sunk into contemplation of our own death, we had come to terms with it and dismissed it. But we both shared a sense of the ultimate indignity of being executed in a strange building within four enclosed walls. That would be worse than death itself.

The floodgate began to open. We eased ourselves out of our quiet and unspoken apprehension of one another. We began slowly, carefully but honestly to tell one another of the things we felt, the things we thought about, and our experiences during that time alone.

It is always difficult for two people to come together and talk openly about those experiences that might normally be termed religious. But once we had begun and realized that each was listening to the other, then there was no need to hold back. Sometimes the words were inadequate to what we needed to share. This inadequacy was always overcome by a sense that we each understood, whether the words or the concepts were correct or not. We admitted to moments of weird religious mania. Perhaps our intoxication with deep and profound things in isolation was misconceived by the conscious mind as a sort of religious fervour. Maybe in its own way it was. But such fervour seems always to speak more about our needs than our beliefs. In that emptiness, memories and delusions piled one on top of the other until they seemed to fill the vacuum. We both spoke about the voices we heard in our heads, and in being so frank we returned to a kind of childlike innocence that absolutely believed in all these imaginary things.

At times God had seemed so real and so intimately close. We talked not of a God in the Christian tradition but some force more primitive, more immediate and more vital, a presence rather than a set of beliefs. Our frankness underlined the reality of our feelings. We were both still trying to deal with the force and the weight of them. We prayed unashamedly, making no outward sign. We simply knew that each of us did pray and would on occasion remind each other to say a prayer for someone in particular among our families and lovers. In its own way our isolation had expanded the heart, not to reach out to a detached God but to find and become part of whatever 'God' might be. The energizing experience of another human being did not allow either of us to dwell too long on these matters, which were deep and unresolvable. We gave honestly of ourselves and of our experience and each received from the other with gratitude whatever was given. On occasion there would be discussions on vaguely religious themes, but they were certainly not confined by the dictates of strait-laced doctrines. We had each gone through an experience that gave us the foundations of an insight into what a humanized God might be.

We talked frequently of where we might be, how we might get out of this place and where we could go to ensure our safety. We structured different plans and went through them in meticulous detail only to find that they could not succeed. On going to the toilet each morning I would cover my face with a very old tattered towel which was so worn with washing that I could see plainly through the threadbare material. We were quick to look around us on this short walk and gather what information we could. We pooled that information and hoped that one day it might give us an escape route.

High up in the corner of one of the walls, just below the ceiling, there was a large air vent. It was impossible to get one's body through it. Curious as a cat, McCarthy would frequently climb up on top of the old filing cabinet, lift out the grille and peer out into the room beyond. He would give me daily reports after the guards had left the building on what they had left behind them. There were always the inevitable Kalashnikovs and hand guns in the room where they slept. On the table just outside the door were cigarettes, bread, and other items of food. We noticed that one guard left the key in the door after locking us in. There was a gap of about five inches between the bottom of the door and the floor itself through which some of the guards would simply push our food without bothering to come in. This was extremely distressing to John, to have his food shoved across a filthy floor. But as we realized the implications we were not displeased any longer. It would be easy now to remove the key and bring it under the door.

For many days we had been collecting bits and pieces which we thought might be useful at some later stage. Foolish things: I had been ripping threads from my bed and making lengths of string; a coat hanger we found hanging in the tin cabinet; and I had finally revealed the piece of electric wire fitted to the socket on the wall and attempted to pull it out. John was not happy about this, thinking that it would make our captors very angry, to which I could only respond 'I don't care if it makes them angry, John, I'm not going to make it easy for them'; and so I ripped it from the wall and hid it under an old piece of raffia carpet on the floor. We had by this time obtained some old magazines. They were several years out of date, and of no importance or value to us, except that they were something to read and talk about. One of the magazines had a full-face cover picture of the Shia spiritual leader Fadlallah. There were two other magazines, one in French, the other in English. When one of the guards discovered that his friends had given us this particular magazine with Fadlallah's face on it he became angry. It was clear that those who were holding us had some connection with the fundamentalist leader.

We had, while squirrelling away the bric-à-brac of our possible escape attempt, assiduously cultivated the guard who called himself 'Joker'. When he first told us this we burst out laughing, much to his delight. Joker was the man behind the trembling hand who pointed the gun at us and told us to pray to God. If we could overcome his fear life would be much easier for us, and less difficult for him. And so we had over the weeks chatted with him, built up his confidence until he would come into the room, sit and talk and leave again feeling happy and confident.

We had planned, when Joker would next be on duty and had left the key in the door, that we would poke out the key and let it fall onto some pages of a magazine that we would slide under the door, and then drag the key back into the room. We talked while we were planning this and we would start panicking about what we would do once we got the door open. We resolved we would deal with that when it was necessary to do so.

What few clothes I still had, my father's shirt, my trousers and new shoes, I had carefully washed and put away in that tin cabinet so I could at least leave without being too obviously half dressed. John's observations through the air vent high in the wall had also told us that Joker arrived by bicycle. We laughed long into the night at the thought of us cycling through the most dangerous part of town in this most dangerous part of the world on Joker's bicycle, one pedalling and the other sitting on the handlebars or on the saddle. The laughter deflected from us the real fear of what we were planning. How fast we could pedal, and to where, we never considered.

The day came. We awaited the arrival of Joker and his friend. The daily ablutions were over and we waited for Joker to leave. Some nights, particularly when Joker was supposed to be on guard with his friend, he would simply go home. He was fearful of staying overnight. And so everything was set. We heard the door closing and the silence enveloping the building. We waited patiently with suppressed excitement. Like children waiting to raid a neighbour's orchard. Then as the noise of the streets died, it was time. We weren't fearful. We just wanted to try this thing out, to get it done. If the worst came to the worst and we thought we couldn't get out of the building, we could simply go back to our room and lock ourselves in. How we thought we would do this we didn't know.

The final dilemma of this escape plan had been cleverly resolved by John some days earlier. How could we ensure that the key was turned in the right position, so that it could be pushed easily from the inside of the lock and fall onto the newspaper, allowing us to slide it under the gap in the door? As resourceful as ever, John had taken out one of the drawers from the filing cabinet and broken off one of the long metal runner bars. He twisted and bent it into shape. We had left it hidden inside the cabinet. Previously we had persuaded Joker that we had not seen ourselves for a long time and asked him for a mirror, which he forgot, as we hoped he would, to take back from us. So we were equipped with all we required.

John lay on his back on the floor and with this extension to his arm he could reach out under the door, and holding the piece of metal in his hand, bend his arm upwards and jiggle the key in the lock, pushing it ever so gently and slowly. On the floor just outside the door lay the mirror guiding him as he painstakingly nudged the key. There was no way, of course that he could turn the key completely in the lock. He pushed, and looked in the mirror, and sweated until he said 'Right, I think that's it,' quickly pulling the mirror and the piece of metal back into the room. With the piece of coat hanger I poked gently at the key and pushed again, tenderly, as though I was dismantling a detonator. 'That's it, John,' and the key fell on the paper. We looked at one another, huge childlike excitement beaming from our faces. We shook hands and burst out laughing. It seemed we had stolen the apples from the orchard and were in fits of laughter at our daring deed. I pulled the key swiftly underneath the door and lifted it up calmly and looked at John. The glint in his eye and probably my own sent us again into fits of laughter.

John was enthusiastic. 'Come on, hurry up, let's go.' I thought to wait a moment, to ensure that no-one heard, that no-one was about to come in. So we both sat on the edge of the bed in silence while our minds raced at the audacity of what we were doing. 'Okay, let's go,' I said to John. Gingerly he stood up with the key and went to the lock. I waited as he fiddled and then exploded 'Fuck me, this key doesn't fit.' 'How can it not fit?' I answered. 'It's one of those bloody stupid locks you can only open from the outside, this key doesn't fit from the inside, it has to be reversed.' In disbelief I took the key from him, tried and it was true. This door could only be opened from the outside. That so much careful planning had come to such an abrupt and disastrous end was difficult to deal with. Disbelief silenced us.

After so many days filled with the idea of escape, it was not possible to stop thinking about it. We still had our crude tools, the steel arm of a sliding drawer, and our bits of wire, and perhaps if we prised off the wooden door frame and hacked away at the keep of the lock we might still make it. It would take some weeks and we could cover up the work every day by replacing the wood. Eventually we should be able to force the door open as there would be no retainer to hold the lock. We tried carefully easing off the wooden surround which made up part of the door frame, exposing the bare wood underneath. We slowly hacked and hacked until our fingers ached. Finally the impossibility of what we were trying to do dawned on us. We could not continually be doing this, for it was not every night that the place was left empty and weeks could become months and months a mass of frustration, especially if near the end we were discovered.

With this deflation came panic. It would be impossible to reinsert the key into the lock. We had to get it back outside on the table where they would expect to find it the next morning. Dear God, we thought quietly, if we don't get this key back we will be in very serious trouble. Again McCarthy's resourcefulness pulled out the only solution that might work. With pieces of string I had been collecting and weaving from wool in the bedcover, we very gently and loosely tied the key to the end of the broken piece of metal. John climbed up onto the filing cabinet, removed the grille and I handed him the length of runner with the key attached. Out went his arm and shoulder and half of his head to look down onto the table. He carefully slid the steel runner down the wall as far as his arm could reach and then by shaking his arm sharply, the key would come loose from its mooring at the end of the piece of steel and fall three feet to the table. If it fell on the floor, too bad. If it fell on the table, all was safe.

With a moan from the pain in his shoulder and the exertion of trying to shake his arm, half caught in the opening of the air vent, John quickly pulled out his arm, I heard the key rattle, and he handed me down our steel implement and said 'Quickly, give me the mirror.' I gave it to him. He held it out, pointed downwards onto the table to see where the key had landed. To our great good fortune it was back on the table and had not rolled to the floor. John climbed down and we hurriedly hid our bits and pieces in their hiding places.

We sat down back to back on the bed and for a moment were quiet; then with an affectionate pat he said 'At least we tried, that's what's important,' not allowing despair to detract from the excitement of the past fifteen minutes. We thought of ourselves as two heroes in a *Hotspur* comic attempting this escape, and laughed again at our bicycle ride to freedom. I reminded John of my own failed attempts in the last prison. He said 'I don't think the man upstairs is on our side after all.'

We would not allow this failure to diminish us and we both agreed half-heartedly that perhaps there would be another time and another opportunity. We grabbed hold of a future we could only half believe in and insisted that it would happen. The following weeks we spent devising games, for they would not give us books and we had read the two magazines so many times that to read them again only made the monotony worse. They brought us processed cheese regularly, wrapped in little foil triangles; sometimes the cheese was wrapped in gold and sometimes in silver foil. I began to collect these wrappings, not knowing why. The mind chooses to do strange things without reason. John would look at me. 'What are you keeping all those bloody things for?' he would ask. 'I don't know yet,' I answered. The question was always the same, the answer was always the same and my collection of coloured paper kept growing.

One day it struck me. I took one of the empty plastic bottles which we used for drinking and managed to tear the bottle in half. John sat in silence and watched me. I then rolled up the silver and the gold foil in two separate piles, rose from the bed and took my half-bottle over and set it against the wall. John eyed me, I returned his stare in silence, sat on the end of the bed facing the bottle and with a fistful of little balls of gold and silver slowly aimed and threw them at the bottle. My first attempt was disastrous; I managed to land three out of some thirty pieces inside the bottle. John was fascinated. I went and picked up the scattered pieces of paper, returned to my bed and tried again, and scored a more miserable one out of twenty throws.

As I went to pick them up, John said 'You're bloody hopeless, give me those things and I'll show you how to do it,' and thus it began: constant competition for hours and hours each day, attempting to land tiny balls of foil into a broken plastic bottle. The weeks that followed made us quite expert and the fierce competition we insisted on maintaining was full of vicious but good-humoured banter. Expletives rolled off our tongues with such fury that we entertained ourselves doubly. Our language was a rich, colourful, foul and imaginative counterpoint to our pellets of silver and gold dropping and rattling against the empty plastic bottle. 'John, you blind bastard, stick your blindfold back on. You might have more luck.'

The size of the room allowed us sufficient space to exercise. We would walk around it in single file and often in silence try to measure out the miles that we could walk in a day. For the sheer hell of it we would argue about who had walked furthest in the past week, always insisting on a competitiveness that was never really competitive. Neither of us sought to outdo or diminish the other but simply to set a challenge for ourselves. A small orange, which at one time in the prison had almost mystical significance for me, we kept as a simple handball and tossed it back and forward and back and forward till it became uninteresting and we put it aside. We would talk into the small hours as we fantasized our bottle of water to be a very strong red wine. Our imagination had performed a Cana-like miracle. We babbled drunkenly.

Our life histories were no longer exclusive preserves. For as we told our different stories of friends and of families we exchanged each other's friends and families until they became our own. People we had never met became vividly real to us. We began to move into each other's lives.

A chequered bedcover became a draught board. With our silver and gold pellets we would shuffle them across a square of this folded sheet and engage in another kind of struggle through which we could climb out of the always threatening vacancy of our imprisonment.

On another occasion two new guards arrived. Like Joker they seemed apprehensive initially. They had no English and very poor French. We tried to engage them in conversation but it was impossible. They were frightened to come into the room to serve us. These men would simply shove food under the door. It was always a trying time when these two guards were in sole charge. Their fear of us was always most apparent when they had to take us to the toilet. On the second or perhaps third occasion on which they were on duty, they came one morning to take John first. For some reason, perhaps because they sensed our confidence and that we had no fear of them, they entered the room shouting noisily. John got up to go and a gun was poked fiercely at him. One of them said something abusive. John quietly answered 'Okay my dear fellow, do be calm.' This seemed to be of no avail. I heard him being shoved through the door. Some minutes later he returned and said to me across the room 'Be careful of this man, Brian, he seems very nervous and he's got a gun and he's extremely edgy.' I could only say 'Okay' and was myself taken off at gun point.

It was my habit when things became tense to break into song. I did so on this occasion. On entering the toilet, I took off the pair of shorts that John had given me, stepped into the shower and began my sing-along. This seemed to cause some distress. I heard loud bangs and shouts from beyond the door. But I continued singing. I must stand firm, I thought. If I allow them to silence me and implant in their heads the idea that I am afraid they will continue to abuse me. I sang on. The door was then thrown open, something was hissed at me in Arabic, and three shots from a revolver were fired. I stood with my back to them, unmoved. The door was closed. I finished drying myself and knocked on the door for permission to leave.

I was walked back this time and now the man was even more fearful than he had been before. I felt his trembling hand on my arm. I was returned to my companion and the door locked. John quickly lifted his blindfold. 'My God, I thought you'd really had it that time, you'll have to be careful about being so cocky, Brian, these guys are not very stable.' I could only shrug my shoulders. There wasn't an alternative, I thought. From that day forward these two men were known to us as the Brothers Kalashnikov.

The Emperor's New Clothes

The relationship we formed with the guards during our six weeks in Abed's Hotel was based on polite curiosity on our part. The one we called Jeeves was always a gentleman. He spoke English much better than I did, was always polite, always dignified and would come to talk with us for fifteen minutes at a time. He had been to London. He commented often on the beauty of the place, so vastly different from the ruined hotchpotch of buildings that the city of Beirut had become. After perhaps twenty minutes he would apologise, excuse himself and say 'Now you are tired, I must leave.' Abed would try to tell us jokes. They were the equivalent of the Irish jokes in England or Polish jokes in the United States, only this time it was the Syrian who was seen as the dumb and stupid buffoon. He told us of his family life, how his father had been killed in a carbomb explosion and how he himself was a student at the University at which I was teaching. Sometimes his garrulousness would frighten even himself and he would suddenly stop, saying 'I have spoken too much.'

Joker was the house pet of our prison. The man who had originally in terror pointed a gun threateningly at us was now a man of childish innocence. He was fascinated by the world we came from. I remember him asking John what he would do instead of being a journalist if he could choose. John simply answered that he liked being a journalist and would like to remain one. When the same question was put to me I said 'I'd like to be a millionaire,' at which his eyes would roll and a grin would spread across his face.

Joker's ambition was to marry a German woman and live in Germany. We asked him why. He told us he would have many children and German children were very clever. But on one occasion Joker came to visit us, this time waving his gun under the towels that covered our faces, and whispering insidiously into our ears 'You believe evil is good.' Such a profound statement from such an innocent mind was difficult to find an answer for.

On another occasion Joker brought us an English translation of the Koran. But in his innocence he asked us to promise him when we read we would not let our fingers touch the holy words. I pointed to a ring on his finger, a silver signet ring with a deep red stone and some Islamic symbol cut into it. As I reached out to point to the ring, he gasped in shock and horror and pulled his hand away from me. Sacred objects were not for our unclean hands to touch. The absurdity was beyond laughter. It filled me with a kind of sadness, and a pity for him. I wondered if these holy things were more beyond his reach than mine. For I had become convinced that whatever life is it is for living fully, without fear or doubt.

The Brothers Kalashnikov were an odd couple. Communicating with them was difficult for they had no English and only rudimentary French. Often we would ask them the time and the answer was always 'Dix.' It seemed we lived in a permanent state of ten o'clock. We sensed that these two men came from an extremely poor background. They enjoyed coming here to guard us not because of any commitment to a holy war, but because they could feed themselves much better than they could at home. They were still afraid of us. When they entered our prison room, they entered into a world unknown to them: two men, their faces hidden, talking in a language they couldn't understand, seemingly unafraid of them and always trying to talk to them. Here the Brothers found themselves exposed to a world they had only seen through the television. In us they confronted the myths of their own propaganda. The reality of our presence was very different from the images of Westerners that had been imprinted on them. They had a hunger to communicate, to know the intimacies of our lives.

Constantly, we were asked whether we were married, had girl-friends, children. With these questions they were expressing the hunger of their own lives. Marriage and family were the first and almost the only important thing to them. As time went on it seemed this curiosity and hunger became a need for affection. I often asked myself if our own need for affection, for human warmth, did not in some strange way communicate itself to them and meet with their own inarticulate and desperate need to be loved. Occasionally one of the men would sit beside me on the bed. He would tickle me under the chin, the way one would a child, saying softly 'We like you, we like you.'

John and I spoke often about the reason why we had been moved and why we had been put together. We could never have known the reason for the move but came to believe that it was in some way related to our imminent release. Out of the timeless capsule of isolation, we began to think that somewhere in the very near future our captivity would come to an end. But my ultimate conclusion was always 'Hope for everything, but expect nothing.' Sometimes I made it my night-time benediction to John. Hope should always be restrained by objectivity lest it leads one off on a dance into a fairyland, which is the final delusion. If that hope is somehow shattered then the level of despair becomes unbearable.

The dashing down from that high ground of hope to which we would often take ourselves with humour, with vicious banter, with the exhilaration of exercise, was soon to come. During one of the routine changes of the guards Abed came in, pleasantly announcing that today we would be getting new clothes. Depression flooded me with that news. I quickly asked what kind of clothes they were, to which he answered 'Pyjamas, maybe shorts and a T-shirt.' I tried to grab hold of myself before I fell too far. I sat in silence letting a kind of slow-burning suppressed anger buoy me up. Abed left and locked the door. John began to talk about our new clothes and I calmly insisted that these new clothes were not a good sign. We discussed what they could mean. They plainly implied to me that we were staying for a much longer time than our hope had led us to believe.

Flatly I announced to John 'I will not wear these clothes.' John was anxious at my refusal, appreciating the problems it might cause. He was also anxious because my own decision committed him to making some decision about this matter. He said 'At least these are clean clothes, we can't be sure that just because they give us clean clothes we are going to spend an unknown number of years in here.' I welcomed his easing of my own anxiety and admired his attempt at rising above the bleakness of what to me was inherent in these garments. But I still flushed with suppressed anger. 'John, you're not facing reality.' My anger built itself into a kind of white-hot Irishness. I said to him 'To put on these clothes is an act of submission . . . it is a capitulation and an acceptance of something that we are not and of which we are not guilty . . . I will not wear these because I cannot.' I remember almost spitting the last words out of me, less with anger than with an upwelling of frustration.

To calm myself, maybe to strengthen my resolve, I talked with John at some length about the 'dirty protest' in the prisons of the North of Ireland. They were an act of defiance and resistance, a means of holding yourself together against an absolute condemnation. It was a way of insisting more to oneself than to the world that one was innocent. I wanted to affirm that I was myself and would not allow my integrity to be taken from me by a surrender to what another believed or would make me be. Perhaps, as I think back on it, these fiery words were not helpful for John. This was not a choice he had ever thought about making. Would my decision force him to follow suit, and if he chose not to would the relationship between us deteriorate?

Something in me – Irish stubbornness, the refusal to surrender no matter what the consequences – meant I could not take and wear these clothes. I walked around the room in slow silence trying to fix my resolve and John lay quietly on the bed trying to prepare himself for what he must do. After perhaps twenty minutes of this sombre but steely silence he spoke. 'Let's worry about this thing when it happens, Brian, okay.' I quietly answered 'Okay.'

Some time later the door opened and Abed and Jeeves entered, cheerfully throwing down our new clothes on the bed beside us. A pale blue T-shirt, clean white shorts. I pushed them from me saying nothing, only taking a deep breath. I could not capitulate now. Abed, unaware of my decision, said as he lifted me from the bed 'You take shower.' Quietly I nodded and moved towards the door. He stopped me gently, handing me the clothes, saying 'You put on after shower.' I handed them back to him and said 'There is a problem, I will explain when I return.' A silence followed after in which he simply answered 'Okay,' half puzzled and half unconcerned.

I showered quickly and returned, seating myself on the bed while John was taken for his shower. The door was locked and I was alone. I sat and stared at the clothes, trying to allow enough of the anger to possess me so that I could follow through what I said I would do and be strong enough to face the consequences. Hearing the door open I shielded my eyes again with the blindfold and prepared myself with another deep rasping breath. I heard John move to a position behind me and Abed the master chef approach and say gently 'New clothes, put on, put on.' He sat them gently on my lap and I with equal calmness placed them back on the bed and said 'No, I will not wear these clothes.' I waited for the burst of anger I was expecting, but nothing happened. I wanted to fill the silence with more words. To wait on a blow and not know whether it is coming is more terrifying than the blow itself. 'Why don't you wear?' came the question from Abed. And then I began to stand on my defiance and with my stubbornness crush out any fear that might be lurking there. I said 'I have done nothing . . . I am innocent . . . but you keep me as a prisoner . . . I will not wear the clothes of a prisoner . . . I will not become what you want to make me . . . I am Irish . . . many men in my country are sent to prison and they are innocent men . . . they will not wear the clothes of a prisoner . . . they will not become that thing that they are not . . . I will not wear these because I cannot wear these . . . this is my tradition . . . you can do with me what you like but I will not wear these clothes.'

Abed was silent and then whispered something to Jeeves. It was too late now for fear and I stood up. Abed answered, nervous, confused, 'This is very bad, you very bad man.' I turned and felt my way back to the bed, and sitting down said 'I am not a bad man.' Another silence and then the door was closed and locked. A kind of exhilaration slowly crept over me. Maybe it was just a relief of the tension that my words had smothered, or maybe it was the feeling of victory. I turned slowly to look at John behind me and saw him dressed in the new clothes. I said nothing. John simply said 'You're a very brave man,' at which I smiled and replied 'No, John, I'm just fucking stubborn, it's nothing to do with courage, it's got something to do with keeping hold of what I am and believing that I am something worthy.' John, while I had been in the shower, had explained to Abed that I would not wear these things and if he tried to make me or if he beat me for it then he, John, would not wear them either. I thanked him quietly and he knew that I meant it.

For the remainder of our time in that place I sat with only a ragged towel around my loins. I suppose the arrogance of it really gave me strength. Each day when Abed brought us food he would say 'You bad man,' but never pushed the matter beyond that and my answer was always 'I am not a bad man.' This act of stubbornness rather than strength became, as the days passed, emotional reinforcement for both of us. We had learnt that if we stood by what we believed and were unafraid, then the guards became hesitant and unsure.

Being exposed to my own articulation of what it was to be Irish, John in his own way felt a new kind of strength in himself. I always like to think it was the Irish in him that began to come out when he found himself being treated in the way that the Irish throughout history have often been treated.

In the days that followed we talked animatedly about Irish history and culture: the politics and the people, and the places that were important in that history. Sometimes seriously, and sometimes with black comedy, we laughed at the outrageous characters that peopled the streets of Belfast. I talked about situations that were not described in the newspapers but that spoke a great deal about the cultural differences between Ireland and England. John listened carefully and with real interest.

My own background, so different from John's, now became an object of fascination for him and no longer a simple item of news. Unconsciously he had entered into it. The incident with the clothes had strengthened us and given us a new kind of confidence against the mundane repetitiveness of each day as it settled on us. We felt we had restored choice to ourselves by this refusal.

We would talk long into the night about long-forgotten things in our past that emerged now, when the mind had little else to occupy it. John's fascination with my tales of Ireland was mirrored in me as I hungrily swallowed his stories of his own home life: the beautiful Elizabethan farmhouse, its herb garden and orchard, the massive timber-beamed building which had once been his family home and which was in such contrast to my parents' backstreet terraced house. So many times, as he talked, I could imagine myself being there. I saw myself walking past the little herb garden which might have filled the skirts of Elizabethan ladies with its aroma.

John's stories of his days at an English boarding school were very different from my own in my Belfast secondary school. I was very grateful that this man was so different from me; without knowing it, he was an enrichment to me. But even in these long nights of quiet conversation and quiet fascination there was something that held us apart. Had my own cocky stubbornness allowed John to see me as some kind of hero figure which he himself was unsure of being? The path connecting us was as yet incomplete. We both still felt an insecurity about each other. But we held onto the value in each other's life experiences.

There was another occasion in Abed's Hotel that for me was a turning point in that relationship and in the process of coming together.

Another morning, and we awoke. I told John how I had awoken in the early hours of the morning and turned around to face him in that half-sleeping, half-awake state, and looking over saw a huge headless chicken devoid of feathers squatting on the floor in front of me. I remember freezing for a moment in fear and looking at this grotesque hallucination and then closing my eyes to confirm if I was dreaming or sleeping and opening them again slowly, to focus on this monstrous thing in the shadow of the room. As I looked and my vision cleared with my sleepy state sliding from me, I saw not a huge headless chicken, but John lying on his back with his legs and backside raised high in the air so that his legs almost hung forward into his face. With fear gone I became curious to know what he was doing.

As I related my vision of the night to him, he burst out laughing and explained to me that he had trouble sleeping. He would often raise himself high in the air, lying on his back and thrusting his legs forward until his backside was pointing at the ceiling, and prop himself up with his elbows on the floor, his hands in the middle of his back. 'It's simply a way of stretching my damn back. I get so cramped at nights, I often have to twist and turn and exercise this back to rest it.' 'Well,' I said, 'you still look like a fucking headless chicken to me.' We both laughed that lunatic laugh that was so often to be ours.

That same day as the laughter diminished we waited for breakfast. It did not come. Nor did any other meal. No guards came either. We were not taken to the toilet and as evening came our eyes were heavy from our long conversation and sleepless night. The hunger began to gnaw. We slept again to await the morning, unfed, unwashed and untoileted.

The next morning we were ravenous but the hunger was not yet deep enough to anger us. We expected that today someone would come with food. That day was as the last. No-one came. There was no toilet, there was no food. We were now seriously hungry and anxious that our supply of water was running low. How many days would we wait here? So again into the long night. This time angry not because we were hungry, but angry that we were forgotten. And as the third day slowly arrived the need to excrete was coming with it. For hours I had lain trying to hold in the urgency of my bowels and to sleep and forget the demands of my body.

The sunlight shone into the passageway outside our door and filtered in a crack of light. A thin sheet of dim light seemed to divide the room and told us that the full morning was approaching and we were not going to eat. I could no longer hold or forget my need. We were talking now in this haze of light and even with the conversation I could not dispel the cramp and pain. I wondered how I could shit in front of John. But there could not be any embarrassment here.

In the middle of something that John was saying I rose from the bed, saying 'Well John-boy, I'm sorry about this, but I've got to do what I've got to do.' I walked to the corner of the room, lifting one of the old magazines that had been lying there for weeks and tore from it the two centre pages. I walked naked into the thin sheet of light, thinking how unbearable it was that I had to sit in the light and relieve myself in front of a man a few feet from me. I squatted as filaments of dust held my attention, placed carefully the double pages between my legs and slowly enjoyed the release from the pain in my bowels. Defecating in full view, my need and agony greater than any embarrassment. Without saying anything I cleaned myself as best I could and as I had done in the previous prison, which seemed such a long time ago, quietly folded up the excrement and threw it away in a corner. I walked back to my bed saying without guilt or shame 'I'm sorry about that, John, but I needed, needed to go.' John did not reply for a moment. Perhaps his own embarrassment for me silenced him and then I heard him say 'Well, perhaps the smell of it might stop me thinking about food, I'm fucking starving.'

The day continued. The guards did not come. We complained half humorously, half-bitterly to each other as if this treatment was worse than anything we had previously experienced. 'I think we should write a letter of complaint to the management of Abed's Hotel about this,' I said to John. 'Never mind writing letters of complaint to the management, I think we should burn some fucking buses,' he said, taking up one of the Belfast colloquialisms that I had been feeding him recently. I laughed at his eloquent English voice catching almost to perfection my plebeian Belfast accent. So the hours passed. We tried to sleep, and to talk between our dozing fits. There was a feeling in this friendly exchange which was not the usual banter but in which the humour was more tender than it had been before. I felt a kind of warmth, almost a pleasure that I had done what I had done and had been seen doing it and had felt unashamed.

After some hours John rose and saying nothing walked into the light where I had recently been and with the same action squatted over a piece of paper and relieved himself as I had done. As I sat looking at the silhouette squatting there I felt something that even yet is hard to explain. Maybe it was the way a father might feel when his son executes a piece of work that he has taught him to do. Maybe it was the kind of feeling that two friends might have after having gone through some ritual initiation into adulthood: a sense of deep joy, companionship, brotherhood. Simply in that moment to know it is there, and that it is a complete thing and that it requires no words.

John duly delivered his parcel near where mine sat and perhaps because I was anxious that he might feel awkward I said 'I bet your parcel's bigger than mine, Johnny-boy.' John, sitting down on his mattress on the floor, replied 'You must be joking, your Irish arse is much bigger than mine.' We both laughed but this time the hysteria had gone. It was a knowing smile. We were now and would always be somehow without shame or guilt before each other.

That evening food arrived with Joker. He told us it had been very hot and he had run a cold bath and fallen asleep in it. We laughed at the idea of a man sleeping in a cold bath for two days. The laughter pricked at Joker's guilt. We got double rations of food. Joker complained that his friend, the teacher, should have come to feed us. We said nothing but ate the food feverishly. Joker again complained about his friend not feeding us, his complaints betraying his own guilt. He quoted from the Koran the prophet's words 'You must feed the people,' and he gestured proudly: 'You too are the people, you too must have food.' His excuse had its own kind of appeal and it was exactly in tune with his own innocence. That evening, perhaps seeking to atone even further, Joker arrived in our room. He sat on the bed beside me and said 'Look, look what is this? What is this?' I pulled the blindfold out from my face, peering beneath the fold and gazed on a whole barbequed chicken. I immediately exploded 'It's a fucking chicken, it's a fucking chicken.' Joker joined the laughter, he understood my swear-word but perhaps understood even better my utter amazement. For so long our food had been bread, cheese and jam. John's disbelief was apparent in his words 'You're joking, you're joking.' I could only answer 'Smell it, can you not smell it from there, John?' Joker was delighted with our amazement at this single small chicken, and delighted with himself.

We enjoyed a rare delicacy. A time of enjoying the rich first fruits of each other. Our companionship had put up a barrier between ourselves and the awful pressures of our captivity. With a new confidence we began to plan our next escape. This time we had no alternative. It would necessitate physical confrontation and Joker was the target.

There was one bed and a mattress on the floor. Every two days we took turns on the bed. Always when Joker came to talk he sat on the bed beside whoever had been sleeping on it. We made a point of always shaking hands with him when he entered. Our plan was that when Joker turned to shake with the person sitting across from him, his hand would be grasped and then jerked forward. The other person, sitting beside him on the bed, would immediately thrust himself over him bodily, containing him. We agreed it would be necessary to physically frighten him, to beat and punch him and to threaten him. Silence was the ultimate necessity. Silent violence we knew about, and we knew its power.

For days we exercised furiously, preparing ourselves for this physical abuse which we both secretly feared. We practised the handshake which would contain Joker over and over again. We changed positions, each playing Joker and testing the plan on one another. We agreed that whoever was positioned to take Joker would do so. The other would complete the immobilization. We had enough hand-made pieces of string and wire and finally our blindfolds to tie and gag him.

'If you keep grabbing me like that you're going to pull my arm out of my shoulder, then we're both fucked,' John said. Both he and I knew that there could be no limitation to the violence once this thing had begun. We were going to have to beat this man into silence. To beat someone physically appalled us both. Finally we were convinced that the overpowering of the guard would take a maximum of three minutes. We could train no further.

It was time for action. I loved this man who was now so determined partly because of my own stubborn antics. I knew he drew strength from me and his belief in me in turn gave me strength and determination. The day was agreed: whoever was in the best position to begin this 'capture' would be decided by chance. We had built up a regime of each sitting in a fixed position. A change would make the guards wary. We had everything stuffed into the mattress or under the raffia carpet. This was to be the day.

We were both confident and frightened – that mix that raises the adrenalin and which we had to hold in check to let the energizing effect of it empower us. We each acknowledged that if this escape failed we were most certainly finished. But we dismissed the fear and told ourselves recklessly that such a daring escape was worth the consequences of failure. We placed everything out of sight but close enough to be able to grab it swiftly and tie Joker up when he arrived. As I think over this episode now and how we sat there waiting for the key to turn and the guard to come in, I think that the desire to escape was secondary to an unspoken need to prove ourselves to each other. Here was the primary unconscious motivation. The initiation ritual was as yet incomplete. The key turned and the door opened. We each sat tense as cats waiting to pounce on their prey.

Then a voice spoke. A voice that wasn't Joker's. It was a guard whose habits did not include sitting with us or talking with us. He simply left the food and turned to go. For some unknown reason the guards' routine had changed. The Brothers Kalashnikov were here. All our tension suddenly left us as the door closed and the key turned. We looked at each other in silence, in relief and desperation. Our escape plan had come to nothing. 'There is definitely something in this,' said John. 'The man upstairs isn't playing the game.'

These men with their Kalashnikovs and their prisons and their blindfolds seemed to us to be servants of a fate whose purpose was that we must remain hostages. We never saw Joker again and with his departure was removed any hope of ever getting out of this room.

The House of Fun

We had been in Abed's Hotel some six weeks. Our companionship had bred new confidence in each of us. The size of the room and our ability to walk and exercise in it helped us in controlling our hopes. But it was not to last. Sitting one afternoon, talking about old friends, we heard movements outside. The key turned in the lock and we calmly took our positions: one of us sitting on the bed and the other on the mattress on the floor. One of the Brothers Kalashnikov rushed to me and thrust another towel over my face. For the first time, I became aware that they knew I could see through my threadbare blindfold.

Before he had completed his action, I saw a tall, stout man dressed in full Arabic costume with a turban on his head. I knew that this was someone very important. The kind of excited homage, almost fear, with which the guards approached him confirmed this. He quickly opened the tin cabinet and took from it what clothes we had there. He threw them at us, with an order to dress. The door closed and he left. We looked at one another and wondered without speaking what was going to happen. At this stage in our captivity every new event caused us to believe that perhaps finally it had come, and freedom was only a door's width away. We dressed and repositioned ourselves, hearing again the key turning in the door. The tall, stout Arab came over and tied two towels tightly about our faces. He never spoke. We were then ushered out of the room and made to squat on the floor in the hallway outside.

For some five or ten minutes we sat in silence and then the outer door opened and we were quickly rushed into an enclosed area beyond it. Again many voices whispering. Car doors slamming. We were walked to the rear of a car and the boot sprang open. Cautiously but without real care we were helped into the boot, first myself and then John. Someone hissed at us 'No speak, no speak,' and the boot slammed. Another car journey began. For the first few moments we said nothing. Then, to comfort and reassure each other we spoke

softly. We patted one another to further the reassurance and said no
more, wondering how long this journey might be and where it might
end.

For some twenty minutes in the darkness of the boot, we travelled
like two silent foetuses. The journey was by now monotonously
familiar. We travelled through the night streets of Beirut and caught
occasional echoes of the city quieting itself for sleep. The car stopped.
Car doors slammed and again we heard men around us whispering.
The boot opened. We lay there anxious and tense. Arms reached in
and pulled us from the boot. We were led stumbling into a building. I
waited while John joined me. Then both of us were walked quickly
through what seemed to be a long passageway. We were jostled and
pushed and then abruptly stopped. Rough hands bundled us into a
manhole-sized opening in the ground. We were lowered helplessly,
and some hands beneath us caught our legs and feet and guided them,
step by step, down a ladder.

It was like my dream of birth in reverse. The hands that pulled me
into that womb-like hole hissed and cursed at me as they laboured to
receive me. The encouraging, reassuring words of the midwife were
now replaced by abuse. I knew from the tenor of the voice that I was
not entering into a new life as a child does but entering into some
unholy underground; away from the sun, from light and from any
sense of life.

I had always been afraid of heights and wondered curiously if I
would have been so calm had I been able to see the distance I had been
dropped. Reaching ground level I was sat in a corner. A guard stood
with his hand on my shoulder. In the darkness I heard John being
similarly handled. He was put next to me while the men who had
brought us climbed down to join us. We sat quietly for some minutes.
Then I felt myself being slowly lifted and walked across the floor.
After some ten or twelve paces I was turned abruptly and stared, half-
seeing, into an area of bright blurred light. The threadbare condition
of the towel covering my head allowed me to see more than they
suspected. Horrified, devastated, I looked into what I knew to be
another prison. Slowly, even gently, I was guided into its corridor. I
counted each prison door as I passed it. The voice of the guard behind
me spoke softly 'Hope to go home soon.' I remember how the
softness of his voice and the sincerity of it held me back for a moment
from the great rush of despair that was welling up inside me. Again he
spoke. 'Your friends from the other place at Rauché have gone to their

home.' It would be many months before my suspicions about Douglas and Padfield were confirmed. But there was something in the way it was said: not threatening, yet somehow ominous.

At the fourth cell I was stopped, turned quickly and guided in. The door behind me closed. I slowly lifted my blindfold. I was in a bare cell. It was six feet by six feet with walls of about the same height. It was completely covered, walls and floor, in white tiles. The ceiling was also painted white. 'Jesus, I'm in a bloody sugar cube,' I said aloud, remembering the last lonely cell in which I was kept, my dread of isolation resurrecting itself. At the far end opposite the door was a shelf. I sat on it and looked at the white emptiness about me. 'No, not a sugar cube, it's an ice cube,' I said, the chill of my despair transforming my first impression. I sat in the white silence and tried to compose myself and control the panic eating into me. Moments passed and again I heard footsteps near my cell door. They stopped. A key turned, and I slowly lowered the blindfold, covering my eyes. I heard someone enter and the door close quickly and lock. I lifted the cloth from my eyes and saw John still blindfolded standing with his face close to the door.

His hands were spread, feeling around the door and walls. I watched him for some moments and then said 'Welcome to the house of fun.' John turned, quickly raising his blindfold. He saw me sitting looking at him. He ran to me and flung himself in an embrace upon me. 'Thank God,' he said, his voice full of despair and gratitude. I choked back my own emotion, sharing his thanks. I patted him comfortingly on the head. In that still cameo of affection between us the icy fearfulness of the cell melted. In that moment I thought of my father and felt a surge of fatherliness well up in me.

The moment passed for both of us. We perched side by side on the stone shelf and wondered what future now awaited us. Our buoyant humour had gone. The white oppression of the cell pressed in on us. 'It's too small for two people . . . Do you think they will keep us together?' This question dominated everything else and we feared the answer to it. I began taking off my clothes and wrapped the towel around my waist. The heat was overbearing. I knew that if I cared nothing about my nakedness, which was an affront to my captors, I could remain defiant. I was still self-chosen: I chose to sit like this, it was a silent insult I slung at them. They had made it like this – the arrogance of my flesh always confronting their zealous puritanism.

When a system of belief is challenged by its own dictates it begins to question itself. The confrontation of innocence nakedly demonstrating itself as defiance and absolute resolve throws that same system into self-questioning disbelief. I was convincing myself that I would not be overcome and broken. Pavlov's dogs were only so because they could not find a way to be unconditioned. Man has choice; even reduced to nothing, he must still choose. Resistance may be passive, but its power breaks chains and changes minds. The unquestioning acceptance of those who walked naked and unashamed in fearful quiet to the final places of Auschwitz or Belsen was ample testimony to the power of renunciation and fortitude. Cruelty and fear are man-made, and men who perpetrate them are ruled by them. Such men are only half-made things. They live out their unresolved lives by attempting to destroy anything that challenges the void in themselves. A child holds a blanket over its face in fear. A fear-filled man transposes his inadequacy onto another. He blames them, hates them, and hopes to rid himself of his unloved self by hurting, or worse, destroying them.

We sat on that stone shelf persuading ourselves to hope, but always silently anxious that we might be separated again. We spoke about the journey and comforted ourselves with the words of the guard who had walked us to this cell: 'Your friends have gone home.' We needed to believe him. We sat asking desperate questions and knowing that neither of us had the answers. One thought always remained unspoken at the back of these questions: Would we be separated? Again we heard feet approaching the cell. A key turned and the door opened. A voice spoke. 'You want anything?' Our minds raced. There were many things we wanted. Most of all we wanted to know where we were and when this absurdity was going to end. But these were answers we knew we would never be given. After some moments I stood up and said 'Yes, I want a colour TV set, a bicycle and a grand piano!' Silence. The guard spoke again. 'Speak slowly, what you want?' Again I said slowly, very meticulously and menacingly. 'I want a colour TV, a bicycle and a grand piano.' The guard muttered something to the men who stood with him. I could hear him laughing briefly. The others stood in silence, then walked off and the door closed.

We lifted our blindfolds and John looked at me, a smile on his face. 'What in the name of Christ ever made you say that. . . ?' 'What else do you say under the circumstances,' I answered. We both knew that these men had little in the way of a sense of humour. When we did speak in this manner, they found our comic dismissal distasteful. Humour was no part or condition of their lives. They could not understand why men in our plight chose to laugh in the face of what might ultimately happen. We ourselves did not know. I only knew the necessity of it and the strength that lay in it. Within moments of the door closing, someone passed by our cell. A hand came in through the grille over the door; a pair of shorts were flung in at us. 'Well, those are obviously for you,' said John. And I said 'Yeah, I expect so.' I lifted them, looked at them and slowly put them on.

I knew John was silently perplexed at this seeming submission. After my fierce refusal to wear prison clothes in Abed's Hotel, here I was quietly accepting these clothes.

In the intense heat of the small room I had removed my clothes. I was unsure what was to be our fate. Would we be separated? How important was my protest if there was no witness? The guards in this place were all new to us. My protest was only meaningful if my captors understood it. I had first to take the measure of this new situation and respond accordingly.

The ominous statement about 'my friends' and my own shock at arriving in another prison had begun to take its toll. I needed time to reassert myself. I was sure we had somehow changed hands again, from one group to another. Who these men were or what their intentions were I could not hope to know. I needed to base any protest on knowledge. I would not walk naked to the toilet until I was sure that these men knew the significance of my protest. Too many confusing questions and emotions were racing blindly around my head.

I was grateful for John's silent acceptance. He knew I was troubled and I knew that to share my thoughts would weaken us and add to our confusion. We both instinctively knew never to share weakness until you understood it. 'Share only strength' was an unspoken motto between us.

In the days that followed we adapted ourselves to the new routine. Always trying to glean information about where we were being held. We took surreptitious looks about us as they walked us from the cell to a toilet at the end of the corridor. All the other cells seemed empty. Yet we frequently heard other doors opening during this morning walk. The guard who led us to this cell told us that we would be fed three times a day, that we would have some light and that they would try to make us comfortable. What comfort in a white stone cube, we thought. The mattresses they gave us took up the whole floor space. We could neither stand, walk nor exercise. Each day we had to lift the mattresses and lean them against the wall: the undersurfaces were always damp. As the days passed the smell of the mattresses and the odour of our body sweat became part of this new home of ours. We were shown a bell in the cell which we might ring when we needed to go to the toilet. I felt like a child in primary school raising my hand to say 'Please Sir, I need to go.'

In those first few days I talked with John of how sometime in the future I thought perhaps to marry. I explained that I doubted my ability to live in intimate association with someone else. Confused about what I was saying, I said I felt that fate had somehow brought me here to come to terms with this inadequacy. I knew of John's relationship with his friend Jill. Indeed we had often talked about past lovers, love's failure or its half-success. John quickly answered my own interpretation of this new confinement: 'What woman would want to live with a black Irish bastard like you anyway?' The intensity and constancy of John's joking rebuffs of my own analysis of our situation underlined his anxiety at our enforced intimacy. There was no room in this place for any distance between us. We lay or sat side by side all day, every day. Like lovers in bed. There was little that could be withheld for long. Some days after our arrival John drew his finger along the line where our mattresses met. 'There's a dividing line here, that's your half and this is mine.' Only then did I begin to understand how stressful it was for John to be so confined. What did he fear was hidden in himself and that he did not want discovered? What had I revealed of myself that made him anxious about being with me in this small cell? Was I secretly just as afraid of the closeness with which we were confined?

Each morning it was necessary to lift one of the mattresses to allow the cell door to open. Every day we asked for games and books. Always the answer was 'Bukkra.' Which translates from the Arabic as 'Tomorrow.' With each tomorrow neither books nor games nor anything that might entertain or stimulate the mind was forthcoming. John's benediction as our day drew to a close and we lay down to sleep was the lines from Macbeth, 'To-morrow, and to-morrow, and to-morrow, Creeps in this petty pace from day to day'. It was becoming increasingly difficult to entertain ourselves. There was no room for silence or retreat. The smallness and the heat of the place oppressed us.

The white walls and the constant repetition of square tiles seemed to hammer home its awful monotony. Like those tiles, our conversations became repetitive. Oddly this was our only escape. While each talked, the other, half listening, could think his own thoughts far removed from captivity. But it was not possible for us both to sit in meditative silence. I often thought of this place as the white emptiness that the lunatics of some old bedlam might find themselves subjected to. I dreaded to be alone in that emptiness.

We often talked of our schooldays. John's life at a public boarding school still intrigued me, but more intriguing was his own dislike of that school. He felt himself an outsider and as a consequence of this in his later years was a kind of rebel. Here was something that I could appreciate. I too was always something of an outsider, always distancing myself from people and situations. Whatever I was engaged in, I always wanted to go beyond it. I was impatient without understanding why. My impatience must have seemed like an arrogance to people. Maybe I was simply afraid of them. Such were the self-doubting musings that the mind wallowed in.

I remember telling John a story of how, when I was about eight or nine, I took pennies that my mother kept in a glass jar in the cupboard beside the gas meter. On occasion I'd sneak into the parlour to this jar and pinch one or two of them. I told him how I never spent the pennies and he was surprised. I simply took them and kept them. It must have been something to do with childish insecurity. Perhaps with these unspent pennies I would feel secure. It was some kind of childish fetish. 'Why did I want those fucking pennies anyway?' I would insist on asking him, knowing that he would not have the answer. The question was so persistent that I felt he should answer it. I had no answers in myself to the many niggling and irritating questions that began to flood into me.

John seemed to understand this. He told how he had felt like an outsider during his university career. 'Hull was not the place to be with an accent like mine . . . The local students abused my la-de-da . . . There was always an air of aggression about them . . . I took refuge in alcohol for three years. I was the university's upper-class piss-head . . . how in the name of Christ I ever got my degree is beyond me.' I answered him 'You're still a piss-head from what you told me about your job.' 'An occupational hazard, old chap . . . we journalists are under great stress you know . . .' 'Bollocks,' I answered.

Our childhoods and the memory of them fascinated us. There were so many things that we didn't understand. We both felt a great need to talk deeply and affectionately about our parents and those puzzling incidents in our childhoods which returned to perplex us. With the realization of that need and the fact that there was no-one there with whom we could resolve these things, we were overwhelmed with fear that our parents might die before we got home. It held us frozen and every night we knew that each prayed for the comfort and survival of our families.

We spoke voraciously of international politics. John's appetite for my fairy tales of the troubles at home seemed insatiable. I laid on my Irishness thick and creamy. John would listen for long periods, then suddenly attack with a barrage of questions. I had to struggle to answer them. Our imprisonment had given us a capacity to think deeply and comprehensively. In the nothingness and those excruciating hours of mind-wrecking isolation from which we had both to climb and fall back and climb again, we had each brought with us, unknowingly, an intellect honed and sharpened. These profound meditations often degenerated into an exchange of foul-mouthed banter. 'That's the problem with marley mouths like you. You write about news you have no understanding of.' John giggled. 'Marley mouth?' he asked. 'Yes, you talk like you were born with marleys in your mouth . . . I don't know how you ever got the silver spoon in.' 'Marleys?' he asked again, his laughter rising; 'What in the name of fuck are you talking about, you ridiculous Irish aborigine.' 'Marleys, you brain-dead piece of shit, are little coloured glass balls that children play with . . . I would have thought that a boarding school pimp like yourself would know all about playing with balls,' I retorted. John's laughter was feverish. 'My dear fellow,' he said in the most precise and mannered English, 'you mean marbles. It always amazes me that the race of apes from which you descended should ever have acquired the basic rudiments of language. As for my manner of speech, your own diction is unfathomable. It is only matched by your audacity, you maggot-faced, pea-brained piece of pus.'

Both of us were now in hysterics. The rich elaborations that we slung at one another endlessly with childish competitiveness intoxicated us. It was heady, monstrous and foul. But it was gloriously imaginative and unfettered. We hurled this abuse with such pretended vehemence and at other times with such calm perverse eloquence that the force of it and the laughter pushed back the crushing agony of the tiny space. 'John-boy, if I get out of here before you I am going to go and see your mum. I'm going to tell her the truth.' I paused. John looked, screwing up one eye as if to say; what are you at, Keenan? I continued 'I'm going to tell her that your language is appalling. You swear like a trooper and your imagination belongs in a dung-heap of a camel overcome with diarrhoea.' John answered 'My dear fellow, if you do I'll tell you what she will say.' He paused. ' "You are a fucking lying Irish bastard, now buggah off," that's what she will say,' he concluded. And again we were off laughing uncontrollably and the laughter of each affecting the other. The way the laughing sailor dolls in fair grounds and fun-houses have everyone who pays to hear them laughing uncontrollably along with them.

In a moment of quiet John would ask 'Do you think God minds us swearing?' The innocence of the question stunned me. 'I don't think so,' I slowly answered. 'Anyway if he does it's too late for both of us, especially you. The stokers in hell will be working overtime awaiting your arrival.' John would not be knocked down, he replied calmly 'Well in that case they won't find an oven big enough to get your fat arse through.' His smiled widened with that remark. I came back at him. 'I'm convinced that the noise and smell of your farts will ensure your own arse is permanently employed as hell's own bellows.' The train of humour and abuse was steaming along again and we rollercoasted recklessly with it.

When we were not butting one another with vicious humour we talked about pleasant moments in our lives. John seemed to be quite a charmer and to have had his fair share of female companionship. I was less fortunate or perhaps had chosen not to pursue commitment too enthusiastically, always having my eye fixed on another horizon or another country. Travel fascinated me and I had done much in the years prior to coming to Lebanon. Even in this talk of travel we would revert to descriptions of the women we had met or simply admired in the different countries we had visited.

Strangely enough there was never any discussion of intimate moments with female friends. We felt no need to talk about the physical side of relationships. We preferred to talk about the comical situations. I often wondered why our relationships had ended in the way they had. Perhaps we had both learned much about ourselves in that long period of isolation, delving back into our history and stopping abruptly to confront the full meaning of a specific incident. In such confrontations we had seen and perceived and understood so much more of what had been happening, what people were thinking and how they were feeling. It seemed as I thought back over the poignancy and vividness of these memories that I had been more blind then than I was now even in the darkness with this piece of cloth perpetually confining my eyes. I turned to John one evening before going to sleep and said 'John-boy, I'm really glad you told me about all those girlfriends because I've been running out of women to think about and now I've got all yours to sleep with for the next week or two.' Sardonically he answered 'You'd be so lucky, they wouldn't have you. These women like class and I'm it.' We both laughed and lay back in the darkness understanding perhaps as we hadn't before our need for love.

For many days we talked of how we'd like – one day, if fate reversed itself – to become fathers. I spoke again of my daydream of birth, during my time in solitary. John didn't comment but only listened, intensely fascinated. We talked of our dreams, trying to understand the significance of what we remembered from them. There were nights that we both remembered, in the early hours, when one of us would hear the other moaning deeply and fearfully. A moaning that sometimes lasted for fifteen minutes. The listener lay wondering at the agony of it. I had my own share of these horrors and would sometimes even in my sleep hear myself moan. It seems that in nightmares we cannot cry nor scream. It's smothered in the dream or in the nightmare itself and it will not come out. On those occasions as I lay shivering with a fear bred in my sleeping mind I would feel a hand gently on my shoulder, shaking me tenderly and whispering 'Brian, Brian wake up, wake up.' I would wake and know that I had been dreaming. John would simply say 'Are you okay, you seemed to be having it rough there.' I would answer, still half asleep, 'Yeah, I'm okay. It was fucking rough I can tell you.' We would both lie back in silence, and perhaps talk of the last remnants of the images and the horrors that had so disturbed us, and then fall back into sleep.

But this madness was not confined to the night or to the sleeping mind. We both lived at such an intensity of mind and of emotion that we knew an exhaustion beyond a physical one. The conscious mind needed rest from the way it was being driven and abused. It needed rest from our separate attempts to contain it with humour or amuse it with story-telling or with that kind of confessional sharing that was so much a part of our bonding together.

Many times we sat staring at the wall or tried to sleep during the day. On one of these occasions while I was dozing after a lunch of rice and spinach, I felt John shake me, not in the gentle manner he would use if I were dreaming but this time urgently. 'I'm not sleeping, John what is it?' There was silence for a moment and then he answered 'I'm going mad,' and again 'I'm going mad . . . I'm really, really going mad . . . what am I going to do?' I knew that this was not a time for humorous rebuttal. I had known these moments, as I'm sure John had before, but in isolation you understand them differently and have to deal with them alone. I sat up and looked at him. He looked pale. I hadn't noticed until now the black circles under his eyes. This thing had been coming at him for days.

He looked at me. 'Talk to me, tell me something, tell me what to do?' he pleaded in desperation, the words faltering from him. 'You're not going mad, John,' I said. 'It's one of those bad patches that come at us.' 'But I can't get rid of this, my mind is breaking up,' he said. I felt in the air the desperation that he was experiencing, as I desperately sought to find an answer for him. 'Listen to me, John,' I said firmly. 'Listen?' He looked at me. 'Try to imagine something.' He stared at me intently. 'I'll tell you what I do,' I said: 'I get these moments as well, and I try to imagine a room, any kind of room anywhere. I think of two things in that room and then I try to build a story around why those things are there. What happened in that room?. . . Where did these things come from? . . . Who lived in there? You've got to build a story in your head.' I saw him look at me now more intensely. 'I'll tell you what. Here's a room. There's a table in it, a few chairs, a fireplace filled with ashes. There's the peelings of an orange. There's a pair of shoes on the floor . . . There're no laces in the shoes.' I looked again at him, his intensity was driving into me. 'Come on, John . . . see that room in your head. Now I've told you two things. I've put two things in that room . . . You put two more in . . . Put them in that room. Think of why those things are there? Why did they get there? Who put them there? What happened in that room? Build a story around it, John. Create a room that you can go into so that you understand why everything is as it is in that room. Search out in your mind all the reasons why that room is the way it is. But first just pick two things completely disassociated from one another and put them in this room. Tell them to me now. What are those things?'

His staring face changed; I felt he was becoming intrigued by my suggestion. 'Come on, John, I've done it lots of times . . . You'll find it's fascinating and you'll find it's interesting and it will bring you

down. Think of it, think of that room, think of those things. There's
an orange peel. There're shoes with no laces in them . . . Put two
more things in that room, any two things. Go into that room and find
out what's happening in there . . . Who's been there . . . What did
they do? . . . It helps, John, it helps.' He looked again at me, very
softly and very slowly he said 'You and your fucking rooms.' Forcing
a gentle laugh I replied 'Rooms are what we know lots about.' I lay
back and John continued sitting against the wall. I lay awake and
wondered would he do as I had suggested or would he sit in silence
trying to crush out the insanity. The moment passed.

I slept and awoke early. John was deep in sleep and I was grateful. I
felt the huge relief that a parent might feel when their child has passed
through some crisis of fever. But the dread of what had happened
hung about. What if we were both to lose control, or if one of us was
to let go and fall permanently down into that pit of mindlessness,
could the other bear it? But what was the alternative? To be separated
would be worse. No, there was no alternative. We were responsible
for each other; no matter what happened we must not be separated.
Our strength lay in one another. As I thought these things I looked at
the little fan turning in the bottom of the door. Its blades were
exposed. If things got too bad we could always ram a hand or foot into
the blades. The guards would have to do something. I heard John
wake, I kept my thoughts to myself.

'How's the raving lunatic?' I asked. I saw the weariness in his eyes,
but it was not the weariness of sleep. I felt guilty and tried to cover up
my guilt and embarrassment with idle talk. 'It gets very rough
sometimes, the mind just goes galloping off, it either leaves you
empty or it trails you helplessly after it.' John looked up. 'It's been
galloping around in circles for days until nothing made sense,
everything was just a mess of everything else. Sometimes there was
just nothing . . . How long do you think we are going to be here?' he
asked. 'Until the man upstairs says your number is up.' I could say no
more. I knew John was only half listening. It was better in any case not
to speak. To cover up and pretend that these things are insignificant is
an injustice and is selfish. Soon breakfast would come and we would
be taken to the shower and maybe things would lighten up.

The food was ample but hardly nourishing. Breakfast was bread,
tea, cheese and jam. Lunch was a mixture of rice and spinach or rice
and peas and carrots. Occasionally we had a coarse stew. They gave us
hard-boiled eggs frequently. Supper was always a repeat of breakfast.

Sometimes we would be given sandwiches brought in from a shop and with them some pastries. Such food was a delight. The sandwiches often contained meat or chicken heavily spiced and filled with hot chillies and pickles. The pastries were often cloyingly sweet and we could not eat them. We knew that lunch was always cooked by a woman living nearby and brought in to us. The food that we could not or would not eat we deposited in a plastic bag that was given us each day for rubbish.

We often noticed that food we handed back, such as hard-boiled eggs, was thrown into the guards' rubbish. Our unclean hands had touched it and thus it was forbidden to the zealots that held us. Each time I saw this I was angry. To be considered unclean and untouchable was a humiliation I would not stand. This absolute judgement was without logic, reason, understanding or humanity, and devalued me beyond all comprehension. To concede to this was an admission of defeat. I hated the waste. I remembered what they had said to me in my first imprisonment when I had refused to eat and they simply shrugged their shoulders saying 'There are many people hungry in Lebanon; if you do not eat, we do not care.'

As we sat in our cell passing those long hours, John and I often discussed the Lebanon we had got to know before we were taken captive. During my four months teaching at the university, I had been fortunate enough to travel around the country, usually going out with a colleague for dinner and driving up into the hills, or perhaps to Sidon. I had seen much of how the land had been devastated and was aware of the grinding poverty with which the people from the southern suburbs had to contend. Lebanon is a country of vast extremes, of great wealth set side by side with the most abject poverty. Its different religious groupings, each of them insisting on the absolute correctness of its own system of belief and way of life, had made impossible the kind of compromise and acceptance of each other's traditions that could have more equitably distributed the country's wealth. Lebanon is crippled by a kind of tribalism, its peoples afraid of one another though they live so close together in this tiny land mass.

I remembered talking to a Lebanese in a hotel one evening and asking him why it was that Lebanese who suffered collectively should choose to kill one another rather than come together and face their common enemy. I couldn't understand the huge arbitrariness of the slaughter that continued between men who after all shared common political beliefs and aspirations. My friend answered in the curious way in which the Lebanese sum up all their problems, in one sentence. He said 'In Lebanon it is not who you kill, but how many.'

I told John a story of the Turkish villa in which I lived before being taken. It was set high off the ground and surrounded by its own gardens. Beside the entrance steps was a small Christian grotto. The Virgin stood angelic in her blue and white. At Easter-time I watched old women walk past and push lighted candles through the gate and rails that set the villa off from the street. They left them there, crossed themselves and prayed. I used to stand and look out of the villa at this. I wanted to open the gate to let them walk through the garden and pray beside the object of their veneration, but I could not. I was living near the Green Line that divides Christian East from Muslim West Beirut. My self-interest prevented me from opening the gate for them. I felt deeply ashamed. Behind me lived poor Armenians and near them even more impoverished Shias who had been dispossessed of their homes in the south of Lebanon. Overnight they had become urban citizens. Their whole way of life and their traditions had been stolen from them, obliterated overnight by the gratuitous and monstrous slaughter of the Israeli invasion of 1982. The city was a refuge but it was also a place alien to them. They were literally strangers in their own land. The distance between the rural population and the city life of Lebanon is immense. You can drive for a half-hour out of the city and into the hill villages and feel that you have driven back generations. John told me stories of the wealthy Lebanese drug barons he had met while working as a journalist, and of their complete lack of interest in and apathy about Lebanon and its problems. Their wealth and their power set them apart and they were untouched by poverty and suffering.

It is always the case when a people feel themselves so totally dispossessed, so unjustly condemned to a condition of absolute poverty that the anguish of it forces them to seek an escape. The need to escape becomes stronger as each community acknowledges its dispossession. Such acknowledgement always carries with it, hidden beneath the surface, a kind of shame and guilt, an admission of loss of identity, of full humanity, and that shame and guilt grows into anger. When the anger can find no outlet, when there is no recourse within the social structure for redress of grievances, the anger turns inwards and festers. They cannot find value in themselves; they reject and loathe themselves. A man can then no longer surrender to such a monstrous condition of life. He seeks power, power that will restore his dignity and his manhood; that will let him stand with other men and know himself to be their equal and restore him to the community of humanity. But so filled with anger is he that he must act to reclaim meaning and purpose. With one great leap he tries to exorcize his fury.

The man unresolved in himself chooses, as men have done throughout history, to take up arms against his sea of troubles. He carries his Kalashnikov on his arm, his handgun stuck in the waistband of his trousers, a belt of bullets slung around his shoulders. I had seen so many young men in Beirut thus attired, their weapons hanging from them and glistening in the sun. The guns were symbols of potency. The men were dressed as caricatures of Rambo. Many of them wore a headband tied and knotted at the side above the ear, just as the character in the movie had done. It is a curious paradox that this Rambo figure, this all-American hero, was the stereotype which these young Arab revolutionaries had adopted. They had taken on the cult figure of the Great Satan they so despised and who they claimed was responsible for all the evil in the world. Emulating Rambo they would reconquer the world and simultaneously rid themselves of that inadequacy which they could never admit.

I told John how, one evening, I had gone with some friends to a cinema near where I was living. They were showing a war film set somewhere in Vietnam. It had a story which was not a story about men killing each other to no purpose. There was no meaningful exploration of the war or the inhumanity of it. We sat there in the darkened cinema and as each character pulled out his weapon and began firing furiously, the young Arab men around us would groan and moan in a kind of ecstasy, crying out the names of the weapons. All around us in the cinema we could hear the words 'Kalashnikov, Kalashnikov; Beretta, Beretta.' These young men knew the names of every type of gun, even the names of mortars and rocket-launchers. The cinema rang with a chant of excited worship.

John was keen to listen to my stories of Beirut. Although my stay there had been short it was still much longer than his.

My life in Beirut before my capture was full of insistent exploration. Unlike many of my professional colleagues I could not bear simply to go to work and return home and lock myself in until the next morning. I had visited much of the city. The Green Line was a division I could not accept. How could I accept the absurdity of such a barrier when the students I taught came from all parts of this divided community and mixed with one another without fear or suspicion?

I told John how, when I came to work at the American University, a French colonial-type mansion with various American additions of the 50s and 60s perched on a hill overlooking the sea and laced with glorious gardens, the faculty administrator lectured the new staff that on no account were we to discuss politics or religion with students. 'An impossible situation,' I explained, as I was constantly asked by my students 'Why have you come here? . . . Everyone is killer.' I could only answer I was from Belfast and let them draw their own conclusions. John smiled remembering my tales of Belfast and its rich and violent tapestry of personalities and conflicts.

John asked whether I enjoyed teaching there. I told him that I used to awake early in the morning excited about the day in front of me. The students were very keen and their enthusiasm made me work.

One young woman, one of the many strict Muslims who attended college, her head shrouded in a chador, told me one day she must go to a hospital as her sister had been shot at a wedding. I reached out instinctively to wish her well. 'I cannot,' gasped the stunned student. But her companion nodded encouragingly. She reached out and accepted the proffered hand saying 'This does not matter now.' I was delighted, I explained to John. That one gesture was worth twenty lessons.

But other students were less open. One of them, a young man, invited me to take coffee in the student restaurant. I joined him and when I responded to his question was I a Christian that I did not believe in God, I was subjected to a lengthy disclosure of Allah.

'Where do you come from?' demanded the student. 'From the womb of my mother and the delight of my father,' I riposted. 'And your family?' my interrogator continued. 'It really doesn't matter. It's the present that matters and what you do with it,' I answered, increasingly aware of the clusters of students studying me.

Later, having escaped this interrogation I was approached by one of my students, Mustapha. 'I am with the troubles of your people,' he said. He handed me a crucifix. He explained it was for his girlfriend. But he was a Muslim and they must keep their relationship secret. 'We can never marry,' he said. I could only squeeze his arm understandingly, knowing the chains that people put on themselves.

One story of my short-lived career in Beirut had John laughing uproariously. One evening I had been visiting a friend. During my absence armed men raided my apartment, tying up my colleagues. Some days later Shamir, a young male student, called me to his car, insisting I sit on the passenger seat. He offered me a handgun, saying 'Mister Brian, I know you have troubles . . . Please give to me again when you leave Lebanon.' My refusal of his offer perplexed him but he persisted. 'I have something else,' he continued, handing me two hand grenades. 'What would I do with these?' I questioned. Shamir excitedly explained a Heath Robinson contraption for attaching to my door. If anyone opened the door they would be blown to bits. 'What about Mr Usher?' I asked, remembering my flatmate. 'Halas, Mr Usher' grinned Shamir, dusting his hands fatalistically.

But this academic garden was a thorny one. The disappearance of Leigh Douglas and Philip Padfield had caused much anxiety on campus. At a faculty staff meeting to talk about the situation there was some discussion, and a vote was taken to close the University for a short period. The whole faculty sat there afraid to speak and obscuring their faces behind their hands, for some students took photos, supposedly for the student newspaper. I could not believe the unanimous show of fear in that gesture.

At another staff meeting some days later the University's Senior Administrator expressed deep concern about the danger of strike action. Though I argued demonstratively against such an overturn of the original decision, I saw again the faces hidden behind hands or newspapers and knew it was pointless. The decision was reversed and fear and apathy won the day.

Thankfully things were not left to the staff. The student body argued that a demonstration was necessary. I felt that those staff members who had originally supported strike action should join the students. After all it was the kidnapping of staff members that they were protesting about. During the demonstration I found myself sitting beside a student holding a placard saying 'Who is next?', 'If I had known, John, I don't know if I would have sat there.'

But for all my enjoyment in teaching at the University, it was the life outside that defined Beirut.

On another occasion I recalled having lunch in a friend's apartment. The noise outside was the typical raucousness of the city. Then sudden gunfire, loud and crackling. This was nothing unusual either. I ambled slowly out onto the balcony of the second-floor apartment. I watched the cars like dodgems screech and race along the Corniche road below me, occasionally crashing into one another, driving furiously into oncoming traffic, all fleeing from the gunfire. But below us as I looked down I saw several young men jump into Mercedes and BMW cars and drive off towards the sound of the guns. They could not have been more than eighteen or nineteen and they hung from the cars, sitting inside but winding down the windows and pulling themselves through to rest with their backsides on the windows and their bodies leaning out holding onto the roof rack with one hand, a Kalashnikov jauntily carried in the other. From other directions men were running with guns, shouting excitedly, almost deliriously, heading towards the fighting. My friend called me in from the balcony. 'Look at them,' she said. 'Every one of them masturbating. They're all running about there with their hands on their penises exciting themselves, only their penises have become pistols.'

There may be some justice in taking up arms to resolve one's loss of power. History has seen such revolts again and again. Some might say that whatever we are as civilized beings is built on the blood of generation after generation and it may be true. But here in Lebanon there was another dimension. These people sought power, sought to be at home in the land and the community in which they lived. Yet they had taken a quantum leap. Though they might achieve power, though they might murder or slaughter each other, or chase out their foreign overlords – Israeli, Syrian or American – they themselves had no understanding of power or its uses: how to devolve it, how to share it and thus increase it. The warriors may, on history's balance-sheet, win the wars. But they are rarely leaders in the peace, and these young men sought a solution to their problems in a Ramboesque fantasy, not yet understanding that the true revolutionary is a lover, whose passion is creative.

One of the saddest stories I remember from my teaching days in Beirut was that of a young Maronite boy who had been working for one of the many press agencies in the city. His sister had a relationship with a Muslim youth and had become pregnant. When the family heard that their daughter was pregnant by a Muslim their hatred for her was unfathomable. She had committed the ultimate disobedience to the family, to God, to herself: she carried the child of a Muslim. In that male-dominated society she was an outcast from her own family and from her community and friends. The rage festered within the family. The young woman could neither be kept at home nor sent away to have her child. So deeply embedded was this vindictive morality that the father's rage turned into the most perverse determination, and he ordered one of his sons to kill the daughter. After the daughter was buried the family claimed that she had been murdered by Muslims.

The community of grief for the loss of this young woman was so vast that even the son, her brother who had killed her, came to believe that Muslims had murdered his sister. He returned to work in the Beirut press agency and everyone felt great sympathy for him. This reinforced his self-chosen belief that a Muslim had murdered his sister. One night, when all the staff in the office had returned home the young man took a gun from his bag and sat quietly in the evening, waiting. As the people began clearing the streets to go home he opened fire, randomly, shooting anyone that came within range. They were Muslims, they were all the murderers of his sister, they were all equally responsible. How many he killed or how many he injured one cannot be sure – the numbers always changed. But some time later, when the journalists returned to work one morning his own mutilated corpse was found in the office. He had obviously been murdered, probably by the families of those he had killed, perhaps by some organization seeking revenge on their behalf.

Months after the whole bloody affair, the story came out. The young man really did believe that Muslims had murdered his sister, and the love and sympathy of his friends and colleagues and community reinforced this. This kink of mind that confuses love with power and equates power with aggression and domination remains a painful sore under the skin of Lebanese society.

John and I often spoke about the guards, and how the word 'terrorist' seemed totally inappropriate. It is a term too frequently applied by people to certain others and serves only to shore up their own prejudices. 'Some terrorists wear pin-striped suits John,' I would argue; 'They hide their terrorism behind institutions of law or social regulation that have more to do with control than liberation. This terror maintains the status quo and power brokerage in the hands of a select few. Democracy has become a myth-word. It has a magical quality. One has only to speak it and people bow down to it and worship it without knowing their own surrender.'

The men who kept us were far from the cliché image of the terrorist. They were a composite of different needs and motivations. Imagine a man aged twenty to thirty, but with the maturity and intelligence of a thirteen-year-old, a mind steeped in fundamentalist and medieval suspicion, a mind propagandized into a set of beliefs and values which it was not informed enough to understand, but weak and fearful enough to accept unquestioningly. The natural and healthy instincts of youth are twisted and repressed by a religious and moral code that belongs more to the days of the Inquisition. Then, imagine the final absurdity. Into the hands of such a person someone places a machine gun and tells him to take his freedom. This was the kind of person to whom we were subject and the contemplation of it was disturbing.

The Devil's Barber-Shop

Our understanding of the guards, which was not one of spite or hatred, was soon to be overturned.

After many requests we had obtained from them a set of dominoes. Still they refused us books. Seventeen-hour marathon games of dominoes began, with an earnestness that was necessary to keep the mind from strolling off down dark passageways. Again I was collecting the silver and gold paper in which the processed cheese was wrapped. I also kept storing match boxes and cigarette boxes. Eventually I had enough material to make a chess set. I was able to hide this whole chess set inside a match box. We knew that games were forbidden and whenever the guards found any they immediately confiscated them. But as needs must we continued to make them and to create totally new games. I remember one game I invented called 'Escape From Beirut'. It took me several hours to explain the rules. When I thought we both understood the game, we began playing. In the course of playing situations arose which I had not devised a ruling for. John would appeal to my rules and I had to reply that I would think up a new rule for the new eventuality, at which John would look at me in surprise, the laughter rising in him, and say 'You dirty cheating bastard, you devise new rulings every time you think I'm winning and you're losing. The rules only favour you.' I would respond with something like: 'You must understand, John-boy, we Irish are more imaginative than you mongrel race of Brits. It's obviously better I devise the rules, having a much more subtle and more elaborate mind.'

One morning after being brought back from the toilet we settled ourselves down to replay our long game of dominoes. Then we heard a noise, a buzzing sound. We were careful not to be seen looking out, John tried lying on the floor and peering through the fan as the blades whirred. We could see little for the fan was at ground level and it was difficult to look up. We both realized after a little while what the buzzing noise was. It was an electric hair-clipping machine, the sort that I remember being used in the barber shops of my childhood.

I lay back and felt panic and anger and fear beginning their slow, taunting rise in me. I had little vanity, I cared nothing about my head being shaved, but I would not let them shave my beard. I lay quietly thinking what I was to do. I turned to John. 'I don't like this one, John-boy,' I said, as his eyes raised in puzzlement. 'I'm not very happy about getting my head shaved but I'm not going to let them shave my beard off.' He sat silently listening. After some moments he said 'I don't fancy having my head shaved to tell the truth.' I replied 'Well, you are a prisoner after all. I'll be able to call you Papillon now.

'What does it really matter,' I asked him. 'There is no one to look at you down here and there's certainly no women about that you need to fancy yourself up for . . . no need for vanity in this place, John-boy!' He snapped back 'Well what's so fucking important about your beard then. If I can't keep my hair, why should you keep your beard.' We were both being affectionate and joking with each other. I explained 'I've had a beard since I was sixteen and I've never shaved it off. I'm fucking well damn sure that this shower of shits isn't going to shave it off just because they want to.' I looked at John's face and I knew he saw the anger rising in me. John ran his fingers through his own bushy growth. 'Well I'll be quite glad to be rid of this anyway, it's so annoying . . . its too hot in here and you're always scratching and itching.' I looked across at him; he reminded me of the old sailor's face on the packets of Senior Service cigarettes I remembered from the 1950s. I thought he looked quite handsome and mature. The boyish good looks that I had first noticed had been changed powerfully by this thick bushy beard. 'We'd both be a lot cleaner without these things,' John affirmed. I turned, anger mounting. 'What the fuck do you mean, cleaner . . . we get a shower every day, we can't be much cleaner although with the sweat and stink in this place the shower hardly merits very much after a few hours. But that's not the problem, there is a principle here, we've got to hold onto principles. I've had this beard for too long for some halfwit who thinks he owns me to make me what he wants me to be.' I was losing my coherence, becoming angrier at the thought of having to sit through this humiliation. 'These bastards don't even shave themselves,' I spat out.

John sat quiet for by now he had learned to let me ride out this anger. I was full-fired now and he let me rant on. 'This is the last remnant of who I am, of my identity, John. They have taken everything from us, everything, everything by which we defined ourselves . . . clothes, money, jewellery, possessions, letters, liberty, the whole fucking lot whipped in a matter of hours and locked up in this stinking hole in the ground where you have to, hour after hour, day in day out, reaffirm to yourself that you are someone and that you are meaningful and that you are bigger, better and beyond their futile stupidity.' I was flying now. John remained silent. 'We can't give in to everything. We have to stand firm on something that gives us back who we are, we have to say no. We have to be self-choosing. We have to keep hold of ourselves or sink forever in this fucking quagmire.'

'Okay old man,' said John, reaching out patting my shoulder. 'No need to blow a fuse . . . It's time to put a leash on that Irish temper of yours.' He smiled. 'Perhaps if you just simply tell them you don't want to have your beard shaved they won't shave it . . . I don't think it's any big deal, maybe there are more important things to get angry about.' I looked up at him. 'There's nothing more important than one's identity and how you maintain and how you hold it and what you do with it because once you let it go you've got nothing and nothing's worse than that,' I said slowly, calming myself, knowing that I must be determined, that determination must be the greater part of my anger at the gross indignity I was about to undergo.

We sat waiting, nervous tension thickening the silence we were enveloped in. Then finally we heard the feet shuffling in their plastic sandals towards our door. The key turned and I heaved a deep gulp of air. I was taken out from the cell and walked towards the shower and toilet. I washed quickly, wanting this confrontation to be over with. I finished drying myself, knocked on the door, and turned my back to it, fixing the blindfold over my eyes. I was walked out and into the guard's room. They told me 'Today you haircut, you shaving.' I stopped, stood straight and said 'You will not shave my beard. I have had this beard all my life. You will not shave it.' The guards were perplexed, not fully understanding what I had said but I knew they understood my refusal. Quickly they ushered me back to the cell and John was taken.

The door was locked and I sat down exhilarated, believing that I had won and that they would not shave me, but I was frightened that this would not be the end. In the minds of our guards, prisoners could not be allowed to refuse. I sat thinking through all the possibilities of what might follow and what I would do and say in the face of the consequences that kept tumbling through my head. John seemed to be taking longer than usual. Then I heard him return. The door opened, I shielded my eyes again with the towel over my face. The door locked. As I removed the towel John hissed at me 'What the fuck have you done . . . you're going to get us both shot.' I stood up. He was talking quickly. 'Those boyos seem really excited about something . . . what the fuck did you say to them?' and as he spoke, for some reason, I don't know why, I stood and stretched my arms and made as if to unleash an arrow from a bow. John made the same gesture in response. We were both two kids in that instant. Perhaps we were David and Jonathan. But that instinctive mimicry, with excitement, the fear, the adrenalin coursing through our bodies, was an inarticulate gesture of mutual support.

'I'm not going to let them shave me,' I said, deliberately emphasizing every word. 'Okay,' John said and as he spoke we heard the guards coming towards the cell. This time there were several of them and this time I had gone beyond the point of retreat. I had no choice but to stand firm, take what was coming and resist it if I could. We quickly pulled the blindfolds down over our eyes and I pushed my back firmly against the wall, squatting but upright. A voice said 'John come,' and I felt John move away from me out into the corridor.

As he went several men entered the cell. I could hear what I thought were four voices. Someone knelt in front of me. I knew this man to be a senior officer. At first he spoke softly. 'Why you don't clean this cell?' he asked; I answered equally slowly 'This cell was like this when we came here.' He was silent for a moment then touching my hair, 'Why you don't have hair cut?' Then his hand slid from my head, down to my chin and tugged at the beard. 'Why you don't shave?' I answered taking hold of my defiance, 'I've had this beard for a long time, since I was a young man, and I will not let you shave it!' I knew he felt the defiance, his hand was now on my wrist and he started to twist, slowly at first. I twisted forcefully against him. He spoke again saying 'We are army, every two months you must haircut, you must shave,' still twisting my wrist and I resisting him. I said 'I will not be shaved.' The whispering voices of the guards behind the man who was speaking with me fell silent. He leaned forward and said 'This is very bad, you know what will happen now.' I sat for a few seconds thinking of an answer and could only say 'Yes I know . . . you are going to beat me but I am not going to let you.'

The man barked an order to one of the guards behind him. I knew the Arabic for pistol. I heard a gun being handed to him and heard him snap and prime it ready to fire. I felt absolutely and completely calm for no matter what he did to me I had already won. Death was nothing and I was already past it. A gun was pressed against my head. His voice again saying 'You know what is going to happen now.' It was softly spoken, but I could feel the tension in it. I was still calm. I said slowly 'I am not afraid of you and I am not afraid of your gun.' This time he exploded with more fury than before. I heard the gun drop on the mattress beside me and the man launched into a furious attack, punching and beating me about the head, my face and temples, screaming something in Arabic. The shock of it and the adrenalin of the last few minutes made it seem painless. It was just a knocking and the jerking of my head. I felt like a kind of marionette being handled by some inexperienced puppeteer. I kept silent. I must not show fear, I must not show pain or cry out.

For how long he rained his blows upon my head and face, I cannot remember. So many things coursed through my mind; perhaps that is how pain is obliterated. At the end he stood up. He seemed exhausted and tense. He barked something to the guards and they bent down, trailed me from the cell, pulling me along the corridor. They sat me on the low wall that ran down its middle. I heard him shout orders or shout at me, I could not tell. He came over to me and I knew I had to say something to keep face, to maintain identity. He said something in Arabic, I knew he was speaking to me. I raised my head, unseeing, and simply said 'You are a very brave man.' I knew the insult of it and I didn't care whether he did or not, for things had taken their course and we would each complete it in our own ways. He struck me hard on the head and walked off again snarling orders. Two of the guards followed hurriedly after him and one stood with me. His hand gentle on my shoulder. He patted me. Maybe he admired my defiance or sympathized with me, I could not tell. His hand on my shoulder made me feel less alone. Perhaps it was to tell me it was over. Yet I felt that what had happened in the cell was only the beginning of something worse. My premonition was to be confirmed in the months and years that followed.

I heard the feet hurrying back. I was lifted out of my sitting position and marched to the guards' room. I was pushed into a chair, my arms held by guards at each side of me. I heard the electric clipper begin its buzzing and with it felt the fall of my hair onto my naked shoulders. I sat in silence, the hair continued to fall. My head was pushed forward, my chin resting on my chest as the clipper crawled up the back of my head. I attempted blindly to blow the cut hair from me. A voice hissed at me. I continued to blow.

To complete this operation they had removed the blindfold from my head and sealed my eyelids with pieces of scotch tape. My head was forced back and over to the side. The tape was pulled from my eyes and a voice hissed at me 'Do not look, do not look.' I held my eyes closed. I felt the clipper run down my temple onto my cheek. I screwed my eyes tightly closed, thinking I must find a way to express resistance, to express defiance even though they were doing this thing to me. I could do nothing more than sit erect trying to force power into every muscle of my body so that their hands tight on my arms might feel the anger boiling in me. It's hard to work one's muscles in a sitting position but the grip of their hands on my forearms and shoulders gave me something to press against. Quickly the clipper trimmed my beard. I felt the coarse hair, different from the hair on my head, fall onto my chest and my lap. I thought it was over and wondered what was to come. Perhaps they would separate me from John. They would not like this defiance. They would seek a way to punish me; possibly I would be beaten again. But I consoled myself that I still had a stubble. The hands slackened their grip on my arms. I sat still, waiting for the blindfold to be put back on my face. Instead I felt the soapy warmth of a shaving brush covering my face and chin with lather.

My immediate reaction was one of awful self-pity but I could not allow it to engulf me. Then I felt several of the guards come close to me, whispering in my ear, softly, slowly but insidiously: 'You Esa, you Jesus, you Esa,' different voices echoing the same words 'Esa, Esa, you Jesus.' Each of them in turn scraped parts of the remaining stubble from my face. I sat straight, the humiliation almost breaking me, and I tried desperately to hold myself together. Around me still, that soft insidious chant of 'Esa, Esa, you Esa.' The razor blade stroking my face and being passed hand to hand. Another man taking his turn to strip me, to rape me of myself. Tighter and tighter I screwed my eyes, feeling something huge and piteous, that pendulum drop into harrowing humiliation. I would not surrender to it and I squeezed my eyes tighter, feeling tears coming into them. I cared nothing now that they were shaving me in this obscene ritual. I cared only that I should not be seen to weep. I squeezed my eyes tighter and tighter and clamped my hands onto my knees. In horror I felt a tear come, caught between my eyelashes, and hoped it wouldn't find a course down my face, wetting their stroking razors.

And then it was over. Someone knelt before me on the floor. The other guards stood behind me. 'Open eyes,' someone said sharply. I sat still and waited. 'In your own time, Brian, let no tears fall,' I thought to myself. 'Open your eyes,' a voice barked, more insistently, and I slowly opened my eyes. Before me a man squatted. He held a large mirror in front of his face so that I could not see him. I looked at my fractured image. For some seconds unmoved, unflinching, showing no expression in any way, I stared at a man I did not know and then said slowly 'It is not me.' I raised my head up from the reflection and closed my eyes, sitting, waiting, uncaring. My eyes were dry.

I waited, they talked about me and around me. The towel was carefully put over my eyes and knotted tightly at the back of my head. I was lifted from the chair. I brushed the hair from my chest and shoulders. My hands were wrenched down by my sides. I stood stiff, awaiting a continuation of what happened in the cell, but I was moved away from the chair and guided towards the passage. This time with one arm twisted fiercely up my back.

I was happy that they still felt the need to punish me. They still knew I was resistant. My cell door opened and I was pushed in. It was banged behind me. I stood and slowly untied the blindfold. John looked up at me and I at him. I felt his great sympathy surge towards me and I felt embarrassed and I didn't know where to turn or what to say. He looked in silence for a moment, then away, understanding my embarrassment. 'Are you okay?' he asked; 'Yes, I'm fine,' I said slowly. Silence again separated us. I continued again after some minutes 'That was a bit of a fucking close shave.' John looked up, I knew the sympathy and the hurt he was feeling for me but he took hold of the humour I tried feebly to offer, and said 'You look like Enoch Powell.' John had his hair cropped but they left him with a neat goatee beard and moustache. Regaining confidence, grateful for his warmth I said 'Well, you look like a cross between Jimmy Hill and Sheikh Yamani.' He stroked his beard and his chin. 'It was a bit of a shock.' I nodded in agreement. 'Van Dyck you are definitely not. I suppose I am going to have to put up with living with Sigmund Freud for the next few months.' We both eased into a soft laugh.

Perhaps because this place seemed to be a purpose-built prison, the routine was more organized. Though we often looked across the wide corridor we could never see anyone. Yet we knew that there were other prisoners. We were sure one of them was a person from the first prison. We heard him occasionally speak with the guards in a high-pitched voice. He had muttered something about being able to speak English, German and French. We thought we heard him give his name as 'Sontage', or something similar. At night we would hear him mumble or cry out in his sleep. He was in a cell opposite us. Occasionally when he was being taken to the toilet we would lie on the floor and peer through the fan, which was about the size of a saucer. We could see he was old. The guards would make fun of him, push him and slap him, in the way one might goad a donkey.

The folds of flesh on his body seemed to hang about him. It was a pathetic sight to watch him being so abused. The indifference to his condition and the callous pleasure our guards took in mistreating him made them more like bullies in a school playground than so-called 'warriors'. Sometimes during the day we would hear him babble incoherently in his sleep. His old squeaky voice echoed in the long stony corridor of the prison. The guards would rush towards his cell, banging and hissing at him to be silent. But in his sleep he was helpless. Their banging only served to wake him and silence his dreaming for a few hours, and then he would be off again gabbling, shouting and snoring.

Some days the guards would come and talk with us after they knew our names and where we came from. Their questions were always about our families, and they constantly asked whether we were married. When we explained we were not they wanted to know why. We were very old not to be married, they said. Did we have girlfriends? How many? Did we sleep with them? We would not answer these intimate questions.

But it was only the beginning. We were to learn more in the years to come of their fixation on sex. 'Why in England and America everyone is fucking? . . . In the American universities they are fucking in the bushes . . . In America men are fucking men . . . In America everyone has AIDS . . . How many times you can do with a woman in one night?' and so it went on, always the same. Their obsession betrayed their own repressed desire. And they were boring. When they began on the subject of sex we simply passed their questions back to them, or made a joke of it. 'Brian, how many times you can do with a woman in one night?' and I would always answer 'You mean how many women in one night?' Their reaction was always the same, silence followed by admiring laughter. Often they would feel the muscles in our arms or with their thumbs and fingers press savagely into the sinew running from the base of the neck to the shoulder. Sexual potency was measured in muscle. Muscle was power. A powerful or strong prisoner they admired but secretly feared.

Allah, the God of retribution and judgement, dominated their minds. How can a man love the thing he fears? When fear commands the mind then the heart is imprisoned. In time I came to understand the greater and more profound prison that held our captors. For years we were chained to a wall or radiator, but they were chained to their guns; futile symbols of power, not power itself. This was something these men could never know: real power embraces; it cannot destroy.

Their poor English limited the scope of their questions and their comprehension of our answers. Occasionally they would talk of politics. Their detestation of Israel was absolute. It was justified by the Koran and it was even more justified by the internment camps set up in Israel to hold and torture many innocent Lebanese Shias from the south. They told us stories of men who had returned from these places, how they had been fed on a starvation diet. How they had been beaten and tortured with electric cattle prods applied to their genitals. The rapture with which they spoke of this sadistic practice again expressed their fascination with sex. Their loud condemnation of this torture was an inverted reflection of their own impotence. With a scream they would tell us 'Never can these men have babies!' Manhood was measured in sexual potency. There was little of real pity or sympathy for their tortured comrades. The relish with which they spoke about torture made me think how much they secretly enjoyed reflecting on atrocities. Even as they spoke a part of them became the torturer. Without acknowledging it they were awed by the barbarity and intoxicated by its power. In their unconscious they were at once the victim and the torturer. I pitied and despised them. 'We treat you better than the Israelis,' they would say, and I knew that some of them would like to do just what the Israelis were doing.

During these talks, or more correctly infantile inquisitions, our guards would frequently ask us if we had heard anyone else. Did we know if anyone else was being kept in that place? To lie, or worse, to be caught lying, was an admission that we were afraid. We simply answered that we heard nothing, only doors closing. We spoke the truth but revealed nothing. It was enough. These men's need for secrecy and security was paranoid.

One night and every night for the rest of our time in that prison the guards hung a small transistor radio in the passage outside our cell. It was turned up to the limit and tuned to static. The constant fuzz and buzz and crackling screech bored into our heads like a needle. At first we tried to forget it and ignore its pressure but it was useless. The mind was always drawn into it. It seemed to be inside us, recklessly slicing and gouging with a rusty broken scalpel. Every fibre and nerve of the body felt plucked and strained by it. Hour after hour, night after night. It tore at the very membranes of the brain. There was no possibility of rest or sleep. It ate into you, devouring all sense and sensibility.

I tossed and turned, clamped my hands over my ears. Nothing would quell this crazy static. I stuffed balls of paper into my ears. I wrapped my towel around my head, and still the noise was unbearable; how long could I endure this. I rocked, slowly at first then savagely trying to create a rhythm beyond the noise. I tried to sing, I tried to pray but my efforts only added to the torment. I tried sitting on the cold damp floor with the foam mattress wrapped about me but there was no protection from the high-pitched screech. My head was burning inside, my body sweated in the heat. It was relentless.

Only in the morning, when the guards prepared breakfast, would the noise be silenced. I walked exhausted to the shower. The luxury of hot water and soap could not refresh me. It merely cleansed the night and nerve-shattered sweat from me. I returned to my cell and slept, dog-tired. For days this discordant pandemonium screamed at us. I could bear it no longer. One evening hearing it start up again I jumped to the door, kicking it and hammering it and leaning in fury on the bell.

Guards rushed quickly to our cell. I stood back as the door opened. Facing them, weary but resilient with anger I waited. 'What you want?' 'Turn off the radio,' I answered with slow, barely concealed anger and deliberation. 'I cannot sleep with that noise, turn it off,' I continued. 'We cannot, is orders,' came the simple reply. John's voice came from behind me, calmer but still insistent 'Then turn the thing down, we have not slept in days.' There was silence, then one of the guards entered and spoke in conciliatory tones. 'But it is same for us, we sleep here also.' I let loose a massive sigh of exasperation. 'It is not outside your door.' John followed my words quickly, finding some humour to defuse the situation. 'If it is the same, then you sleep here and we will sleep in your room.'

Puzzled and silent, the guards stood looking at us. Then again that phrase which was the standard answer to every request: 'Bukkra', tomorrow. I sank onto the floor in silence. 'Those brain-dead pieces of rancid shite wouldn't hear an elephant's fart in their ear while they're asleep. There's nothing inside their thick skulls but congealed emptiness. How could nothing hear anything?' I spat at the four walls. John's voice came from behind me again. 'Well it doesn't seem to have affected your vocabulary any.' We both laughed quietly, exhausted by the sleepless nights and the futility of speaking with these people.

That night I slept fitfully, overcome by exhaustion, both physical and mental. On occasions I woke, the noise continually wrenching me out of sleep. Even in that darkness I could feel the whiteness of the walls blinding and burning me. I wondered then as I do even now how noise can affect our perception of colour. The whiteness had become deafening.

During the days that followed we complained frequently about the noise. It seemed to have some effect. The volume of the radio was lowered. But too late: I was already beginning to experience an irritation in my ear. Unthinking, as we played dominoes, I would push my little finger into the nagging ear and vigorously satisfy the craving to relieve the itch. This itch was with me for days. I felt an almost sexual pleasure in satisfying it. But then early one morning before the dawn call to prayer came undulating into the hollow cells I awoke with an excruciating pain in my inner ear. Tears filled my eyes with the intensity of it. For hours it crippled me then slowly died away. I lay awake until breakfast came. Pain experienced in conditions such as those in which we were held moves out of pain and into panic. What is this illness? How will it affect me? Will it get worse? Such questions were insistent. But there were no answers, no reassurance. Not knowing was more frightening than the pain itself.

For several days this pain attacked me, moving from one ear to another. The night was torture. I had either to be on my back or on my face, smothering it in the pillow. For long periods I was deaf. The inside of my ear was fat and swollen. John's comforting reassurance that I should not worry and everything would be all right did not calm me. Was I becoming deaf? A deaf man cannot teach. He is locked in a world of silence. The comfort of companionship is removed. The world is a silently moving image which he can only stare at and half understand. Such was my panicking thought, as if rocks were being piled on my chest, holding me in this silence. I tried to calm myself by saying it would clear up in a few days. But instead the pain grew worse

and the deafness more complete. I complained to the guards. They
listened and left. Their lack of interest compounded my panic. John
too was becoming anxious. I could barely hear him speak. I tried
joking 'At least I won't have to listen to your bloody idiocy.' He
would crack a barely audible joke in response. 'See, what splendid
relief not to listen to you.'

My complaints became more earnest. I now wore twists of tissue
permanently in my ears to protect them from the dust and irritating
heat. When the electricity was turned off we lay, unmoving and in
silence, our bodies glistening with sweat and grime in the rising
temperature. My deaf ears pounded and throbbed. I tried to imagine
my life in this shroud of silence. What would I do without music? I
could never speak to anyone because I would not know if they heard
me. All the insignificant noises of humanity would be denied me. This
self-pitying introspection annoyed me as much as it worried me. I
needed some medication but more importantly I needed someone to
tell me what was wrong with me. Fear is diminished when we give
something a name. By simply naming it we take possession of it. I
needed knowledge to break me out of fear. I resolved I must have
medicine.

Every time the guards entered and tried to speak to me I sat in
silence or asked John what they were saying. He answered me loudly,
his face close to my ear. Again I told them I needed medication. One of
them sat close to me and said 'What is your problem?' I shrugged, John
again spoke loudly in my ear. In detail I outlined my 'problem',
making a point of blaming the radio for damaging my ears. He
listened in silence and then rose to leave. 'I will speak with my chief,'
he said and left. Two days passed and nothing happened. The routine
of complaint and silence continued.

On the third day I waited for John to return from the toilet. He
returned and I was taken. In the small washroom, which contained
only a wash hand basin and a shower head over the hole in the ground
where we squatted and defecated, I washed slowly, careful to keep the
water out of my ears. Having finished, I knocked on the door to leave.
Slowly I walked back to my cell led by a guard. Inside it was strangely
silent; my hearing was impaired, but not absolutely. I felt the
emptiness rather than silence. I lifted my blindfold. John was gone.
One mattress, one urine bottle, one bottle of drinking water
remained. Each object emphasized the emptiness. To my surprise I
did not feel shock or fear. The sudden vastness of the tiny cell

hypnotized me. But slowly the emptiness pressed in on me; what would I do? How would I pass the days on my own? Quickly, almost instinctively I jumped up and began running on the spot. It had been weeks since I had exercised. Faster and faster I ran then slowly trotted myself to an exhausted collapse. I lay sweating and panting, my mind still racing, seeking some resting place.

The Hammam Mail

When lunch was brought I asked where John was. 'I do not know,' came the reply. 'If you have hurt him . . .' The door banged shut before I could finish my intended threat. I passed the day thinking of our time together. Occasionally I stood, hauling myself up to look over into the cells opposite. Nothing, no movement, no noise. I called out his name softly, then louder, fearless of the consequences. Still no answer. That night I prayed for my companion's safety and comfort as I knew he would be doing for me. We were apart but somehow we were in communication. A compassion greater than our need for each other created an invisible presence, shared experiences and memories filling the cell. I slept alone yet somehow not alone. One question preoccupied me: what would I do if I learnt John had been executed? I remembered the words of the guard as he walked me into this prison many months ago. 'Your friends have gone to their home.' I know he was referring to Peter Padfield and Leigh Douglas and I was beginning to suspect that their 'home' was a final and not a family one. My prayers were no longer requests. I demanded his life and safety.

Morning came. This time I walked awkwardly to the toilet, the calves and muscles in my thighs screaming from the punishment I had subjected them to the previous night. I entered the tiny shower exhausted from the short walk. My ankles felt as though they had been smashed with a hammer. I waited for the pain to ease, looking up at the bulb that lighted the toilet. Suddenly it hit me. Without thinking what I was about to do I committed myself to it.

I turned on the cold tap of the shower and cupped my hands under the spray filling them with water, then threw the cold water against the hot bulb. Explosion and darkness. Hot pricks burnt my shoulders and feet as the glass fell around me. I stood motionless, waiting and afraid to move. Would I be trailed out of this place and beaten again?

The door opened slightly, a hand reached in with a small piece of candle burning on a saucer. I set it on the shelf above the grimy wash hand basin. As the door closed a voice spoke 'Douche, quickly.' So far I was safe. I looked about me. My eyes fixed on a piece of shattered glass. I picked it up and placed it inside my cup. Quickly I finished washing and folding the glass inside my towel, knocked on the door, informing the guards I was ready to return. I was led back to my cell.

Crouching in the corner I felt excited by my scheme. A long day and night passed, my mind turning over what I was going to do and what the consequences might be. Early in the morning before the guards arrived with breakfast I took the glass fragment in one hand and with the other spread my toes open. Wincing and hesitating I cut the flesh until it bled. Hurriedly I took the twists of tissue with which I plugged my ears and dabbed them in blood. I set them on the stone shelf. I put more pieces of tissue between my toes to staunch the bleeding. Carefully I placed the glass into a tear I had made in the mattress. By the time breakfast arrived the small wound between my toes had stopped bleeding. As the guard set the food in front of me I took the pieces of tissue from each ear and showed him the bloody ends. He took them from me asking 'You have blood?' I pretended not to hear him. He held the twists of tissue under my blindfold. 'Blood?' he said inquisitively. I simply replied 'Medicine; Doctor!' As I expected he took both my hands in his, turning them over and scrutinizing them. 'Okay' he said and left.

Each night and morning I carried out the same routine. After a few days, one of the guards who spoke good English informed me he had told his 'chief' of 'my problems'. His chief had told him that after one week if my 'problem' continued he would come to see me. I knew now that the ball had started to roll; where it would stop I did not know. I only knew I had to go with it. I continued my ritual incision, daily becoming more worried that the glass might be discovered. I knew that there were days when my cell was searched as I showered. I could not explain or lie my way out of the severe consequences if it was found.

After five or six days of this game I sat one afternoon, trying to calculate mathematically the sum total of all the chapters and verses in the Bible, which had been given to me some days before after repeated pleading for books. Suddenly the door rattled open. I sat unmoved. I had always, in the presence of the guards kept up the pretence that my deafness was worse than it really was. A man whose voice I did not know squatted in front of me. He took my hand and shook it. 'How are you?' he asked.

I leaned forward, lifting the blindfold from my ear, gesturing that I could not hear him. He said something in Arabic to the guards who stood behind him. He put his face close to my ear and asked 'What is your problems?' I explained the great pain in my ears and that I had difficulty eating because as I chewed the pain became worse. I showed him the bloody tissues and told him I could hear what he asked me but his voice seemed to be far away. He asked me what medicine I needed. I answered that I did not know. I had never had such problems before, and emphasized that the noise from the radio had caused this. He listened, asking me if I had other problems. I told him that living like an animal was a problem. He spoke to the guards, then, patting my shoulder and again shaking my hand, got up and left. I had no idea of what would happen next. The longer I persisted with this gamble the greater the danger of them finding the sliver of glass. Worse still, what if I got an infection in the cuts in my feet? How could I explain that? I could only wait and see, but the waiting was agony.

Two nights later my cell opened. One of the guards handed me my clothes. Trousers, shirt and shoes. 'Quickly, put on,' he commanded. There was laughter in his voice. I remembered to play deaf. He tugged at my shorts. 'Dress, dress,' he said and left. I dressed and sat, again waiting. After about ten minutes the door opened and several guards led me out. As I passed one of them said 'You have ID?' I answered that my passport was in my apartment. He laughed and I laughed with him.

I was ushered along the prison passageway and hoisted up through the hole I had been dropped into, seemingly so long ago. Out into the warm night air. Things were happening fast. I was surprisingly calm. They jostled me into an old van. Several men were there and I was pushed onto the floor. The van stank with the smell of sheep or goats. A gun was placed at my temple. The thought of the dark tunnel when I was first taken came rushing back to me. The filth and stink of this van was such an undignified place to die in. I wondered where and by whom my body would be found. Then strangely I thought perhaps it would be better for my family if I was buried here. Having to go through the suffering over my death and then dealing with the agony of bringing me home and burying me would be too much for them. For a moment I despised these men for the anguish they had visited on my family. The great well-spring of compassion I felt for them drowned my fear.

We travelled bumping and jostling for fifteen minutes and then came to a halt. The men in the rear jumped out and I was taken from the van. Quickly my blindfold was removed. 'Close eyes,' a voice said as two men took me by the arm and walked me into a lighted building. I was walked swiftly along a corridor and into what was obviously a doctor's surgery. I squinted about me. My guards pushed me onto a chair. Another man, presumably a doctor, addressed me. He was extremely nervous, speaking quickly, his voice shaking. I described my condition and before I had finished he placed an instrument in my ear. I flinched with the pain. He spoke in Arabic and was gone. I sat with the guards' hands clamped on my shoulders. A few minutes passed then I was taken back to the awaiting van. Another journey. To where, I wondered? Again I felt myself being dropped through that hole in the ground. Quietly I was walked back to the same cell. I sat again where I had always sat. My plan had failed. But I was untroubled. I felt only a great relief that a doctor had seen me. Now they would do something about my ears. One of the guards entered. With real surprise he said 'Why are you here?' I shrugged, then asked him about what the doctor had said. He did not know. 'Sleep,' he said, and left.

I was too excited and too relieved to rest. When I was sure the guards had settled themselves in their own room I stood and peered over the top of my cell door. To my astonishment I saw in the cell opposite a man staring back at me. Only half of his face was visible. We stood transfixed by each other, entranced and silent as though watching a miracle performed. I came to my senses and gesticulated with my hands telling him to wait. Rapidly, I dropped to the floor and grabbed one of the tissues. There had been a pen in my clothes, which they had given back to me. Quickly I scribbled on a piece of paper in large capitals 'I AM IRISH'. I scrambled up to the door again. The other prisoner was standing, waiting. I held up the tissue for him to read. He signalled that he could not read it from his cell. I knew it would be extremely dangerous to cry out to him. Instead I thrust my hands and arms outside the bars and held the note to him. It seemed he was taking an eternity to read this simple message.

My legs ached and trembled with the effort of standing so long on my toes with my arms outstretched. 'Hurry up, you fool; if the guards see this we will both be in trouble,' I said quietly to myself. Then I saw his face change. His eyes seemed to light up. The frown from the effort of reading vanished. His eyebrows raised and his forehead wrinkled with surprised delight. Suddenly, ecstatically he was throwing me kisses and shouting in his old squeaky voice 'I love you, beautiful, beautiful, I love you,' his strong French accent betraying his nationality. He continued blowing kisses and exclaiming his devotion. I panicked and gestured furiously for him to be silent. But he continued, oblivious of the danger. I dropped to my knees in desperation. 'The crazy old fool,' I muttered, excitement and fear filling me. I thought if he did not see me he might shut up. I stretched out on the floor and looked through the fan at my new-found friend's cell. He was silent now but still watching.

Again I stood, signalling him to be silent. He blew me kisses and I returned them. The pathetic foolishness of what we were doing made me laugh, nodding and waving and blowing kisses to this old man. I was beginning to feel tears forming in my eyes.

I suddenly saw in the cell next to this old Frenchman's, a figure move and another face appear. I had always known there was someone in that cell but had never seen him. Perhaps he had been too frightened to look out. It was obvious that the old man's cries had caused this other prisoner to look when he thought it safe. I looked at this new face. He looked back. Then he raised his hand and waved it slowly like a metronome. I waved back. Three of us like silent marionettes waving and blowing kisses, caught in an awful wonder. I signalled to the old man that the person in the cell next to him was waving. He nodded and clasped both his hands over his head in a victory salute. I gestured to the other man to wait. I repeated what I had done with the message I had held up to the Frenchman. He nodded and began spelling the word 'American' with his finger, tracing the letters in the air. As he was doing this another face appeared alongside his. We exchanged waves. On another tissue I wrote 'My friend is English.' Again they nodded and began to spell their surnames. Sutherland and Anderson. The old Frenchman, understanding that I was communicating with the cell next to his, began crying out again, 'Beautiful, beautiful.' I watched the two Americans rapidly disappear at the sound of his voice. I laughed loudly. It was like watching coconuts knocked from their stands at a fairground. I signalled the old man to be quiet and waved to him as if to say goodnight. I signalled goodnight by resting my head on my hands, and sat down knowing there would be little sleep. My cell was filled with invisible strangers.

Next morning I breakfasted with my secret knowledge. I knew John was in one of the other cells. I wondered if my new comrades might know if he was near them. I was anxious to communicate with them. When my turn came I washed quickly. I had counted the number of doors opening and closing before the guards came for me. It seemed that there was one more door banging closed than had been the case before John's move from my cell. I was sure he was still here, though the appearance of two Americans in one cell cast some doubt on my assumption. I stood waiting as my cell door was unlocked. I walked in and heard it bang behind me. I lifted my blindfold and saw the smiling face of John McCarthy. 'Couldn't stay away, could you!' I said with smiling nonchalance. John returned my greeting. 'I was convinced you had gone home, I recognized your shoes passing my cell door.' 'Peeking through the fan again, naughty!' I joked back.

I told him the events of the night before, my visit to the doctor and my contact with the other captives. John knew they were Americans. He had been kept in the cell next to them and heard them talking to the guards. 'I have some bad news for you,' he said slowly. 'We are with Islamic Jihad.' We both knew the consequences of this knowledge but chose not to speak of it.

I continued to complain of my hearing. I knew that the visit to the doctor must have some outcome. I was sure the doctor was terrified but believed that he would at least provide medicine. Three days after we had made contact with the Americans one of the guards came to our cell. He presented me with a course of very strong anti-biotics and promised to return in some days with ear drops. It was ten days before they arrived. However the penicillin and the companionship of near faces worked their own magic.

The next days and weeks were spent signalling to the Americans. It was a long and difficult process, spelling out words letter by letter, but we persevered. The need to communicate was greater than the risk involved. After a few days of this laborious activity I suggested to John it would be less complicated and no more dangerous to secrete written messages in the toilet overnight and the Americans could pick them up the next morning. We conveyed this to the Americans. There was a hole in the wall high above the sink. We would leave messages there for collection. We would also leave the pen so the Americans could return a message. They had told us that they had no news of events outside since their capture. We had lots to tell them, too much for hand signals.

It was necessary to write very small and on thin paper. Too much bulk would be discovered and hard to transport. The tissues we intended writing on were too soft. They either tore, or the tiny script became illegible as the pen imprinted onto it. We discovered a method of hardening the paper, thus allowing us to write as small as we wished. We separated the double layers of tissue into a thin single sheet. This sheet we soaked with water and held in front of the fan until it dried. It was now hard and resistant to tearing. We penned voluminous notes about world events, and the continuing campaign in America for the hostages. I was able to tell Tom Sutherland about his wife, as I had worked with her at the University. John and Terry, both journalists, had lots in common. The finished letter was then rolled around the pen and tied tightly with a thread pulled from our bedcover.

We each took turns delivering and collecting the correspondence. With our first message we instructed the Americans to let us know the following morning that they had successfully collected the letter. Confirmation would be conveyed by rattling something against the spinning blades of the door fan. Every morning we sat waiting for that noise.

Our anxiety about this exchange of letters soon made us change the hiding place. The wash hand basin rested on two hollow steel pipes. Into this we inserted the pen with its message tied around it. A short length of thread was left hanging out of the pipe so that the pen could be drawn out. For over a week the pen passed secretly across the prison. We devoured each letter as it arrived, but there was a limit to the amount of new information we had to exchange. Even the attempt to play chess by post soon petered out. Each letter ended with the words 'Coppula eam, se non posit acceptera jocularum.'*

As the week progressed the letters were becoming more dangerous. Sooner or later someone would be caught. Then one morning John returned to the cell with a letter. There were only a few words on it. The pen had dried up, and it was impossible to replace. I felt empty and angry. Our game had come to an end. The little piece of victory that each letter represented was taken from us. For hours I sat with the pen trying to make it work. It was hopeless. We began again spelling out conversations.

Terry Anderson came to the rescue. He had devised his own version of the deaf and dumb alphabet. He taught it to John and John passed it on to me. It was like learning to read and write again. For hours John

* 'Fuck them, if they can't take a joke.'

and I would sit silent in the cell practising this strange hand-language. So intense was our concentration that frequently as we spoke we would automatically signal words. Our hands had become our mouths. They danced in the air, telling silent stories and jokes.

But our written communication had not ended with the pen. We had continued to save the silver paper from the packet of cigarettes we were given every three days. The foil from the cheese we also squirrelled away. I would store anything and everything. 'This place is like a rubbish tip,' John would complain. 'What are we going to do with all that silver paper? You've already made three chess sets and all those other daft games that only a daft Irishman could think of.' 'Well I might make some Christmas decorations. But I am seriously thinking of opening a shop!'

Amongst the 'pruck'* as I called it was a cigarettebox and matchboxes, cotton buds for my ears, dead matches, stubs of candles and candle wax. One day I took some of the silver cigarette paper and a match. I was just about to begin imprinting some crude design on the foil when it struck me. 'I've got it John-boy, I've got it. Fuck the bastards, we've beaten them again' I burst out excitedly. John looked at me. He was used to what he called my 'homebred Irish insanity'. 'What are you raving about now? No, don't tell me. I don't want to hear. You are more crazy than these halfwits who have locked us up. I am going to sue you for mental torment when I get out of here. Now what is it?' John was fascinated. 'Simply a piece of exquisite Irish genius,' I said, mocking his accent. I handed over the cigarette foil with the words 'Brits out' scrawled on it. 'Look, with this match, or anything pointed, you can write.' I reached over and flicked my fingers against the fan. Tom Sutherland stood up across the passageway. I signalled the words 'Tomorrow a letter.' His puzzled expression made me laugh. Again I signalled him to watch. I held up the cigarette paper and the match. He could not see the match. 'Wait,' I signalled again. 'John, quick, give me a cotton bud.' He handed it to me and I held it up for the Americans to see. Terry Anderson was now also looking across at me beside Tom. I held up the silver paper again. They nodded. Then with my other hand I held up the cotton bud; again they nodded. I tore the cotton end off and pretended to write on the foil. Anderson instantly understood. His eyes blazed, he raised his two fists above his head, puncturing the air. His delight was rapturous

* Pruck: a Belfast term for odds and ends.

and infectious. The postal service was re-established with tubes of silver cigarette paper being delivered to and collected from our hiding place under the sink.

Our days of finger talk and the 'hammam'* mail service slowly petered out. Again we had exhausted the news we could meaningfully share. Days went by when we did not bother communicating across the 'Great Divide' between ourselves and the Americans. John and I once more retreated into our endless games of dominoes. Long intense discussions on English and Irish politics were always given some light relief by our 'telephone conversations': John and I, sitting in separate corners of the cell with our hands on our ears holding imaginary telephones, as Margaret Thatcher and Charlie Haughey engaged in long exchanges.

Charlie: Hello, hello, oh hello, Margaret . . . What's that, Margaret, you wanted to speak to me about something important. You mean you're thinking of . . . No, no of course you're not thinking of resigning. I know, I know, Margaret, you don't believe in that word. Yes I remember what you said about the divine right of Prime Ministers . . .

Thatcher: Charlie, you do remember Boadicea?

Charlie: Of course, Margaret . . . But she was a Celt and overcame the alien invaders. She was . . .

Thatcher: An inspiration, Charles. But history has been rewritten since the British Empire. I am the new warrior queen and I will . . .

Charlie: Yes, yes of course you will, your holiness . . . Now what exactly was it you wanted . . . at 4 o'clock in the morning . . . Yes, yes I know time stands still when the Queen is on her throne. But we lesser mortals need our sleep . . . There is a difficult situation in the Middle East, of course, Margaret. It's been there since the British Empire. How can the Irish help you, Margaret?

Margaret: There's an Irishman who's an Englishman who's been kidnapped.

* 'Hammam': Arabic for toilet or bathroom

Charlie: A what, Margaret? An Irish-Englishman, kidnapped . . . What's that you say Margaret? The British Government's going to take care of everything? Margaret do you think you should have a wee think about this first? The British Government's been looking after Irish problems for a long time and there seem to be more of them than when you originally started out. Maybe a little bit of Irish charm might sort it out.

Margaret: No! No! No! I will not tolerate . . .

Charlie: Now, now, Margaret, don't be getting yourself all worked up. Think of your poor husband. He's too old for this. Do you think, maybe if we gave them a couple of hundred tons of Kerrygold . . .

Margaret: No talks, no deals, no compromise, no surrender.

Charlie: Easy now, Margaret, easy, easy. What about a few hundred cases of Irish whiskey or a few thousand gallons of Guinness? Do you think that might do the trick? And Margaret while we are at it, you know the new house you are building? How about if we sent over a few labourers to lay the drive, build a few walls and a few observation posts? Sure it would be a grand place. And haven't the Irish been building English castles for centuries . . .

And so we continued, crazily demolishing the hours. Occasionally we might pick up some snippets of news from the guards' radio. This was eagerly transferred across the 'Great Divide' to our companions. On one such occasion we heard that the British representative at the United Nations had put forward a proposal that the Israeli Army should withdraw from the occupied area of Lebanon. The resolution was passed unanimously. Our hopes soared. We were convinced that this was directly related to our imprisonment. What more could these men hope to obtain from our respective governments? But we knew nothing would happen immediately. It would be weeks before any release could be effected. We were prepared to wait without expectation, allowing hope to carry us through. But another event was to quell this new hope.

It was late afternoon. The sudden noise of approaching guards made us alert. They often patrolled the passageway to ensure we were not looking out, but always one at a time. But now we heard several men approach. They spoke softly in English to someone. A deeper, more mature voice answered 'I'm okay.' The newcomer was locked into the cell next to ours. The prison was filling up, not emptying. The latest arrival made our numbers eight, of whom we could communicate with only three. That evening as the guards slept, our neighbour began knocking on the wall. We knocked back. It was enough. We knew that in the morning we could establish some communication with him via Tom and Terry. But we were wrong. For days the man in the next cell did not show his face. Fear and confusion, even more than the cell that held him, imprisoned him. We knocked a nightly reassurance to him and he returned it. Each of us in our separate cells tried tapping messages but they were incomprehensible. In the early hours of the third morning after our neighbour's arrival we heard him call out through the bars above his door. 'Is there anyone Lebanese here? I am Lebanese. There are thousands of us.'

The voice in those early hours was eerie, and so was the message it carried. Who could the thousands be? We had seen the pale skin of this man's feet and legs as we looked through the fan as he passed our door each day. How could he be Lebanese? But more worrying was his attempt to communicate aloud to us. We would all be punished if he was heard. The guards still came to talk with us occasionally. But always we were instructed to speak in whispers. We tried listening when we heard them entering the next cell. We picked up only a few words. But why was this Lebanese man always speaking English with an American accent? We knew from Tom and Terry that David Jacobsen, another American, was in the first cell on our side of the prison. He had been brought with them but after a few days he had been removed to a cell of his own.

Jacobsen, Anderson and Sutherland had spent a lot of time together since they had first been taken hostage. They had also shared cells with Ben Weir and Lawrence Jenco, two American clerics who they knew had been released. Sutherland and Anderson were sure that Jacobsen's separation from them had nothing to do with their personal relations. Perhaps he was being made ready for release or the group may have wanted him to make a video message. The guards who visited us never mentioned the other prisoners to us. Whatever brief conversation we had was always limited and always terminated with 'You want anything?' We had long since learned that no matter what we asked for, we rarely received it. But there was one guard who we often heard in the passageway but who as yet had never come into our cells nor spoken with us. We always knew when he was about. He would parade up and down imitating the sounds of the cartoon character 'The Road Runner'. 'Meep, beep, whoosh' would constantly echo throughout the prison. Other half-learned phrases from cartoon characters were added to his repertoire. The guard was called Said, as we were later to learn. He was the authority in the prison, a lower lieutenant in his group and extremist in his religious beliefs. He had a curious psychology. He told us some months later that he made these noises because he knew that in our condition we would find them frightening. It was strange reasoning, and as we were later to learn Said was a strange and frightening man.

Occasionally our complaints about the food worked, and sometimes we regretted our requests. Fresh fruit when we were given it still delighted us with its colour and texture more than its flavour. Most times, though, the fruit was ripe rather than fresh. The ripeness was a condition that made the fruit unsaleable. Passion fruit I came to hate with a passion. It was given to us often with the usual lunch of rice and some vegetable or other. One day I rolled the soft fruit through my hands. It was more interesting to play with than to eat. It had lost its firmness and its sheen. It felt like a lump of rubbery dough. I broke it open to bite into its soft flesh. The skin repelled me. I told myself it had vitamins I needed. The slithery softness of it made me gag. I swallowed it quickly. 'If these Muslims ate pork they'd probably feed their pigs better than us,' I gulped, throwing the remains of the fruit into our rubbish bag and wiping my wet stained fingers on my towel. 'There is as much passion in that piece of mush as there is in the dried up dugs of a witch's ditty.' I tried to bury my revulsion in language as foul as the fruit I had just eaten. 'Can you really imagine anything sexual about this?' I continued, tossing the other passion fruit into the rubbish. 'Well not with these particular fruit,' said John, holding his broken fruit before my face. 'They're full of maggots, look! And you just ate one of them.' He was already roaring with laughter before he had finished his sentence. I began to burst into vituperative abuse but the infection of John's laughter swept it from me. I joined him and laughed until it hurt.

Our laughter soon degenerated into a childish malice. 'Go ahead Brian, give the Americans a call and ask them if they enjoyed the fruit,' John suggested, his eyes laughing more than his face. I grinned in return. 'You filthy malicious bastard, you ask them. I wouldn't be able to keep my face straight,' I admitted, collapsing into laughter at the thought of what the Americans might reply. We were filled with comic impersonations of the Americans. That night we planned the next day's entertainment.

The following afternoon, as John signalled the question 'Did you enjoy lunch? How was the passion fruit?' I sat in the corner choking with laughter as John stood straining and giggling surreptitiously while translating the answer signalled back to him. 'Yes they enjoyed them. A little on the ripe side and a bit messy to eat, but a welcome change.' John could hardly hold himself upright. I was already prostrate on my mattress in torments of laughter.

This was only the first occasion that the Americans' misfortune caused us to collapse in laughter. Our silent conversations with Tom and Terry had told us that their cell was extremely damp. They had spent several mornings mopping up the pools of rainwater that seeped in. After several days of continual rain the Americans demanded to be moved to another cell. We watched through the fan as they were led to another room carrying their mattresses, bed covers and piss bottles. Dressed only in shorts they stumbled out in their blindfolds, tripping on their dragging blankets. It was a pathetic sight. For some reason the children's song *Three Blind Mice* came into my head. I hummed it as I watched the macabre procession. But my tune changed within the next half hour as I watched this same procession returning to the cell they had just vacated. This time I hummed *The Grand Old Duke of York*. We laughed cruelly at the senseless comedy that was being played out before us. We learned later just how black this comedy was.

Signalling to us, Terry Anderson explained that they had been taken to a small room. After the guards left them and they lifted their blindfolds to see where they were, they were shocked at what confronted them. The cell was filthy and alive with cockroaches. Terry Anderson lost control. He banged and banged on the door until the guards returned. With his nerves frayed and anger choking him he told them he was not an animal and would not live in such filth. 'Go ahead, why don't you shoot me. You enjoy killing Christians. Your religion permits you to kill. Go ahead, shoot me. I am just an animal to you people.' Such was the force of his despair that he challenged them and was fearless of the consequences.

I watched his face as he silently signalled to us an account of this confrontation. In that silent exchange I felt guilty at my mocking abuse of his misfortune. I also felt his despair in myself. It was true: we were treated like animals. But self-pity is a measure of defeat. One has to overcome it with humour or with anger. It had long been apparent that the men who kept us feared both: they were confused by our laughter, and our anger about our conditions made them guilty. The worst of them, unable to bear such guilt, turned aggressive. We were prisoners, therefore we were evil, and if they felt guilty about what they were doing they displaced it into anger. Soon their anger was to work itself out in violence.

Our silent hand signals across the prison passageway had become fewer as the weeks passed. There were weeks when nothing happened. We had nothing to talk about. Occasionally we would pass on odd snatches of news we had picked up on the radio. On other occasions we spoke of the guards, sharing our separate impressions of them.

Tom Sutherland had a particularly stressful time. They frequently accused him of being an agent of the CIA. Their hatred of this organization was intense and Tom took the brunt of it. Tom was a man who had spent all of his life in the teaching profession and nothing in his past experience had prepared him in any way to deal with the abuse that was now laid on him. Talking with us one day, signalling in the air, he informed us that the guards had proposed to the Americans that they be given a new cell. Tom was greatly distressed about this for it seemed to imply that they were to be separated into individual cells. Being alone is the most difficult situation to deal with as a hostage. Tom had not yet been held for any long periods on his own, and in the time he had spent with Terry Anderson he had become reliant on him. Both John and I tried to allay Tom's fears. But we knew that our jailers could do as they wished.

And then the dreaded day came. We were all unprepared for it. The usual routine of going to the toilet and being brought back changed suddenly. I sat one morning waiting for John to be returned from the daily ablutions. To my surprise the guards came back without him, telling me to come to the toilet. I wondered what had happened. It was normal for John to be taken and returned and then I would go after him. I walked along the passageway into the guards' room and then up the high step into the shower room and toilet. I searched the toilet for any sign of what might have happened. There was nothing. I thought perhaps they had simply taken John off for questioning. If they wanted to question anyone they normally took them off on their own. They would not be questioned in the presence of another prisoner. I took a leisurely shower, deciding that whatever had happened I would learn of it soon enough. I was led out from the shower and began my walk back to the cell. But as I slowly paced out my steps I was suddenly stopped and turned into the doorway of a cell which I normally passed on my return.

I entered. The guard stood behind me and whispered in my ear 'Look, look.' I raised up my blindfold to find myself in a double cell. This was the cell in which our American friends had been held. The wall separating it from the cell next door had been knocked out. Before me on the floor was a mattress with a brand-new light cotton bedcover. On the stone shelf was soap, a red toothbrush and to my surprise a bottle of eau-de-Cologne. I glanced into the other cell and saw John sitting, his blindfold still down over his eyes. The guard asked from behind 'You like? . . . You like?' I nodded, yes. How could anyone say they liked this place? The guards thought that we should be delighted with our new larger accommodation. With the new bedclothes and eau-de-Cologne we were being treated like kings. But to us it meant nothing. If you put a diamond collar on a dog it's still a dog, made more ludicrous by the diamonds around its neck. The guard patted my shoulder thinking he had performed me a great service and left. I sat down on the mattress and looked at John sitting in his cell. It was as if I was hypnotized. We sat in silence looking at one another. His cell and his bed and the accoutrements on the shelf beside him were an exact replica of my own. It was like looking at ourselves in a mirror.

John took no joy in our new accommodation. He was beginning to feel now as I had felt when they first brought us new clothes to wear. I had refused, knowing that those new clothes meant we were to be staying for a long time. John's sense of this new cell was that there was nothing awaiting us beyond the continuing monotony of this place. The thought struck us both at the same time: what had happened to the Americans? We dared not look out through the grille while the guards were walking about, taking the other prisoners to and from the shower. There would be time enough after everyone had been brought back and locked up to see if we could still communicate with our friends. 'Poor old Tom,' John said, 'he's not going to find it easy being on his own.' I nodded but there was nothing more to be said. I did not want to think about Tom's situation or to dwell too much on that isolation, which both John and I had experienced when first captured.

Later that afternoon, when everyone had been returned to the cells and the guards had retired to their own room, we thought it safe to look to see where everyone was.

Tom Sutherland's face peered from behind the grille of the cell that John and I had recently occupied. He signalled to us that Terry was in the cell next to us. As we began our slow hand-talking a face appeared in the cell next to Tom Sutherland's. It was Frank Reed, another American – the man who had been brought some weeks before, and with whom we had exchanged knocks on the wall. Tom was already despairing. He did not know how he would be able to manage on his own. We knew he was afraid of the guards. He had previously been badly treated and now felt greatly threatened. We could only talk with Terry by passing our message across to Tom and Tom passing it back to Terry. These conversations naturally took longer. But both John and I knew that we had to keep contact with the others. If it were us in their situation we would desperately need this silent communication. The next few days we spent teaching Frank the rudiments of our hand-language. Once he had grasped enough of it he was able to tell us about himself and his life in Lebanon and how he had been kidnapped.

Frank was able to confirm what I had suspected, that Leigh Douglas and Philip Padfield had indeed been executed. At first we were unsure what this would mean for us. We sat and talked about it, whispering quietly in the darkness. John and I both acknowledged that the death of these British men had serious implications for ourselves. It told us quite clearly that our captors would have no hesitation in executing who they wanted, when they wanted.

We made a point now of communicating daily backwards and forwards across the cell passageway with Tom and Frank. They in their turn would pass the message to Terry in the cell beside us. But these conversations were too tedious. The longer they took the more dangerous they became for us. It was necessary, we all agreed, for us to re-establish our mail service. For these men now in solitary confinement such communication was essential. As before, we scratched out notes or even jokes on pieces of silver cigarette paper with a match for a pen. They were delivered in the old way and collected the next day. Tom, because of his past experience with the guards, felt unable to collect any messages that were left for him. Consequently someone had to pick up the message, bring it back to their own cell and then send the message by hand-signal across to him. We also discovered that there was another prisoner next to Tom. We only saw his face twice. He never noticed us looking at him or waving, trying to attract him. But he was a Korean diplomat who had been taken some few days before the disappearance of the two murdered Englishmen. For the rest of our time in this prison he sat alone on his mattress. We never saw his face again, only his feet as he walked past our cell each morning.

Frank Reed, the most recent arrival, engaged our attention. He was a new face, and with that new face came new stories. As the days progressed we became somewhat anxious about Frank. Whether it was the shock of being taken captive, whether it was the result of so many weeks alone it would be hard to say, but Frank's stories sometimes seemed outrageous. There is a kind of distortion of self-image which takes possession of a man subject to long periods of isolation. Frank eagerly informed us that he would soon be going home, that he had many important friends in the Lebanese government. We listened and made sarcastic remarks to one another about Frank's confidence in his own importance. We had all learned the lesson that no-one was important in this situation. All men were equal and equally liable to end up dead if that was the will of those who kept us. The Lebanese government meant nothing to these men. Their allegiances lay in a very different direction, to God and to the Iranian Republic. The Lebanese government was unable to ensure our safety, much less our release. Yet Frank remained convinced that he would be going home soon. He would be the first to be released. His insistence on this at first bored us and then made us angry. But we tempered these feelings, remembering the kind of irrationality that we had both experienced in similar ways.

During our first weeks of captivity each of us had undergone a process of denial of the reality we were trapped in; continually we minimized our situation and in so doing inflated our self-importance. We, like Frank, believed absolutely the lies we had concocted about our own importance.

My anger at Frank was more because he had exposed to me that weakness and delusion that was so much part of that early period of captivity; I wanted to turn away from it; I did not want to acknowledge that weakness in myself.

Frank had become me and I could not bear to look at the mirror image of myself.

Late one evening, a fan rattled. It was a signal that someone wanted to talk. We stood up and looked out through the grille to see what eyes met ours. They were Frank's. He was excited and very distressed. He told us how some of the guards had come and prayed outside his prison cell. He knew that he was going to be shot. We tried to calm his fears but our silent finger-talk was meaningless to him. He was caught up in the idea of his own execution. Anxiously he told us to tell his wife and young son whatever happened. We tried again and again to tell him that it meant nothing that the guards prayed outside his cell door. But he would not be calmed.

Another day he told us how the guards had come and had told him that they were going to shoot his wife and son. This for him was further confirmation that his own death was near. We became more certain that he was suffering from paranoia and was full of the sorts of undiscovered fears that rise up in a great rush and fill the mind beyond the control of reason. On other days Frank told us how the guards had come in with whips and beaten him. They had tried to torture him with wires connected to a car battery. We sometimes tried to make a joke, telling him to be careful, and not to give in to such wild imaginings. It was impossible to instil some reassurance or comfort in him across that wide silent passageway. We all need the reassurance of a human voice and the touch of another human to make those words of comfort meaningful and real. The silent hand-talk we shared was inadequate for this purpose.

Each of us had travelled the road that Frank now found himself on. Frank's suffering was not unique to him even now. In the cell next to his we would see Tom Sutherland's distraught face. He found being alone difficult. There were no books, no games to play. I would look every day at these two men and see the face of one man desperate with thoughts of his imminent execution and the face of another man sunk in despair. I began to feel that here were not men's faces but masks of madness, and as I watched their hands feebly spelling out their anguish, I felt myself becoming angry. For it was as if their own distress was a kind of contamination running rampant around the prison. It beat around the walls of my own cell, like those blind birds I had known in my own long period of isolation. Their despair, their fear came crashing in on me and I wanted no part of it.

Occasionally I sank back on my mattress and condemned these men for giving vent to their frustrations and confusions, offloading them onto me when I could hardly deal with my own. Then I would feel the hot flush of guilt at my lack of compassion and my own self-interest. I saw shadows of myself in their anguish. I raged at the futility of trying to signal messages to a man who was desperately trying to kill himself.

How can one make shapes in the air to convince a man that his own death would be a death of part of each of us? That he had no right to ask us to participate in his death? We would all be maimed by it, even in freedom. But I myself had on occasions thought the same thoughts, juggling with the desire to kill myself. My own experience taught me that in such a situation each of us dies many times. But if we can take hold of that moment of death, we go beyond it and pass into a fuller life.

On many mornings I would hear Terry Anderson praying in his cell. He always began by thanking God for the day that had been given him. I remember one day Terry, full perhaps of despair and anger, sat banging his head repeatedly against the wall. The claw of despair and insanity reaches deep down into the very bowels of a man and wrenches all life from him.

These were hellish days for all of us because in that silence each of us shared and partook in each other's suffering. We breathed in great lungfuls of it, and had to regurgitate the foulness of it and find some way to protect ourselves from it: in so doing, hopefully protecting those who had become engulfed in it.

The only thing in our prison cells with which a man might end his life was the plastic bag which we were given every day for rubbish and the remains of food. I thought often of a man lying alone in that tiny emptiness, so full with black imaginings. How could he take a plastic bag and place it over his head and block off all air from it and lie and hold it there and hope that he might soon die? It was not possible. Surely everything in the body and in the mind and spirit of a man would rebel against such a thing.

The fury of life is always stronger than the compulsion of death. From somewhere John remembered an old axiom as the means by which we sought to forge our way out of this hell-hole: 'Exercise, the companionship of friends and above these the gift of the spirit which is divine' became for me and my friend John an oft-quoted phrase in which we would lay a claim to life. We had the companionship of friends in each other, outside our cell we had other friends. We each felt we had come to know, with meaning and real purpose, the gift of the spirit. Because we had found that gift understood by another person, it became more real.

Exercise, which had for so long been denied us in our tiny cell, we could take up again in our new double cell. As before, in those marathon games of dominoes, we insisted on maintaining a fierce competitiveness. It didn't matter that the room was only twelve by six feet. To us it was panoramic. Every day we would walk around this space, each trying to gauge the miles and always trying to better the previous day's walk. It was the same with the press-ups and squats that we devised for this small area. They were fierce and demanding; we constantly pressurized each other as we tried to outdo each other's best efforts.

By this we could energize the mind and move it out of maudlin preoccupation. It was refreshing and life-giving. On other days, we would attempt to race around this small space hurling ourselves in a half-demented fury against the four walls, deliriously crashing into them. Sweating and panting like two retrievers, after some ten minutes of this lunacy we would throw ourselves down exhausted, giggling with laughter. We were children playing games. In his foolishness, John, as he raced around, would slap his backside pretending to be riding a horse. On other days we raced around the cell because the cold and dampness of the place had driven us to it. The cold white tiles exaggerated the numb atmosphere inside. But running for warmth was less enjoyable. As always John injected some humour. Strutting the cell and flexing his wasted muscles, he would act out some humorous caricature. Like a drill sergeant on a parade ground, he would bark at me: 'Right you puny little Irishman, I am going to show you what a real man is made of,' and with this he would press his bare chest against the wet freezing wall and to complete the performance would drop his shorts and plant his backside onto the same freezing tiles.

We would imitate different characters as we played, or more frequently we would create characters out of our imagination. With these characters we entertained ourselves for many hours. Through them we brought other people into the cell to be with us, to talk to us or to make us laugh. In that laughter we discovered something of what life really is. We were convinced by the conditions we were kept in and the lives that we managed to lead that if there was a God that God was, above all else, a comedian. In humour, sometimes hysterical, sometimes calculated, often childish, life was returned to us.

However, on each occasion that we found ourselves rising above the grinding monotony, something happened to warn us that reality is not always comic.

Exile

(Dedicated to Brian)

A fragment of sky alone remains
The troubled memory of an Ulster day,
Poised between black-fissured rock and violent sea
Where high above the Causeway's serrated edge
A seagull lost in flight
Endured alone the wind's adversity.

It had fallen from the chaos of the air
In exultation or in pain,
Plummeted downward, searching the perilous rock
Hoping to regain the narrow cleft
That was its home.

Surrendering its solitude
Paddling the air with ungainly feet
It strove against the wind, struggling to touch
The cliffs beneath.
And yet, each time it neared, each time bird
And land appeared to meet,
The wind's malicious hand cast it back
Into frenzied sky,
Barring it from the indifferent shore.

Absorbed by the clownish heroism of its flight,
I watched through an afternoon, that seemed
Suspended in the tangled intricacy of
Wing and wave,
Until, mangled between foam and sky,
Seeking always the comfort of its befouled nest,
It sank beneath my sight, borne down by its
Salt-sodden breast.

No Yeatsian elegance certainly,
No swan-like wing outstretched upon the night,
And yet, like all impoverished birds of air
This too a symbol in its own right,
A metaphor for a rock-nurtured man,
Dreaming of a wind-lashed, bitter land
Not a land of 'saints and scholars' in which the heart
Can find its ease,
But a land from which the wind-crazed eye
Can watch the desolation of the seas.

Trevor Magee

The Great White Safari

We were still sending messages and signalling conversations. One day we had just finished sending a message to Tom and sat down to begin our game of dominoes. We heard a cell door open. I quickly scuttled to the fan and lying on my chest saw Tom being brought out. It was late afternoon. Tom walked past our door and was led to the guards' room. A voice abruptly ordered him to wait. For some moments there was silence, then suddenly the radio was turned up to full volume. Western pop music flooded into our silent prison. We were perplexed. Western music was forbidden to these Islamic warriors. John positioned himself near the door, pressing his ear against it. 'What's happening?' I asked. John hissed me to be quiet. Dire Straits' 'Sultans of Swing' filled the cell. Behind the music, we heard the sounds of a man being beaten. This was the first time since we had been together that we had heard that dreadful sound. We could only sit in silence and try to block out the sounds of the blows landing on naked flesh and the smothered moans of a man in pain. We tried to continue our game, but our black comedy had become blacker and the 'Sultans of Swing' took on a horrible significance. We sat and listened until it was over. Tom was shuffled back to his lonely cell.

We sat in frozen silence. There was nothing to say. Nothing could change what had happened. We knew that now beating had begun, it would continue. The silence was broken only by our commiserations. 'Poor old bastard, hope he is all right,' and then the sympathy was joined by foul-mouthed abuse. 'Those stinking pieces of dogshit. Why did they have to pick on Tom?'

We allowed a half-hour to pass then rattled the fan to try and communicate with our friend. No face appeared. We rattled again and looked. Still no face. 'Perhaps it's better to leave him alone for the evening.' Neither of us wanted to signal a conversation. But both of us felt the need to reach out and touch this man in the only way we could. It struck home to me then that when we participate in another person's suffering, we in part heal ourselves. We needed some way to dispel the alarm and fear that was beginning to take hold of us. We had been suddenly wrenched out of our laughter and security. We needed the reassurance that talking to Tom might provide.

The next day, after the washing patrol was completed and the guards returned for their daily dose of TV, we signalled again and stood up to see our friend. Even had he wanted to return our call, he could not. They had placed a metal flap over the grille through which we could see each other. Tom was now in complete darkness, without means of communication with anyone. He was to remain in that dark hole for seven days.

The face that emerged after the week had passed was one which I found it painful to look at. It was waxen and withdrawn, as if some cold fingers had moulded this dreadful face in wet clay and left it fixed. All animation had gone from it. Looking into Tom's dull eyes was like looking into emptiness itself. It seemed all life had been extinguished in him during those long black hours. It was hard to draw him into conversation. I can still see, even now, his fingers signalling out the words 'I can't take any more of this.' Slowly, falteringly, he told us in silent finger-talk that the guards had seen him looking over towards our cell and thought that he had been spying on them. They had taken him to the guards' room and there four of them tied him up and beat him with what he thought was some kind of rubber hose. For a week he had to eat in the dark, not seeing the food before him and only knowing what dish it was by the taste of it in his mouth. The punishment of that black week was greater than the physical beating he had undergone. In those empty eyes and in that fixed coldness of his features I read anew a kind of pain that is beyond any physical hurt. Tom was again hopelessly talking of suicide and we tried to talk him out of such thoughts. We told him how, though we had not been able to see him, our thoughts were always with him and we had prayed continually for him. We talked to him of his family, his wife, his three daughters. We tried to talk to him of what he would do when he was released to make him believe that this ordeal would not be permanent and that it would come to an end. My conversation as I silently fingered the words across to him was made half garbled by the terrible despair that was etched into every feature of that empty face. Slowly as the days passed some small spark of life began to come back into his vacant eyes.

The week of blackness and isolation behind the closed grille that Tom had gone through was to be endured by all of us.

But not as punishment for looking out of our cells. Whatever power was piped into this prison, whatever light we had to eat and wash by was suddenly taken from us. The prison generator either broke down or was switched off for some nine days.

It was not an unusual occurrence for us to be in darkness for a day or two. The first few days of this black-out we tolerated, having had to cope on several occasions already. As time dragged on into the fifth day the strain on each of us was beginning to tell. We persuaded our guards to give us small pieces of candle to eat by. But such was the size of these candles that we could not afford to light them for any purpose other than eating. Long hours of constant darkness seemed, even with the companionship of John, to be a kind of action replay of our first captivity. John found this period particularly distressing. In the darkness we each knew the other was there but we could only hear whispering disembodied voices as we tried to talk away the darkness. When we tried to sit close to one another we could not see but only feel each other. The nights were like the days, and only the regime of meal-times told us that it was morning or evening. The evening cup of tea told us that it was time to sleep.

But for John there was no sleep to be had. This darkness brought with it the night creatures that he found so hard to deal with. Often as I lay trying to sleep I would hear John's excited voice whisper 'Brian, Brian, wake up, wake up, there's something in the cell, there's something in the cell,' and I would hear it. Those huge cockroaches were scratching and crawling their way about the cell and we could not see them. Mice often came in. With the electricity off, the fan that turned in our door to circulate the air had stopped. This provided an opening for these night creatures to enter our cell and crawl unseen over our beds and the floor beside us. At John's insistence I would get up, light the tiny stub of candle and begin to search our prison cell to find some offending creature which, though tiny, to us had become a tormenting monster. For hours we would lie there, trying to sleep, having found the creature and killed it. But there was no sleep for we were tense with listening for another scratching sound, the scuttling of mice or what we most dreaded, rats. The noises in that black silence were magnified in our imagination. Always in the darkness the mind finds free passage to the most awful places. Even though we knew that small mice were harmless their constant presence and the noise of them running about seemed to worsen the sense of terror and absolute subjection in this long night. With what light we had, we tore up pieces of blanket or of tissue paper to block the holes through which these creatures streamed, but it was never enough. Within hours of building these barricades we would hear the scratching and crawling animals in our private blackness.

On one occasion after we had been trying to sleep for some hours, John anxiously woke me. 'Quick, get up, there's something in the cell, quick, get up, get up,' and again we lit the candle stub and began our hunt. These hours we called the 'Great White Safaris', as we hunted in every corner lifting mattresses and blankets, searching out the beast. Finding nothing, John looked over at me and I at him. I saw for a moment his face beginning to break up. He was on the edge of nervous tears. His face spasming as he spat out at me, filled with vehemence, 'They're probably breeding under your bed, you filthy Irish bastard,' and I looked at him and realized how stressful this darkness had become for him. Quietly and calmly I spoke the words that his mother had spoken to his father when his father got angry about something. 'Now, now, we are getting very paddy today, aren't we John?' His eyes caught mine and all the fear and stress seemed to wash out of him, and he smiled, remembering his mother saying it so lovingly to his father.

The first mouse we caught was a pathetic creature. We stumbled in the darkness chasing it with our tiny candle, sometimes leaping in the air with fright as it dashed towards our feet, laughing nervously until finally we trapped it in a corner. It sat and looked up at us. In that moment both of us felt a kind of pity, knowing we were about to kill it. We tried to shoo the mouse out of the cell but it would not go. We watched it flash up the wall and we hoped we could push it out the grille but as it tried to scale that six-foot door it fell back. We knew we could not bear this living creature scuttling in the dark about us and yet we both felt that we could not kill it. It somehow mirrored our own fear and our own pathetic condition. It dashed in under John's mattress and slowly we lifted it. It sat almost on its hind legs as if to beg. What we were about to do was an offence against everything we had come to believe in. How could we take this life? John excitedly said 'Kill it, kill it,' grabbing at the bottle with which we hoped at least to knock it senseless. In that moment some animal savagery in him welled up and was suddenly gone again. I leaned forward as the mouse squatted, looking up at me. Before the blow descended I heard it scream in fear and I almost held back.

It was dead. Picking it up delicately by the tail I deposited it in our bag of rubbish and lay back sweating with tension. I felt a huge guilt and compassion and ugliness in myself. I wondered if that tiny pathetic creature had known what was about to happen? Do all creatures know the moment of death before it claims them?

Having set out so often on these Great White Safaris we became immune to the slaughter and as we chased these creatures in the dark we found ourselves laughing again. It was a diversion from the pressure of so constant a darkness. As we tried to fill that darkness with stories, songs or sometimes with jokes the strain and effort of trying to block it out with words exhausted us. On these hunts we giggled and we killed our prey with sometimes brutal savagery.

We recalled our time in the place we called Abed's Hotel. The guards had woken in the middle of the night and we heard them rummage around their room. They were laughing, they were shouting, chairs were being lifted, tables overturned and we wondered what was happening. For hours those two men seemed to be wrecking the building. Then we heard gunfire and more laughter but could not fathom what was happening until the morning, when the guard Abed brought us breakfast. He explained that there had been a mouse in their room and they had been trying to find it. Was their terror so great that they needed a Kalashnikov to shoot this little rodent? We asked 'Did you shoot it?' to which Abed replied that they had tried but that it moved too fast. 'Did you kill it?' we continued to press him. 'Yes,' he said, and began laughing loudly as he explained how they had eventually destroyed the mouse. They took a syringe and filled it with pure alcohol. Having cornered the creature they had soaked it, squirting the alcohol from the syringe. Then with much glee they had thrust lighted matches into the area and watched it burst into flames, incinerating the mouse in an instant. We laughed at these 'terrorists' who fearlessly hunted mice with Kalashnikovs. We thought how malicious was the mind that would destroy a creature in such a way. Abed's delight as he told his story had the sadistic feel of a cartoon about it. I suppose we felt ourselves quite brave hunting around in the darkness destroying these animals with blows from a plastic bottle.

On another occasion, in another of our prisons one of the guards brought us a mouse which he had trapped, and held it under my nose. I looked and watched it feebly trying to struggle out of the thick layer of stickiness that had trapped it. It could not move its feet. I watched the muscle and bone in the body struggling, trying to extricate itself. The guard was laughing delightedly and I just felt pity for it. I choked back the rising emotion and shook my head, to the guard's surprise. 'Why . . . why you shake?' he demanded. I sat in silence, my pity becoming anger. By this time that glue had became the chains on my own feet and I wanted so much to spit out into his face that his savagery was an obscenity. I wanted to explain to him how that trapped, struggling, crying creature was myself. I knew he would never understand and knew that he could feel no empathy for it or me. Any such response was not a part of what that man knew or felt for us. To him, we were his night creatures to be abused or beaten as fancy took him. My thoughts on that occasion would become literal truth before too long.

As the days of absolute darkness continued we thought that we could not endure much more. Yet something in the human spirit seeks a way to overcome such oppression. There is always something in us that will not submit. In the after-dinner candlelight I reached under my mattress and took out a sheet of the silver cigarette paper that we had been keeping for messages. From inside the mattress I pulled out a stem of candle that we had been trying to save and began slowly and carefully to roll the silver cigarette paper round the length of the candle. John watched me, curious and silent. I looked at him and winked in the candlelight, continuing my delicate operation. Having rolled the silver paper round the candle I melted some wax and dropped it into the seam of the silver tube, sealing it. I pulled this silver sheath off the candle and lifted it up to my eye, peering through it at John sitting opposite. I then tore off a piece of cigarette-packet cardboard and took some threads from my bedcover. I sat in the candlelight and began plaiting them into a single string. With the three pieces of string plaited together I made a tiny hole in the small square of the cardboard and passed the string through, tying a knot in the end preventing it from passing through the hole. John was watching me closely.

I sat in silence, refusing to explain to him what I was doing, teasing his curiosity. 'I thought you were making a skipping rope for a moment,' he said. I smiled back. 'No, John-boy, something far more complicated and far more necessary.' He looked at the piece of card and string in my hands and the silver tube. 'Interesting old fellow,' he said simply. I reached my hand back again inside the torn pillow and extracted chunks of melted candle wax that I had been accumulating over the days of darkness. John's fascination deepened. 'You're a great horder of rubbish, Brian.' Quickly I broke the pieces of melted wax into tiny fragments, and collected them together on my stone shelf. I lifted the plaited pieces of thread and ran them along the pool of wax gathering on our lighted candle. The molten wax seeped into the plaited thread. I held it at each end, blowing on it until the wax had congealed and the piece of string became rigid. This piece of string was passed through the tube of silver paper, blocked off now at one end by the piece of cardboard that was attached to the rigid string. Slowly and carefully I began dropping the pieces of candle wax down the tube of silver paper.

'I'm just beginning to understand how your devious mind is working, Keenan,' John said slowly and I laughed, beaming widely. With the tube packed tight with these crumbs of candle wax and the end of the plaited thread sticking out through them, my task was complete. 'Abracadabra, the ignorant Irishman does it again; magic, just simple magic,' I said holding up my improvised but complete candle. John crawled over to me. 'Mmm . . . very smart, much smarter than I thought you were, Keenan, but will it work?' and I laughed again. 'Of course, you apathetic Englishman, anything I do works.' 'Go on then,' he said. 'Light the fucker.' Delicately I lifted our lighted candle and touched the flame of it against the plaited thread which was now serving as a wick. It rose in flame and as it burned down began melting the broken and crumbled pieces of candle wax packed tight in the silver tube. It burned brightly. We sat and stared at it, hypnotized by the flame and glinting silver. At last we had our light. Quietly, calmly a sense of victory welled up in me and I thought to myself without saying it 'Fuck them, they haven't beat us yet. We can blot out even their darkness.'

The days that followed were spent plaiting threads and making wicks for our improvised candles. Furiously we grubbed about the cell scraping off the pieces of candle wax that had accrued over the time we spent eating in the dark. We began crumbling them and storing them. It was wise not to have a store of such improvised candles but to have the materials at hand. John had astutely begged for and been given a small battered tin ashtray. We now used this same ashtray for melting the crumbled wax and pouring it into the silver tubes. The hours we spent making these candles diminished the terror and monotony of this black timelessness.

Now we could exercise again and slowly we walked around this candle planted in the centre of the floor in a kind of ritual trance of silence. The candle flame seemed to still and calm the mind on those long silent walks. In that soft half-light we would imagine ourselves walking in some favourite place. Occasionally, taking it in turns, we would describe it to each other. Perhaps along a riverside, sometimes walking along a windswept beach or occasionally climbing up some hill that had been a childhood place of adventure.

On one of these walks pacing slowly around the single candle, John calmly asked me 'Do you know I am a Count of the Holy Roman Empire?' I walked along behind him and thought about this. I knew by the manner in which he had addressed me that this was not a piece of John's lunacy. 'You're what?' 'I'm a Count of the Holy Roman Empire,' John said, with some pride swelling his words. Still calmly and slowly pacing along behind him, I said 'You're off your half-empty head, my son.' John stopped, turned around and with the same pride and comic arrogance said 'No, really it's true, I am a Count of the Holy Roman Empire, and furthermore,' he continued, 'you pathetic little piece of nothingness, I think you should begin addressing me as befits my station.' 'I'll station my foot up your backside McCarthy, if you don't start talking some sense.' We both began laughing, feeling that tide of comic and foul abuse welling up. We loved this game. It was like fencing with wooden sticks. But it was competitive and fierce and we found phrases and words and long sentences of the most elaborate invective thrusting out from us, driving us deeper into laughter. 'My dear dog-eared and dopey-dick,' John spat out at me, 'that is not the way in which you should be addressing me in light of what I have just told you.' 'I'll address you with a urine shower if you don't cut this out.'

We were laughing again and this time we stopped and sat down. John explained how his brother, who worked as a Queen's Herald, had examined the history of the family. With a great show of enthusiasm and pride John claimed his descent from the McCarthys of County Kerry and how one of them had at some point in their history been dubbed a Count of what was then the Holy Roman Empire. I listened and was as fascinated as John had been at my stories of Belfast. As he finished this long saga I admitted that I did believe him. I turned to him, looking him straight in the face and with a cheeky grin affirmed to him 'I'll tell you one more thing you are, John.' He raised his eyes. 'You're a shilling-taking shithead.'

He began laughing again. 'What do you mean, my old son?' he asked. I explained to him how with his origins in the McCarthy clan in County Kerry, his now proudly held English Protestant citizenship made him a type of turncoat. 'You've taken the Queen's shilling . . . You went fleeing out of Ireland when times were tough, took the Queen's shilling, changed your faith and now look where it's got you. That will teach you to sell your heritage for a mess of porridge.' He was laughing and I saw him studiously take on board this new term, 'shilling-taker'. 'Shilling-taker,' he said, trying to get my Belfast accent. 'Shilling-taker.' We were both pleased and delighted with this new term that had entered into our repertoire and would remain a constant source of abuse and of affection.

When we were not engaged in our marathon domino games or our candle-making or our discussion of John's ancestry we found ourselves talking of how men could do such things as had been done to us. What was in a man that allowed him to lock up another human being for long periods of total darkness – a human being he did not know or understand, who had given him no offence, nor committed any crime against him. We could never answer the questions we asked ourselves. But as we talked and tried to understand how these men could ever justify their actions, I recall saying to John 'I understand it, I accept it, even though I do not condone it . . . I think I understand it.' John looked back at me, puzzled, and quick as a flash I said to him 'Well in another sense now you know what it is like to be Irish.' He knew what I was hinting at, for so many people in the history of Ireland had lost their lives or liberty and now here was this English man undergoing something of the agony that people were still suffering in English jails.

Another morning came. I lay in the dark silence waiting for my friend to wake, and thought back on the sleepless night I had undergone. Half asleep but with my mind working overtime I had suddenly opened my eyes, and stared into the blackness, listening to the silence made louder by the darkness around me. For a moment I thought how do I know I am alive? I felt my skin and felt my face and it gave me no assurance. I could have died in the night. I might be dead now. Do even the dead imagine living? I see nothing and hear nothing and feel only my flesh. What does it tell me? This kind of self-indulgent introspection fascinated me, yet made me wary. Was my mind so empty? Was I left only with this futile curiosity? For some minutes I lay and thought again about what happens when there is nothing more to think about. Do I reach the edge, and feeling the intoxication of its darkness, throw myself hungrily into it? Would a mind so completely empty feel any pain?

I struggled to convince myself that by thinking such thoughts my mind was not empty. Even if it was approaching a vacuum these questions denied that there ever was or ever could be a real emptiness of mind. I somehow convinced myself that, in some way that I could not explain, the mind could never become a void. I repeated these words lest that insidious panic should take hold again. The mind is endless. There is no vacuum in the mind.

I heard John wake and quickly seized the opportunity to move myself out from this obsessive introspection. 'Good morning, your Eminence. What may I order you for breakfast today?'

It was later that day, as we sat huddled beside our home-made candle playing our usual dominoes, that the light suddenly, blindingly returned. We both started up, dazzled. We looked at one another and held one another's stare and then both simultaneously jumped up raising our hands in the air, jumping around in circles. The light was back on! 'How many days do you think it's been, John?' Looking at him now in the full light, wondering strangely had he changed any. 'I don't really know,' he answered. 'Seven, eight days, now that I think of it it's hard to remember.'

But this surprise of light was to be topped by something which made this place we called the House of Fun funnier and more insane than we could ever have imagined. Days passed with their usual monotony. But then one day we heard the guards coming to unlock the cell. As usual we pulled the blindfolds down. We were both given new shorts and new T-shirts and told to dress. The cell closed and we looked at each other, puzzled. 'I am sure we can't be going anywhere, not in this get-up anyway. What can it mean?' John asked. I simply shrugged. 'It doesn't really matter,' I said: 'At least it's good to have them, the elastic has gone out of my shorts and I have to tie them in a knot to hold them up they've had so many washes, but they are more often around my ankles than around my ass.' Without further conversation we changed and sat down thinking nothing more would happen that day.

We had guessed wrong and the key was turning in the padlock

again. 'Come, come' a voice said to John and I heard him lift himself off his mattress and walk out into the passage. The door closed and I waited. After some minutes I was also walked to the guards' room. It was our habit to tie the blindfold loosely so that we could look down underneath it at our feet as we walked. Now as we stood in the guards' room I looked down and saw spread out on the floor the edge of a new bed cover. The creases were still in it and sitting on top were bowls of fruit and nuts, oranges and apples. I tried to turn my head slowly to take in the area several feet around me and caught sight of other bowls with similar fruit and nuts laid out around the perimeter of this bedspread stretched on the floor. Two hands gently pushed my shoulders. 'Sit, sit' a voice said quietly and I sat down. I could hear John's voice across from me say something to one of the guards. 'What is this?' he was asking. We both feigned surprise for we knew what it was.

It was John's birthday. These terrorists were giving him a birthday party. One of the guards switched on a cassette player playing some piece of classical music and a few other guards arrived and talked excitedly amongst themselves. Then we heard the voice of the officer Said. He seemed angry and switched off the cassette. For this zealot, music was absolutely forbidden. With much enthusiasm we passed the next ten minutes eating our nuts and some fruit and then great slabs of birthday cake were set before us. We ate and tried to speak with the guards who were sharing our birthday meal. I tried to visualize the situation: here were five or six men with guns in their waist bands and Kalashnikovs stashed against the wall, sitting here eating this food, trying to talk normally with us as we sat blindfolded, fumbling with the food that we could not see properly, trying to peel the fruit or to break the shell from the nuts. The House of Fun was restored to its lunacy and the black comedy was began again. John must have been reading my mind. From across the birthday feast I heard him politely ask 'Excuse me, do you think I could have a photograph of this?'

Said, the officer, barked some order and into this bizarre scene there came a chorus of Arab voices singing a discordant harmony of 'Happy Birthday, Happy Birthday, Happy Birthday John, Happy Birthday John.' Our laughter was nervous and forced, though we felt unafraid. This would take some time to come to terms with. When we had finished the meal and washed it down with a cup of Pepsi we were raised from the floor. A handful of nuts and some boiled sweets were placed in our hands and I began my walk back to the cell. The door closed behind me and I sat waiting in confusion for John. I expected him to be brought in immediately after me, but I was left to wait for fifteen or twenty minutes before I heard the door opening and John entering.

I lifted my blindfold and John standing above me raised his. 'Okay, birthday boy,' I said 'what else did you get?' John raised his eyes and his outstretched hands in a very typical Arab manner. He answered 'You're not going to believe this, you're just not going to believe what this bunch of fruitcakes have just tried to do.' I waited for him to continue. 'Well then come on, spit it out, what happened?' I asked. John began to explain and as his story unfolded my laughter unfolded with it. 'They took me a little way down the passage, then spread a blanket on the floor and told me to lie down. I tell you, Brian, I was a bit panicky . . . I lay down on my back and Said said to me "Don't worry, nothing bad, nothing bad happen . . ." I wasn't too sure about nothing bad going to happen . . . I'll be honest, Brian, for a moment I thought these bastards were going to sexually abuse me.' At that statement I stopped laughing for a moment and quickly said to him 'You must be joking, who would want to sexually abuse a piece of rubbish like you!' He smiled and continued his story.

'I just lay there, I didn't know what these cretins were going to do. Next thing I heard all the guards come around me. Said was giving orders and I didn't know what the hell was going on. Then I felt their hands reach under my legs, my backside, then hands on my back and at the back of my head as I lay there. I was beginning to panic I can tell you. Then they started humming something and then they started laughing and Said started shouting and they were quiet for a while with their hands under me and then they were all laughing again. I don't know what I was feeling at that time but I just wanted to get away from those crazy creeps.' 'Well, what was it all about then?' 'You won't believe it, you just will not believe this.' 'Come on, John, stop fucking around and tell me.' 'Well it's simple,' he answered. 'They were trying to levitate me.'

I looked at him dumbfounded. 'They were trying to what?' 'I told you you wouldn't believe it. They were trying to levitate me.' I rolled back on my mattress, the laughter choking me. 'Did it work, John-boy?' 'Did it hell,' he answered. I was laughing again. 'Well I suppose you can always tell your grandchildren that you were levitated on your birthday by a bunch of Arab gunmen.' 'No-one would believe it,' he said dolefully. 'You bet,' I said. 'The inmates of the asylum are the keepers of the sane.'

The return of the electricity and the birthday party had somehow endeared us to these men. In the days that were to follow they would frequently come into our cell and try to talk, and seeing us play dominoes they would join the game. Said, the prison chief, who had beaten me so badly over my refusal to be shaved, now visited us often. He would play dominoes and cheated outrageously. We knew even with our blindfolds that he was looking at the pieces we had in our hands. For Said it was important to win. We knew his cheating and laughed at its outrageousness. Yet this man who walked around the prison making noises and imitating cartoon creatures, in the belief that we were frightened by them, sat and played dominoes with us. The first time that he came he sat for almost an hour with his arm around my shoulder. It was as if I was his brother or long-lost friend. I knew that this action, sitting, almost nursing me or holding me in an embrace, was occasioned by a fierce kind of guilt. There was no other reason why he should display such affection.

For some reason the return of the light had prompted our captors to move the prisoners around. Frank was now brought from the cell opposite and put into the cell beside us, next to the guards' room. Terry was moved across into Tom's cell, and Tom moved into Frank's. The reason for these shifts we did not understand, but they later led to an event which was to remind us that beneath this idiocy and seeming friendliness cruelty was lurking, primed and always ready to be released. We knew from Frank's signalled conversations with us that he had become a Muslim, enabling him to marry his Syrian fiancée. The guards had somehow learned of this and one of them visited him frequently with the Koran and talked with him about its contents, though we could not hear their conversation clearly.

Terry Anderson had been remonstrating with Said for a Bible to be given to us. His persistence had been fruitful and two Bibles were brought, one for John and me, and another one circulating around the three Americans. The blood and gore of the Old Testament stories horrified me and I sometimes wondered how far the men who held us were removed from the mentality of those vengeful days.

John and I both found great solace in reading the Psalms. The anguished suffering mind that had created them and had cried out to God in his suffering reflected much of our own condition. Exhausted with profound questions and never finding an answer, we took relief in devotional moments. It seemed we could meditate on the active nature and qualities of what this God of love could mean in human terms. The gentle eroticism of the Song of Songs delighted me and I read it over and over. The Book of Revelation held me mystified with its elaborate language and symbolism.

It was sometimes disturbing to overhear a man in the next cell pray, speaking only of his own worthiness and his own importance and telling God why God should set him free. Long periods of isolation sometimes puff up the ego to monstrous dimensions. In this place we had only ourselves and choked sometimes with self-pity or self-indulgence, we lost control of our humility. Perhaps the need to keep hold of our identity, the need to reaffirm constantly to ourselves that we had value, and that we were important, allowed us to believe that we were greater than we really were. A man who prays in praise of himself rather than of what he understands to be God puts himself at a far remove from the God to whom he prays.

Sometimes the guards who spoke reasonable English would ask us questions about Christian belief. As far as we could we would answer them and attempt to talk to them about their own beliefs. They seemed amazed that we had read the Koran but they remained adamant that Christ was not the son of God. God was God and needed no sons. But always their belief was undermined by their own repressed sexuality. The idea that God could have sex with a woman in order to have a son fascinated them. But for us these conversations were difficult. We knew that these men cared nothing about scriptural or doctrinal argument. Their minds were simply intoxicated by the idea of a sexual God.

On those occasions when they brought with them a copy of the Koran in English we would turn again to those chapters that we recalled as being significant to our own situation. We would point out the phrases and question them; sometimes they would answer but their minds were not trained to think. They would leave us sometimes angry, sometimes confused. For them the relationship with God was one of complete submission and man should not question the words of the Koran. I could not abide their abject surrender. How can one submit to what one does not understand? Their submission to God was an act of repression. Their God was a God of judgement and of vengeance and they were afraid of this God. And their own repressed fascination with sexuality hinted at none of the liberation that a religion should present to its followers. It held them in bondage.

These men existed in their own kind of prison, perhaps more confining than the one that held us.

Out of the Fairy Cake

The Count of the Holy Roman Empire and I had been talking about house-building. We chose locations high in the hills or near the sea, though we were both city born and bred. The city held no fascination for us now. We dreamt of a quiet rural idyll. Slowly stone by stone and plank by plank we discussed our dream homes. How we might build them and what we might do in them.

Our talk must have affected our keepers. For the past few days they had been painting the walls outside our cell. The work came to an end. We peered out, the walls were a creamy pink and a flat grey. 'It looks like we are living in a fucking fairy cake, John,' I told him. The walls reminded me of icing sugar on a cheap cake. The guards were coming regularly to talk or to play dominoes. It seemed that they were fed up with their own company. During these games if I was losing I would exclaim 'Oh bollocks!' Once, a guard turned to John mumbling 'John, what mean bollocks?' 'It is a very bad word,' he answered. The guard seemed satisfied, quietly repeating to himself 'Bollocks, bollocks.'

A new guard arrived. His English was quite good and his French even better. He told us his name was Abed but this was certainly not the Abed we had known in Abed's Hotel. This man was younger. He was at first very polite, and somewhat shy. He was perhaps overawed by the situation, for here he was talking with foreigners. He spoke slowly, asking us to forgive him for what he was doing. In the days that followed he came frequently, and spoke often of his religion. He told us he had had visions in which he had seen angels, Christ, Moses and the holy Imams. We sat quietly listening and not knowing what to say. He explained how when he had been in the south with the other 'warriors', they had been creeping through the countryside to make an attack on some Israeli installation. Many of his friends had been killed. As they prepared for their attack he looked behind him and saw many more warriors follow him, coming to help. These were the warriors sent by Muhammad and promised in the Koran.

At night we would sometimes hear him crying out or moaning fearfully in his dreaming sleep. Religion had possessed this man with an evil kind of possession. He continued his stories, telling us how his brother who had been killed would come to him in the night and call to him, to come and join him. This man's death-wishing was of the most morbid and fantastical kind. Both John and I pitied, as much as we were a little afraid of, his strange warped mentality.

All of them wanted to die for Islam and each of them in their time told us of the plans they had made for heroic death in the name of Islam. But their dreaming and death-wishing had the quality of a child's wish-fulfilment. Some of them saw themselves driving a car bomb into a crowd of Israeli soldiers, killing themselves and everyone around them. One of them hoped to crash an aeroplane into the heart of an Israeli town. Somehow this was not the thinking of a cold and calculating terrorist mind. They believed fervently that all the warriors of Islam went to an Islamic heaven. 'This life no good,' they would frequently reiterate but their boasting and their dreaming sometimes went beyond storytelling. Many times they would come into our cell brandishing a pistol or Kalashnikov and they liked to show us their guns.

Said, the prison chief, was the most boastful of them all. He had a huge macho dilemma and during these exhibitions he would bark out orders to the other guards until they brought half the armoury they kept in the guardroom. Several Kalashnikovs were shown to us, semiautomatic pistols, a Beretta, hand grenades and a mortar launcher. Said proudly showed us a rocket launcher, which he told us was one of many in their arsenal. We took these guns in our hands and fumbled with them. The magazines were always removed first. Some of these weapons were of Italian or Spanish origin, but the larger weapons like the mortar and the anti-personnel rocket launcher were of British make.

All of the guards crushed into the room and each of them was eager to display his knowledge of these weapons. As we held the large rocket launcher in our hands we would feel several of our guards' hands pull and push at it, each wanting to be the man to show how it worked, and to display what a soldier he was. I heard John ask loudly 'I say, do you fellows know if this thing is loaded?' Said answered 'Of course, it is always loaded, we are always ready to fight!' John and I laughed. Here in this tiny cell, two prisoners and five or six guards were crushed together, all of them grabbing and fumbling at and barely missing the firing-pin on this weapon. If any of us had touched it accidentally then all our troubles would have been over.

Often, after the guards had left, we laughed derisively at these childlike warriors of God. When Abed visited us, we spent some time and energy teaching him English. Unlike the other guards, he was quite adept at learning. The others would give up with boredom after ten minutes, but Abed persisted. We learned that his father was a teacher of French in one of the hill villages, which explained his fluency in the language and why he learned so quickly from us. Often as these lessons came to an end Abed would rise from the position he was sitting in, come over to us and kiss us both on the top of the head.

In our many short conversations with these men we slowly became aware of the dilemma in which they were trapped. Genuinely most of them wanted us to like them. Yet they wanted us also to be afraid of them. They had no meaningful reason to dislike us. They were afraid of us and when they occasionally displayed any instinctual affection towards us, it threw them into confusion and they retreated from us. Somewhere in their minds was the notion that we were prisoners and therefore must be evil. This constant ambivalence played upon them, and we in our turn played upon it – sometimes to extract information, and sometimes when it was necessary to reveal our anger at the way we had been treated. These conversations also gave us some access to their language and with difficulty we would catch words and phrases in Arabic. It was a beneficial exercise, for as the years progressed we were able to pick up things on the radio in the guards' room reporting world news or local events. We were told that the chiefs had specifically ordered them not to give us instruction in Arabic. For obvious reasons they did not want us to overhear their conversations.

On one of these visits Abed and another guard brought us each a small plastic stool rather like an enlarged bucket with a lid. The novelty of this soon wore off. It was hard and uncomfortable. We yearned for a chair with a back so that we might sit properly and relax. Sitting down on a piece of furniture seemed strange. For so many months we had had either to stand up or to lie on a mattress. We were so unused to sitting that after those first few days we hardly bothered to use the stools.

Early in the morning we heard a loud banging noise that woke us from our sleep. We wondered what might be happening and thought to ourselves that one of the guards must be repairing something. We said he must be taking a hammer to the rocket launcher trying to make it work. The banging continued. We couldn't sleep and cursed our captors who insisted on making this racket so early in the morning. But our surmise was incorrect. For some fifteen minutes the banging went on. It was perhaps four o'clock. Suddenly the banging stopped. We lay back to try to catch some sleep before the guards came, and as we lay in that darkness, we heard someone speak to us through the grille above our door. The voice spoke softly, but urgently. 'Hey you guys, I'm going out of here right now, they are going to shoot my wife and my child. I've heard them talking about it. I've got to go. I've got to get to them. Don't worry, I'll get word to your families, I'll tell everyone.'

We knew the voice and we knew that somehow Frank had got out of his cell and was wandering about in the passageway. He was excited and we became tense. He had set in motion something very dangerous for all of us. We began to panic about what he would do next. The entrance into the guards' room was sealed off by a barred gate. How Frank intended to open this we could not conceive, nor why he failed to open the other cell doors. How did Frank expect to run through the suburbs of Beirut in a pair of shorts and a filthy T-shirt? Perhaps panic and fear, accumulating over weeks and weeks, had finally driven him to this action without any proper calculation of what would happen if things went wrong. We heard Frank bang at the gate into the guards' room. Obviously they had not stayed the night. Frank's banging continued and we knew he would never be able to open that gate. We whispered quietly to each other, wondering what the hell was going to happen. Frank kept banging but with less enthusiasm. Perhaps it was dawning on him that this gate could not be opened.

Despair leads to panic and panic drives a mind out of all reason. Frank began shouting at the top of his voice 'Come on you guys, you told me a few days ago I would go home tomorrow, you said bukkra, well it's bukkra now, I'm ready, I'm ready to go home . . . Come on you guys come on, come on and get me, come and get me.' His voice shrieking rather than shouting. All logic had gone from it. Frank would be quiet for a while, sometimes shuffling around outside then back to the barred gate, shouting again and banging and then silence. John and I whispered 'Christ, I hope that he doesn't try and open our cell. How in the name of Christ will we ever get the thing closed again.'

We were now more fearful of what Frank had done and might do than we were of the guards. Suddenly Frank's voice started up again but this time he was not calling for the guards to come and take him home. This time he was praying loudly perhaps knowing that the consequences would be grim, praying loudly, recklessly, fearfully. 'Tomorrow's really going to be an eventful day, the House of Fun will really hot up tomorrow,' I whispered to John. He was silent. We did not want to talk about tomorrow. We needed to think and prepare.

Breakfast came and we were routinely led to the shower and back to our cell. Nothing seemed to have happened. The other prisoners were taken to the 'Shit, Shave and Shower Shop' as normally as on all the other days. Had the guard not noticed that Frank's door had been opened? We knew he had returned to his cell the previous night, closing the door and hoping foolishly that they would not notice.

It was not till the late afternoon that the expected retribution began. Frank was taken from his cell. We heard a voice, which was not one of the regular guards, speak to him harshly. 'Who did you see? Who did you speak with? What did you speak with them?' This was a voice of some authority and of an officer more senior than Said. Frank quietly answered in the negative. 'I did not speak to anyone, I did not see anyone.' Before his sentence was finished we heard the thud of a punch land upon him and we heard him fall to the ground. After some moments the question was repeated. Frank repeated his answer and again the blow landed on him. Then more blows, no questions, only the sound of a man being beaten slowly and deliberately.

After some twenty minutes of this, Frank was locked away in the small cell that adjoined the guards' room. It was set apart from all the others, the same cell to which Tom and Terry had been taken earlier when their own room flooded with rainwater. We heard the door slam, the whispering of the guards and orders being barked at them, then silence again. There were some fifteen minutes of silence, in which John and I anxiously planned what we might say if we were questioned about the events of the previous night.

It was obvious to us that this matter would not be allowed to rest with the simple beating of Frank. We would all be interrogated. We needed to have some reasonable answers that endangered no-one else. Quickly we talked over the possibilities of what they might ask or do. Always in the back of our heads was this thought: will they separate us? They would be worried that they might come in one morning and find all of us loose. It would be very easy for six men to overpower three guards. As we plotted nervously, the silence was abruptly smashed again by Frank shouting and beating on his prison door, his voice loud and hysterical. 'Come and get me, come and get me . . . I'm ready . . . I'm waiting . . . Come and get it over with, come on . . . Come on, do it, do it.' He banged and banged, crying out 'Come on, come on . . . Get it over with, shoot me. I'm waiting . . . Come and do it, come on, get it over with.' The fear and panic in Frank's voice was like a hot poker being pushed slowly into our own flesh.

The shouting brought the guards back. We heard them descend into the room. Two of them, perhaps three, they seemed excited. They were talking quickly. They were not sure what to do. A man out of control with unholy expectations can be a fearsome thing to face. One of them went over to Frank's door and shouted at him 'What you want? What you want?' Frank was silent. His voice lower this time but still the same words. 'I'm waiting, I'm waiting . . . do it, do it.' The short sentence growing louder. 'Do it.' Now the guards were afraid. We heard them lift their guns and noisily slide the magazines into their weapons. Perhaps they were hoping to frighten Frank into silence, and they were really frightened themselves.

Frank's door opened and the guards went in. It was quiet. No more shouting. We could hear the guards talking, the sound of their voices but not the words. Seemingly calm, they relocked the door.

That evening, the expected visitors arrived. John and I were unable to work up any enthusiasm for our game of dominoes, thinking over and over again what might happen and what Frank might say. We heard the shuffling feet approaching, the padlock opening, the bolt sliding back. One of the Brothers Kalashnikov and another guard entered. They spoke to one another, then began rummaging around our cell. What they expected to find we could not imagine. They looked everywhere, tossing cups, toothbrushes, towels about the floor, lifting and throwing the mattresses against the wall, shaking them and throwing them at their feet. John was taken out and I followed quickly behind. We were stood in the passageway. Carefully hands traced over our bodies, searching our fingers and fingernails. Obviously they were looking for cuts or abrasions which would suggest that we too had attempted to get out of our cells. Quickly we were shoved back inside and the door was locked.

Within minutes the guards were back and John was jostled quickly out of the cell. I knew that he had been taken to be questioned.

John and I had decided how to deal with this interrogation. 'Say whatever you like, but whatever you say, say fuck all, John.' That old Belfast axiom was helpful now. It was necessary only to admit that we heard banging and that we heard a man shouting. We knew nothing else, spoke with no-one else and saw nothing. Half-truths are always more convincing than whole lies. So we agreed and I waited. I prayed not for John's strength nor for his courage but for his safety. There is something terribly frightening about sitting half naked and alone and knowing that men around you are about to beat you. You never see the punch coming, never know where it is going to land. The tense nervous waiting is more frightening than actual blows. So I prayed again. One needs to believe that someone, somewhere is thinking about you when you are in a dangerous situation. John was only gone some ten minutes and then he was brought back. We had agreed that if there was any serious physical abuse he would cough as he entered the cell to warn me to be prepared. I listened as he came in and sat down. There was no cough.

The guards marched me aggressively, obviously to impress their waiting chief. I was made to sit down. I knew that some five or six men stood around me. A voice speaking excellent English, very soft and calming, asked 'What is your name?' For a moment I thought, do I crack a joke or do I answer him directly. 'My name is Brian Keenan, what's yours?' I asked. A calm voice replied 'It is not a matter.' I waited. 'What did you see last night?' It was time for a joke. 'It's very difficult to see when you are asleep.' I tried to force a smile. My interrogator seemed nonplussed at my poor attempt at humour. 'What did you hear last night, my friend?' I answered with the story that we had prepared. 'I heard someone banging, I thought it was the guards upstairs. I heard a man shouting, and then I heard a man praying.' I concluded, trying to afford Frank some protection, 'This man is very stressed . . . this man is very confused.' There was a short silence. My interrogator whispered something to the guards around me. He leaned forward and took my hand in his. 'Do you know what we have done with this man,' he said. I said 'I do not, and how could I? I am stuck in a small cell twenty-four hours a day.' I was becoming confident. Again silence. I sensed my interrogator move closer to me, for an instant it flashed across my mind that he was about to slap my face. I held myself still, tried not to let the tension reduce me to a nervous trembling. Again a voice soft and low came at me. 'This man is dead, we have killed this man!'

It was my turn to be silent. I knew they lied and I knew now that they would only try to frighten me. Slowly, speaking softly like the man who questioned me I said with great deliberation 'I do not believe this, for it serves no purpose.' The atmosphere changed. The questioner's tone of voice altered, not yet angry but less relaxed. 'Why do you say this,' he said speaking quickly. 'I did not hear a gun and I did not hear a man scream and I do not believe that you would do such a thing.' My interrogator's hands laced around my throat, his thumbs gently, slowly, pressurizing my adam's apple. His voice was no longer low again as he spoke. 'We do not kill him with a gun, we kill him like this,' and gently his thumbs pressed into my neck.

I thought in that instant that this bastard was a real ham actor. I said nothing. I sat still, tried not to flinch. Again the soft voice came at me, the pitch of it higher. 'Do you want to see this man?' I wondered why he would ask this. I knew if I said yes that it would cause me problems. They would consider my desire for such knowledge a dangerous thing. Quietly I said 'I am from Ireland, I have known many deaths, I do not need to see another. What is a dead man? He is nothing.' The hands were slowly taken from my throat. 'Why did you not try to get out of your cell?' the voice asked. I quickly answered 'I am one, you are many, you have guns, I have none . . . Where can a naked man go if he leaves this building? . . . Where could I go wearing only these rags?' I stopped and paused, then said 'I am not a fool.' Said, standing behind me, liked what I had just said. I heard him laugh and felt him pat my shoulder. But my interrogator was not yet finished. 'Do you stand up, do you look?' Vehemently I answered now 'Of course, I am a man, I need exercise, a man is not made to sit on the floor all day.' 'What do you see?' came the voice again. And I answered 'Occasionally I see the head of a man in the cell opposite as he exercises, but I have not seen his face.' I searched out the last piece of humour. 'It is not possible you know to exercise walking around the cell on your knees, a man must stand and a man must walk.' No-one laughed. I felt a cigarette being pushed between my lips. Through the blindfold I saw the flash of a lighter and a voice saying to me 'Smoke.' I drew in the smoke, it was a Gitane. I commented 'Gitanes, very good! . . . Here I only have Cedars . . . they are the worst cigarettes in the world.' I smiled. Voices behind me laughing slightly. I felt myself being lifted. Two guards walked me back to the cell, and now there was less force, less pushing. I had passed the test.

That night John and I discussed the interrogation. Our stories were the same, and it seemed that we had been believed. The fact that we were still together suggested that the guards had no intention of separating us but the next few days would tell. John told me Frank had been returned to his original cell. We tried knocking on the wall. There was no answer. We hoped it was over for him but hardly believed that they would let him off so lightly. The evidence of this came within the next few hours. Said entered Frank's cell. At first we heard him speak, his voice rising. Then we heard something slapping against skin. Obviously Frank was being beaten with a belt, or perhaps as Tom had been, with a piece of rubber hose. I felt physically sick. I wanted to scream 'Leave him alone, you miserable bastards . . . He's had enough.'

The next day, lying on my chest, looking through the whirling fan at the foot of the door, I saw Frank exchanging cells with Terry Anderson. We heard the guards speak with him. 'Do you want anything?' asked the guard. 'I want to go upstairs, I want to have a bath,' Frank said.

For the next few days Frank's face did not appear at the grille. We speculated on how it was possible for him to get out of his cell. Had he opened all our cells, we might as a group have overpowered our guards. We discussed how we could all have waited in the second cell and when the guards had entered the first, we could have burst out, locking them in. But there was always the problem of clothes. We knew the guards kept the changes of clothes in their room. Would there be enough for all of us? And how would we go, in twos or threes? Would we take guns? Could we kill anyone if it was necessary? In part these discussions were like playing adventure games and in part they were explorations of a very real moral question.

Two days after his first escape attempt Frank again caused havoc. When the guards came to take him to the toilet for his daily wash, Frank emerged slowly out of the cell, then burst loose and ran along the passage, up into the guards' room. The guards ran after him shouting and calling back to one another. Frank had no hope of getting out. Within minutes he was brought back to his cell and locked in. John and I sat amazed. It seemed he was determined to make life extremely difficult for himself. What, we wondered, could have prompted him to commit such a serious breach of their rules?

For this desperate gesture Frank underwent another round of beating from Said.

Perhaps because of these breaches of security involving Frank or perhaps because Said simply enjoyed his new-found occupation of beating and tormenting, he became a more frequent visitor to our cell. On occasion he would stay in the prison overnight, his cartoon noises always betraying his presence. He would often indulge in conversation about Islam, and took great pleasure in describing the punishments to which criminals were subjected. The cutting off of heads. The cutting off of hands for thieves. Boastfully he told us how in Iran, thieves would have only their fingers cut off because they needed their hands for praying. This was much superior to the punishment that was meted out in Saudi Arabia, where the whole hand was removed. Said loved talking of these bloody rituals; he thought they frightened us. Often when he visited the other cells, we would strain against the door, our heads close to the fan to try and pick up some of the conversation. We knew that Said had met the Americans when they had first been taken, and that he would occasionally give them news about their situation.

We were now convinced that the fate of the Americans and our own were tied together. I remember saying to John that he would go home when the Americans' problem was resolved. Margaret Thatcher's ideas about dealing with terrorism were quite redundant. In any case her own engagement with the Reagan regime was so close that she or the British government would do nothing for the British hostages that might reflect badly on the American government.

We listened to Tom Sutherland complaining that he needed another bottle in which to urinate. He had a bladder or a kidney problem and spent hours in pain, trying to hold back the need to urinate until the guards came in the morning. Said listened but did nothing. 'You must train yourself to toilet,' he said.

It was during one of these visits with the Americans that we heard Said read a newspaper report of the visit to Beirut by Terry Waite, the Archbishop of Canterbury's envoy. This visit was to be the last that he would make and it would assure the release of the hostages. Said seemed quite excited as he relayed this news. We were convinced that Said believed that something was about to happen. We were not sure of the significance of this for ourselves, but as the news was also given to Terry Anderson we became more convinced that something was being set up for the Americans. Conversations with Tom and Terry Anderson told us that they had been measured for clothes and shoe sizes.

One night as we settled down, we heard many guards arriving.

They entered the American cells and left clothes and shoes for them. The day had finally arrived for them. We all believed it. Terry was in the next cell, and he knocked furiously and for a long time on the wall. It wasn't a message. It was just sheer joy, exuberance that the moment had finally come. With the same kind of rapture we knocked back to confirm that we understood, and to express our own joy that the Americans at last would be getting out of this place. We felt no pity or concern for ourselves. To know that someone, anyone was going home was a kind of release for all of us. Our trio of friends had been held longer than us and had been through some traumatic experiences. Some twenty minutes after the clothes had been delivered the guards again came in. Doors were banging all around the prison. And then the Americans were gone.

The prison seemed so empty. It even felt colder than before. Only the Korean remained. He never looked out of his cell and we had no communication with him. John and I were alone again. We spoke often about the emptiness of the prison and wondered how the Americans would be dealing with life outside. We convinced ourselves that it would only be a short time before we joined them. The lights went out early and we were left with our stubs of candles and our home-made 'lamps'. These candles reinforced our loneliness. Our thoughts turned more and more to the Korean now. He sat silent and alone, and often refused the appalling food. Few of the guards even spoke to him.

Rape

The removal of the Americans and the reduction in the hours of light prolonged the days. The light we provided for ourselves from the handmade candles did not diminish the long drag of each day. But the news about Terry Waite and our belief that the Americans had gone home was enough to push back the depression that was always hidden in those long hours of darkness. We spoke often of going home and the things we might now do in our lives. We wondered how much had changed, and what had happened to our friends and our families. Surfacing periodically was that fear that members of our immediate family might have passed away; we knew it would take a long time for us to deal with that.

John spoke frequently of his mother and her illness. Sometimes we were convinced that our parents had died and we had to convince ourselves that such thoughts were irrational. But then both John and I were shown a video of his mother making an appeal to our captors. He was heartened by this and we talked about her appearance. He felt she looked a little older than he could remember, but otherwise she seemed to speak with the calm confidence that he had always remembered. I called her 'The Dowager Duchess'. 'Listen, John, how could your mother be dead, after all the Dowager Duchess has become a bloody TV personality and probably a movie star. In fact I'm quite convinced she is paying Islamic Jihad to keep you here, so that she can go prancing in front of the TV cameras.' John would smile.

Cautiously, but with passion, we questioned each other about how our captivity had changed us. We both felt that our personalities had not changed, but the things we desired, and the dreams we wanted to pursue were very different from those we had known as free men. These existential conversations went on long into the night. We were forced to whisper, more softly and lower than we had been used to. With the power turned off and no fan turning and buzzing in the door, the slightest noise could be heard. We talked particularly of how long would it take for Waite to achieve his purpose. Nothing could happen quickly in these circumstances.

Suddenly, in the silent darkness we heard one of the guards cry out and jump up shouting, almost ranting. The barred gate was opened and Said came running furiously down the passage, opening the cell doors. What was happening?. We both knew that this man Said was extremely paranoid and neurotic, and that he frequently underwent mercurial personality changes. This outburst boded no good. We sat in our separate corners, waiting. In the darkness John whispered to me 'Jesus Christ, I'm shaking like hell and I can't stop.' I answered 'Don't worry, the feeling is mutual.' We both sat there shivering, trying to control this seizure of fear. I remembered on many occasions when I had scolded my dog how it would lie shaking and trembling uncontrollably and here I was trembling like an animal. Reason could not calm me. My mind seemed tranquil but no matter how I tried, or what thoughts I tried to force to mind, I could not overcome this trembling in my limbs. I tried to kick my legs and move my arms, pumping some sort of life through them in the hope that they would stay still, but I could not control them.

Then the door-bolt slid back and Said burst in. He stood beside John and said nothing. His silent anger filled the room. Often the guards would come in and stand, saying nothing, and look at us for long periods as if we were alien creatures. It was so dehumanizing to be studied like that. You sat in the silence, knowing their eyes were poring over every inch of you and you wondered what was in their minds, what thoughts passed through their heads as they gazed at you in your naked helplessness. Said lowered the tone of his voice, trying to disguise it. He said something to the guards who were with him. They went away and in a few moments returned. Silence again. And then I heard it.

Said began beating John about the body as he lay on his mattress. The butt of his Kalashnikov thumped into him again and again. John was silent. Said never spoke. He was panting like an exhausted runner. With the acceleration of his heavy breathing the blows became faster and harder, raining down on my companion. My trembling was now gone, my mind was fixed on something else. I could do nothing. To stand up or to protest would only drive this man into a fever that would make the blows more painful and prolonged. I sat listening and screamed silently in the darkness at this monster who thought we were parcels of rancid meat to be kicked and beaten. Then the blows stopped.

I knew that it was now my turn. In a way I was grateful for what was about to happen, for to be on the receiving end of this brutality seemed to me less painful than to sit in that darkness and listen to it happening to another man who had become so much a part of myself. Said quietly walked the few paces over to where I sat. Again I felt that searing tension flash through me, waiting for the blows to come, not seeing them or where they would land. I hissed quietly to myself 'Get it over,' echoing the words I had heard Frank cry out days before. Said began by taking deep breaths, deeper and deeper, faster and faster he breathed in and out. He was working himself up. I sat and listened to him exciting himself into violence. Down it came, hard, on my shoulders, driving into my chest. Then along my thighs, banging against my knees, Said's excited breathing becoming louder. Every part of my body was being insulted. I could feel the heat of this man beside me. I could smell the perfume that he always wore, mixed with his sweat. This man was the violent lover and his abuse of my body a kind of rape. I felt the closeness of him and knew that he was sexually excited by what he was doing. The blows rained down and I felt only anger; to be raped by a man so filled with fear revolted me. A man fascinated by violence and obsessed with sex. In that moment I hated him, I did not fear him. I made no noise as each blow landed and was driven into me. My resistance was a joyful thing. Said became more passionate, more vicious, always seeking out the tender parts and banging the butt of his rifle onto my flesh. He worked himself into exhaustion and finally, as a last humiliation, he pressed the butt of the gun tight onto my neck, pushing down hard till I felt the air being choked out of me. How long would he keep this up, and how long before I would burst out screaming for air? But it was his final insult.

The butt was lifted, and he stood exhausted and panting above me. The smell of him, his sweet sickly perfume, the sweat, the garlic from his panting breath repelled me. The room was pungent with his violent aroma. I wanted him to leave, not because I was afraid of him, but because this man had violated me with a rifle butt and I wanted every trace of him and the air in which he stood sucked out of that cell. His presence was being pushed down my throat and I could not abide it. The anger in me became a volcano in my chest and if I trembled now, I trembled with a subdued fury. It was an elemental anger and had nothing to do with who or what I was or that personality I had insisted on maintaining for myself. This was a rage that was greater than me. How long could I contain myself ? The blows and the bruises and the kicks hurt me but I felt no pain, just this cold anger. And as I felt it gather up its force in me and move towards the moment when it would explode, Said was gone.

The banging door confirmed it. But cautious that he might be standing there, I waited. I sniffed the air like an animal. His smell lingered but it was less strong. He had gone. I slowly lifted up my blindfold and looked at John, he looked at me. We could not see much in the darkness. 'Are you all right?' he asked. 'Yes,' I said and winked. For a few moments we were shocked and too frightened to speak. Then slowly crawling through the darkness towards one another, we felt each other's arms and faces. 'Are you sore?' 'Not really.' 'No, I'm not either but I expect we'll feel it in the morning.' Our voices were now very, very low. We could hardly hear each other speaking. We whispered soft words of comfort and reassurance to each other. 'The man's a fucking head banger! He is a wank-stain, an empty piece of exhausted flesh.'

We both lay back in the dark to calm ourselves and flush out the arrogance of his violence. I thought, as the anger began to ebb back in great torrents, how I would take great pleasure in castrating that man and quietly standing over him as I watched him and made him eat himself. I spat out my anger in silent and foul abuse. This man had ceased to have any element of humanity. I could not consider him human. Twice now he had beaten me and sought to humiliate me and I wondered how many more times before I could contain myself no longer and try to wreak havoc on him. I remembered as I lay there how he had often quoted a phrase from the Koran, one that is copied from the Christian Bible. 'An eye for an eye and a tooth for a tooth.'

As my anger diminished I felt a new and tremendous kind of strength flooding me. The more I was beaten the stronger I seemed to become. It was not strength of arm, nor of body but a huge determination never to give in to these men, never to show fear, never to cower in front of them. To take what violence they meted out to me and stand and resist and not allow myself to be humiliated. In that resistance I would humiliate them. There was a part of me they could never bind nor abuse nor take from me. There was a sense of self greater than me alone, which came and filled me in the darkest hours. Because of it, their violence energized me and I felt nothing. As these thoughts somehow refreshed me, I whispered through the darkness to my invisible companion 'John, don't let this thing get you down, it doesn't mean anything.' A moment's silence followed, then John replied 'I got fed up with him beating and bruising me and I just thought to myself over and over again "That's enough, away over and do that bastard of an Irishman in the corner." ' We both laughed. The moment of violence was meaningless. It passed from us as our compassionate humour came flowing back.

In the morning before entering the shower the guards checked over our bodies, noting the bruise marks on arms, chest, legs and hips, even on our ankles and shin bones and our feet. They said nothing, only whispered to one another as they pointed to each blackening bruise. The hot shower was a luxury, but not against the pain, as I stood in it, I remembered my thoughts of the night before: the stench and reek of Said, his perfume, his garlic breath panting over me, the wetness of his body, the whole sexually charged aura of him that seemed to lay layers of filth upon me. As I stood in that shower, languishing in the steam, I washed him away. I washed myself clean of his brutality and of his putrid sickness.

That day John and I spent joking and abusing one another. It was like a gentle lotion to our bruises. Our laughter rubbed against the ache in our limbs. 'I've got more bruises than you anyway,' John would say; and I would answer 'That's because your fucking white lily-livered-shilling-taking flesh marks more easy than us pure-blooded Irish!' 'What blood? . . . You Irish don't have any, you've just got pig shit and cow dung in your veins!'

Some time later we heard Said walking in the corridor, making his cartoon noises again. He passed our cell, his hands reached in over the grille and he pulled his face up to look in at us. We would not look back at him. He had become nothing. 'Look at me,' he said, 'Look at me.' We did not look. 'Look at me,' he said, 'Look at me,' and his voice was pleading. Said wanted us to recognize him, to acknowledge him. Did he want us to forgive him? But we would not look at him. His pleas fell on our deaf ears. 'Look,' he continued, 'Is OK . . . no problems, no problems.' He was pleading again, John glanced up at him for a second and turned his face back to me. I sat with my back to him, I would not turn, I would not look. He was not there. He was invisible to me and was nothing. He fell down from the door and walked away, whistling softly. 'He's got blue eyes,' John said. 'He looks older than his voice suggests.' 'Yes, a real centrefold that one,' I retorted. We returned again to our dominoes.

That evening I told John of the dream that I had had when I was first kidnapped and held alone. I dreamed that I had been in a café somewhere and that a friend had come to sit and chat with me. We talked of times we had enjoyed together. I listened but as I looked into his blue eyes I knew that this friend had come to kill me. His eyes told a story that made his words lies. He noticed the intensity of my watching, and knowing that in his blue eyes I had read the truth, said to me 'You know! . . . Don't you?' and I said 'Yes, I know.' There was silence as we looked at one another. I was submerged in the blueness and softness of his eyes. Suddenly I saw something in the eyes and heard the bang of his gun as he shot me, then he wasn't there. I was free of him and of his deceit and of his awful betrayal. I felt no pain or fear. If this was a nightmare it held no horror for me. It was so clear and I remembered it after all those months. John sat silently and listened. 'You don't want to read too much into these things, Brian.' 'I know,' I said slowly, 'I don't, it's just a dream I had.'

We saw little more of Said in the days that followed. Whether or not he was frightened of us and knew our anger, he was most certainly aware of our changed attitude towards him. Perhaps he was embarrassed. His violence had been without purpose or meaning. His absence was a relief for us. Had he come to talk or even to attempt to play games with us, the atmosphere in the cell would have told him how much we loathed him. We believed with Said gone that we would be left alone to eke out those long periods of darkness as best we might. We had become accustomed to the darkness. We had our candles and our games and above all we had each other, more defiant and stronger than before.

In those long dark hours we taught each other songs that we half remembered. We made up new lines for them. 'The Boxer' by Simon and Garfunkel became a favourite. We added many additional verses to the original song, extending the story and often drawing on our experience of imprisonment. Our feelings were transformed into verse and harmony, recreating what we believed was a better and certainly a much, much longer version of the original song. In this way we were articulating indirectly to one another some of the intensity and intimacy of our experience. It was a way of speaking confessionally to one another about our deepest emotional responses to what had happened over the past months. But this time of mutual reassurance, of shared imagination which was as comforting as it was stimulating, was to be short-lived.

Sitting in that darkness one evening, speaking of those songs and the music we loved and missed more than we had ever expected to, we promised how, should we ever leave this place, we would each teach ourselves to play some musical instrument. We both believed ourselves hugely impoverished in that neither of us had any musical skill. John was keen to take up the piano, which he had begun to learn as a child. I thought how wonderful it would be to be able to play a banjo and a harmonica. Occasionally when John was asleep I would sit with my two hands cupped over my mouth holding an imaginary harmonica and humming tunes into my hands as I rocked back and forth, its rhythm nursing me and comforting me. I believed myself to be the world's finest harmonica player. I was indeed, in the world in which I was held.

It was again late at night when the key turned in the padlock. The door began to open very slowly, which was unusual. We sat in silence facing one another, wondering who had come in and what they wanted. It was unusual for the guards to visit at night and especially when there was no light in the cell. Someone came in, a voice spoke, one we did not recognize, but it was a voice disguised, just as Said often attempted to disguise his own. It spoke in Arabic.

We didn't answer but we both knew who this person was. It was Abed, the young man of the nightmare dreams: the zealot who cried out in his sleep, who saw angels, who had spoken with Christ and Moses and who had seen the imaginary holy warriors of the thirteenth Imam march behind him as he carried out a raid in southern Lebanon. This was the young man who told us he had hidden in a cave in the hills to experience visions. This was the man who heard his dead brother call to him 'Come, come, come and join me here,' so immersed in the Koran that his mind was contaminated by hallucinations. We had tried to teach him English. When he first came he asked us for forgiveness, and kissed us on the head as he left us, but now he had become someone else.

He stood over John sitting some ten feet from me and I heard again the butt of a Kalashnikov fall repeatedly on John's body. Slowly and unexcitedly the blows continued and then stopped. I heard him walk towards me. This time I cared nothing. There was no trembling. There was no fear. I secretly relished what was about to happen because of the strength it gave me. Here it was again, the thumping down of this weapon bruising my body. Unlike the excited quasi-sexual rapture of Said's rape, this man was frightened, his blows only half as heavy as Said's, slow and deliberate, picking the impact points.

An Evil Cradling

I even felt a smile inside myself. The hot tempest that was part of Said's abuse was not here now. I was oblivious for the duration of this beating. He stopped and walked away quickly, almost running from the cell. I crawled over to John. We were both unhurt and unafraid.

In the morning we were taken to the toilet, our arms firmly twisted up our backs, Abed kicking and pushing at our feet. Both of us laughed.

Abed now became our tormentor every other night. Occasionally in the afternoon he would come in and play out a game, his role as torturer. He would take great pleasure, having beaten us, in jumping up and down on our outstretched legs. We never spoke or cried out. It was becoming apparent to us that this perverse individual had more need of us than he understood himself. He was attempting to make himself a man. He thought by beating and brutalizing us, that his manhood was assured.

We spoke often and at length about Abed, attempting to understand what distortion of mind or imagination could allow him constantly to beat naked and blindfolded men in the dark. What was there in a man that would tell him such things made him more a man? I often thought that he had seen in Said's violence a way of obtaining power and stature and perhaps a way of obliterating his own weakness. In these moments of torture Abed suddenly had had thrust into his hands absolute and unlimited power. He could not resist it. He immersed himself in it. He had become addicted to his own cruelty. But in the compulsive addiction to the power he had over us he was powerless. His need of us made him our prisoner. In our silence and in our strength he felt only his own fear thrust back on him. He knew and was afraid that we cared nothing for him and would not submit nor cry out to please him. As these beatings continued it was as if Abed was feeding off our naked flesh. We were bored by his pathetic need. Our silent resistance made him more fearful, and we felt his fear in the blows and laughed inside ourselves. But not all was calmness and quiet resistance.

John knew the Vesuvius of rage that smouldered inside me. 'John, I can't take much more of this little bastard using me and getting himself off on me. At times I feel like blowing up and breaking the little bastard's neck.' John was always calming. 'I know . . . I feel the same,' he said. 'But what's the point. You do that and you give them what they want, full licence to do anything they want.' What reinforced my anger and loathing at this man's violence was that on other occasions he would come to visit us as himself, Abed, and talk, perhaps play a game and then go off again to return later, his voice disguised, and begin again to take his pleasure, his addiction out of control. I was always sickened when he sat with us to talk of his family and of the politics of Lebanon and then return in the darkness as someone else: the other person he wanted to be but could not be because he was not a hero and we would not let him be one. How long would we have to endure this? I wondered as I tried to sleep.

The answer was to come sooner than either of us expected. After lunch we were playing a game and making up our new songs when we heard several feet come to our door. Quickly we pulled down the blindfolds and the guards entered. Our cells were emptied of everything. We were left sitting on a cold floor wearing only a pair of shorts. We sat in that freezing silence for hours, wondering what was happening. We found some last pieces of candle wax and some threads and made a small candle, and in the white darkness we sat with our eyes fixed on this struggling blue flame, shivering and shuddering in the cold. That little tiny blue flame was like ourselves, struggling to stay alive, and then finally exhausted with the struggle it was snuffed out, and the blackness crashed in.

We lay huddled together for warmth, then heard feet moving quickly towards our cell. The door opened, two sweaters were thrust at us. 'Put on, put on,' a voice ordered. We did so, grateful for the warmth. Then quickly we were taken out and rushed along the passageway and heaved up through that hole which we had been dropped through so many months before, then out along the dark passage and once more into that old Volkswagen van which we had now christened 'The War Wagon'.

For some twenty minutes we careered and bumped through the dark suburbs of Beirut. The van stopped and we waited, expecting to be taken out and delivered to another prison. But the waiting was to be prolonged and for three hours, our muscles and bones aching, we were made to sit in cramped silence. Every time we moved or sought to stretch our limbs or to ease the pain, a gun would touch our chests or heads, and a voice would spit out 'Silence.' But we cared little now for guns and this was an order that could not be obeyed: the cramp needed to be relieved.

The agonized waiting ended. The old Volkswagen engine exploded into life. We drove on for two or three minutes, then stopped again. The door slid open and quickly we were taken from the van and walked awkwardly inside what seemed to be the foyer of an old apartment block. I was left waiting with one of The Brothers Kalashnikov. John was brought quickly behind me. The Kalashnikov Brother seemed genuinely delighted to see me. I heard him announce himself and pat my shoulder, then John and I and Abed were squeezed into a small lift and it ascended. John was shaking, not from fear, it was just his muscles and limbs relieved suddenly from their tense strain. Abed spoke, this time in French. 'Pas bonne expérience.' He touched his pistol to our foreheads. We smiled.

From the lift we were ushered into an apartment, walked along its hall, and into one of the bedrooms. A huge room, perhaps three times the size of our double cell. A carpet filled the floor. Nothing else was there. Within minutes mattresses and covers were brought to us. One of the guards asked 'Do you want a toilet?' I said 'You bet,' and was taken to the bathroom. The door closed, I lifted my blindfold and stood in amazement: a bath, a shower, bidet, washbasin, real soap. I squatted with mystified delight on the toilet seat. Laughing in my confusion at once more sitting on a toilet seat, I quickly finished, knowing that my friend would most certainly want to use these luxurious facilities.

We slept that night side by side, a two-foot gap between the mattresses. We were exhausted from the cold in the prison and the cramped ache from sitting in the van, but the size of the room was a relief. Space to walk again; we cared for nothing else. The windows were covered with sheet steel, but we had electric light with a switch on the wall. This was paradise.

The next morning we discovered what we had least expected. There were other prisoners being held in the bedroom opposite ours. We could not see them but their voices revealed that the Americans were not home, they were here, hostages still. The next six weeks we spent here were comparatively carefree. The horrors of the House of Fun passed quickly from us.

We walked around the room daily, scoring up the miles, and in the evening played dominoes, often talking and reminiscing about that last awful place. Mahmoud, the guard who spoke good English, and with whom we had established a reasonable relationship, was here. Abed was too and so was our friend the Kalashnikov Brother who we now knew as Saafi. Said visited occasionally. We had little to say to him and he stayed for only a few minutes. Walking around the perimeter of the room, John felt a lump under the carpet. Cautiously we lifted it. Underneath was a fat envelope. We opened it. 240 Lebanese pounds. We were amazed. Searching and lifting the carpet in other places we found a letter written in very small handwriting. It was in French and difficult for us to decipher. We knew that this letter and the money had been hidden by some other guest of our captors. We returned the letter, because it would have been dangerous to have it found in our possession. The money we decided to keep. 'This is our taxi fare home, Brian, if we ever get out of here.' I laughed, but it was a spur to hope. We had never given up planning our escape. Escape was never possible when held in an underground prison, but locked up in an apartment there was always a possibility.

Abed came regularly with our food. He had become himself again. Perhaps being away from the confines of the prison and being able to look out from the balcony onto the street below, he, like us, had become more human again. He would frequently attempt to wrestle playfully with John. It was impossible, it was a piece of childish foolishness. John, blindfolded, could see nothing. Abed would laugh. He never played such games with me. He always sensed my antagonism. I think he was fearful. So was I, for if he attempted to play with me I was not sure I would be able to keep it playful.

Southward Bound

The six weeks we spent in the apartment were alleviated when they at last gave us some books. Mostly they were ineffectual gothic romances or poorly written stories dating from the 1950s. Surprisingly some of them were recent works, particularly in the field of international politics. Michel Seurat's name was written in a few of them. We knew he was a Frenchman taken hostage at the beginning of Islamic Jihad's campaign. We also knew, from the Americans, that Seurat had died at the hands of his kidnappers.

We were not disheartened though we knew the three Americans were being held in the room opposite. We knew also, from hearing a chance radio broadcast, about Terry Waite's disappearance. We were still hopeful, we still wanted to believe that our transfer to this apartment was a preparation for our release. We concluded that the kidnapping of Terry Waite was only a measure to ensure the kidnappers' security during the releases. Thus our spirits remained high.

Towards the end of that six-week period Mahmoud, the tall English-speaking guard, came and took away our mattresses, bed covers, the books and everything that we had been given. We were left alone. This was surely indicative that something was about to happen, and we were both convinced that this time it was over. For two nights we lay shivering on the carpet trying to sleep, but unable to for excitement and anticipation. We were always wide awake and talking with one another before the dawn call to prayer. It would have been impossible to sleep in any case. The nights were filled with automatic gunfire and the relentless shelling of a heavy cannon. What radio news we picked up told us that this was an attack by Amal, one of the Shia Muslim paramilitary groups, on the Palestinian refugee camps. All night long this bombardment continued. It became for me the noise of some grotesque monster grinding and slashing the earth outside our four walls. This city was in a perpetual night of warfare and what my

Lebanese friend had once told me rang true once more. 'In Lebanon it is not a matter of whom you kill, but how many.'

For many hours as we walked in circles around the room we argued out why it seemed that the time was right. We had accumulated limited information from the radio besides what we had gleaned from the Americans and knew it was just under a year since our disappearance, since those snatches from the radio allowed us to fix an approximate date. It had been a long year. We always felt that the longer we were held, the stronger our captors' position became. But whatever our expectations, the truth was not as we were desperately believing it to be.

Several men entered the room late one evening. Our hands were taped to our sides, our blindfolds tightened and most of our faces covered. We were given sweaters, and then quickly we were walked out of the apartment and down the six flights of stairs. Outside the air was hot and dusty. We were walked a short distance, then hands took hold of my body and I was slid into some kind of compartment underneath the floor of a truck. John was put in beside me, his feet beside my face. It was tiny and we were crushed together. Lifting my head from the floor I felt the roof of this compartment some three inches above me. We were in a kind of coffin.

We lay in this cramped airless space for perhaps three-quarters of an hour, wrestling to free our hands and pull the gags from our mouths so that we might breathe more freely. Outside the guards talked and then were silent. We thought they had gone away. Were they going to leave us here for someone to come and collect us? What if the people that were coming for us could not find us? The air was thin and the heat would make this coffin an oven. Tormented with these thoughts we heard Said's voice speak loudly. 'John, John no speak.' Then Said informed us that if we made a noise the truck would be blown up: the driver had instructions. We couldn't speak in any case, with the gags on our mouths and our hands tied to our waists. The man was a fool, I thought. Then the engine roared into life and we set off.

We drove for several hours, and all through the journey we were squirming and wriggling to release the gags and our hands and somehow edge up the blindfolds from our eyes. But it was pointless. It was so dark and all the effort was using up what little air there was. As we moved we could see some light filtering in through odd holes in the floor and in the sides of our container. Soon the sun began to beat down and the dust off the road thrown up into the compartment made breathing still more difficult. The pungent fumes from the diesel made the atmosphere suffocating.

The horror of this panic-stricken journey seemed to me indescribable. Fear choking in your throat. The air suffocating and your head banging and bloody against the roof of that shallow space. My attempts at silent song could not calm me. I began to rage and blaspheme man and God. I cursed every one of my captors and searched out every foul-mouthed word of condemnation that I could find. Panic was seizing me by the throat. I felt the pressure of it and I raged and raged and tried to remember those convoluted chapters of the Book of Revelation. There in those apocalyptic words, I found enough violence of expression to condemn these men. Exhausted from my ranting I would try to recall that hymn of William Blake:

Bring me my Bow of burning gold:
Bring me my Arrows of desire:
Bring me my Spear: O clouds unfold!
Bring me my chariot of fire!

I will not cease from Mental Fight
Nor shall my Sword sleep in my hand
Till we have built Jerusalem
In England's green and pleasant Land.

I would repeat it over and over again spitting out the words defiantly, this time hating only myself and wishing that I was not here and being made to endure slow and crippling death in this tight hot darkness. John was silent. I tapped his head with my feet and he returned the gesture. There was no comfort of touch and reassurance beyond this tapping with our feet on one another's heads.

The hours were endless. We were drowning in that airless box. Through it all, the raving, the singing silent songs defiantly and the desperate prayers to end this thing, for death was preferable to this slow, slow poisonous suffocation. In these conditions, there was no way to control the mind. It spun off, launched into some unholy awfulness, doubling the physical suffering. The words and images that flash through the mind in such conditions are not of human origin, and they were beyond my understanding. They crushed me with their horror. It seemed as if hot wires were being drawn slowly through the centre of my brain. My mind was exploding over and over again. Given the chance I would have screamed out and had the van and the horrors that it bred blown to oblivion. It would be over, and the torment would be extinguished. We travelled for about three hours, my head continually beating as the truck bumped and swerved. The man who drove this truck was as mindless as my mind was full of terrifying and incomprehensible things.

Finally the van stopped. My mind jumped with delight and with relief and it seemed that all those horrors were instantaneously washed away, but another kind of panic set in. I was impatient to be out. I could not bear waiting. My mind lay in smithereens inside my skull. I wanted to breathe again and blow away this creature-thing I had become.

The doors opened. 'Hurry, hurry, hurry . . . you bastards, you pieces of filth . . . hurry up.' I snarled to myself 'Hurry up, hurry up' and then like a piece of bread from an oven I was slowly dragged out and carried to the ground. I lay gulping, choking myself with the fresh air. But the tapes about my face still restricted that full sweet inhalation. At last I felt a knife cut the tape that bound my hands and feet and the tapes on my face were ripped off. They bundled me into a corner against the wall and soon John was thrown in a heap beside me. I reached out to touch him 'Are you okay?' I asked. John's answer puzzled me. He asked, with his mind half gone, 'Are they going to shoot us?' Now I understood that he too had travelled further than this truck had carried us. 'No, John, they are not going to shoot us,' I whispered. The guards were sitting around us. They were silent. 'Do you want anything?' one of them asked. 'Water, give me some water,' I answered, angry, not caring now that they should know my anger. They gave me a bottle of water. I gulped it down, almost choking myself with another huge swallow of water. 'John,' I said again, 'here, drink.' I handed the bottle to him. One of the guards again asked 'Do you want anything?' and I answered with loud sarcasm 'Yes, I want a swimming pool!' I wanted to defuse myself in cool, clear, crisp water. I wanted to feel my body languidly move through it, to be alone and free in the vast sunlight with cool water caressing my flesh.

The next few days we were held in the outhouse of a farm in the hills. Said spent all that time with us and revealed more of his paranoia. He could not sit with us in silence. He desperately wanted us to talk with him. He was always asking questions, making remarks or simply demanding 'Talk, talk to me, speak, speak.' It was then I knew for sure that this man was afraid of himself and of being alone with himself. John, having recuperated quickly from that dreadful journey, seized the opportunity, 'Said,' he asked 'why were we beaten so many times in the prison?' Said was silent, then answered, brushing the question away from him, 'This man, he is crazy man.' John coldly, defiantly answered, 'Yes, Said, he is very crazy, he is also very evil.'

Said was silent. Later that day he gave us his own plate of food. Never before had he shared a room with us. It was a gesture of appeasement and an acknowledgement of guilt. We devoured the roast chicken, forgetting nothing.

After two days we were moved a short distance, again in the boot of a car, to a new hiding place. We found ourselves in a very large space, more like a barn than a room. We were placed in the corner, mattresses were brought for us and we were told to sleep. To our surprise the guards slept with us, only a few feet from us. We were warned not to look at them as they slept, but we had no desire to. More and more now we sought to live our lives exclusively to ourselves and as far as possible dismiss the existence of these men and create our own separate meaning.

The next day, sitting, leaning against the wall whispering to one another as the guards watched television or listened to the radio, we realized it would be impossible to sit for twenty-four hours a day blindfolded with the guards beside us. It is difficult to live in a world when you can see no-one in it. Conversation dries up when you cannot see the response or the eyes of your listener. We decided to ask the guards to put a screen around us so that we could exercise and lift the blindfolds in order to eat. If they refused, we could refuse to eat, for we would not be animalized any more. We would eat as human beings and look at what we ate.

Mahmoud, the gentle giant, as we came to regard him, hung bed sheets around us creating a barrier between themselves and us. We were in our own world again. Foolishly at night the guards would sit in the full glare of the TV and the light burning brightly in their half of this barnlike accommodation. We sat in our darkness, but we peered through the coarse weave of the fabric, watching our captors as they sat and stared at the television.

From now until our release, for over three years, we were to be held with chains on our ankles and wrists. They came and drilled the wall, fixing steel bolts into it, to which they attached the chains by padlocks and then put the chains on us. The shock of being treated like this made us furious. We insisted bitterly that we were not animals. But our complaints fell on deaf ears. 'It is our work,' one guard would say, half apologetic, and another simply said viciously 'It is not your business.' These chains made it difficult to sleep and practically impossible to exercise. They were totally unnecessary. We could not escape and even had we done so we didn't know where we were, nor how to return to Beirut.

The proximity of the guards, with only a coarse cotton sheet separating us, was more and more disconcerting. We had to talk in whispers. We had to restrict our conversations for there were many things which we would not want them to overhear; things that we held precious to ourselves.

We were aware that other prisoners were near us in other rooms, but, could not see them, only hear them move to the toilet in the mornings. We were sure that the French were amongst the other captives. The days were crushingly long though we had some relief in listening to the television through the curtain.

We now received our first in-depth interrogation. We were given no warning. On one of those long boring days, the guards came and unchained my feet, and took me out from behind the sheet. They led me across the room where two roughly made long wooden stools had been placed at right angles, and I was put behind them and rechained to a radiator. The man who came to speak with me was polite and well-spoken: his English was almost that of an academic. His accent suggested that he might not be Lebanese. He asked me how I had come to Lebanon, who had interviewed me for my position in the University, what courses I taught. I insisted on asking him why I had been taken and what value was an Irishman to the cause of Islam or the freedom of the Arab peoples. My interrogator was nonplussed by my interrogation of him. He sat silent, fumbling out his answers. In the end I sensed a genuine sympathy and confusion.

'I do not know why you are here,' he said. 'It is not my decision, I promise you I will speak with my chief of your case,' he concluded. 'Do you want anything?' Those words, so often repeated, had become intensely annoying. Knowing I had his sympathy, and that he could not answer my questions, I told him calmly, emphasizing every word, 'Yes, I want something, I want my freedom, I want to live like a man, I am not an animal.' His hand reached out and took mine, he held it for a moment much as a young lover would, then squeezed it firmly in a strong handshake. 'What can I do for you?' he asked. I knew that to protest any more would gain me nothing. 'I want books, many books.' He asked, surprised, 'You have not been given books?' He wanted to know what books I would like. I could not think of titles and I did not expect that a specific request would bring me what I wanted. 'Anything, bring me anything.' He tapped my shoulder again. 'I will return tomorrow.' Across the room I heard him questioning John. He spent a long time talking, seeking information which John did not have.

That evening a television was placed in the far corner of the room. Sitting in diagonally opposite corners, we could see the screen but not each other. The guards were out of sight in another room. The film was the usual Americans-in-Vietnam story, full of macho posturing and constant slaughter. Something struck me as I watched this. I was appalled at the violence of it and yet the movie was no more violent than anything I had seen previously, perhaps even less so; yet the violence in it burned deep into me and sickened me. I could not watch it, I was horrified and ashamed. After it was over I sat thinking why I had found myself so repelled by what I had watched. What had changed in me? Perhaps it was a combination of the futility of the mindless violence in the film and the way these men were entranced by it. But these are the reasons of the mind. Something deeper within me recoiled, aghast and unbelieving at the horror. I could not understand this passionate revulsion in me.

The next day my interrogator brought me a gift. It was a newly purchased book about the history of Black Americans. I was grateful. He apologized for the violence of the previous day's movie. That evening I was returned and chained up again with John. We spoke of our interrogations. John had been quizzed at length about his work, what he knew about the different paramilitary groups in Lebanon, and who his political advisor was in his news agency. It was obvious they considered John to be some kind of spy. We were all tarred with that brush.

When this interrogator returned the following day, we complained vehemently about the chains and the many beatings that we had received. He was genuinely surprised. He seemed also to be angry that they had occurred. His simple answer to our anger at the chains was that they were for our security. His calm explanation that God was testing me brought my anger to a boiling point and I turned on him and asked 'And who is testing you, my friend?' To make God the justification for the way these all-too-human warriors had treated us was more than I could bear. It seemed the ultimate cowardice.

Later we were offered the chance to write a letter to our families. We said we would think about this. At first I was not in favour of letters arriving home a year after our disappearance. It would be unbearable for our families. We discussed whether these letters, if we wrote them, would ever be posted, but concluded after a time that it would be better for our families to have some news of us. At least they would know we were alive. When the interrogator returned to collect the letters we asked him what was happening in the negotiations with our government. He answered 'Nothing, your governments have done nothing for you.'

We sank back into our separate silences. There was nothing to be said. One year and nothing, and how many more years? So many questions filled our heads. We retreated, almost grateful for our blindfolds, and lay back, drowning in our own thoughts. How long could our families hold out? To what extremes would these men go to achieve their purpose? What were they demanding? And what was in the minds of our respective governments, that they would not negotiate? We tried to console one another and compensate for the futility of those questions. After all, would these men know if there were negotiations? Even our interrogator with the authority he seemed to have might not know if negotiations were progressing secretly at a higher level.

The immensity of our kidnappers' conceit was beyond belief. They had murdered, maimed and taken hostage a handful of men, how many exactly we did not know, but we reckoned possibly fifteen. With these fifteen men, some like ourselves chained to walls in apartments, in prisons, or in underground cells, they hoped to hold the world to ransom.

The cotton sheet that separated us from our captors also allowed us a deeper insight into their minds and their behaviour. Every morning before dawn Said would come and sit at the other side of our sheet with a portable cassette player and would play a tape of some holy man chanting and reciting the Suras of the Koran. The tape would be loud and blaring. Said would sit chanting in unison with his mullah and after hours of this he would become delirious. He would begin sobbing, then wailing. This self-induced morbidity seemed interminable. At times he would continue in this distraught and mind-jarring state literally for hours, and when he had finished another guard came. Said made his men pray, and they, like him, would work themselves up into a grief-stricken hysteria. Having to sit listening to this three times a day, day after day after day, was maddening. It was a kind of psychological torture.

Both John and I were driven to distraction by this religious frenzy a few feet from us. It was becoming harder and harder to hold ourselves together. In its own way it had much the same impact as the radio tuned to static outside our old prison cell. It seemed these men could thrust themselves into the most pathetically morbid states, effortlessly, like throwing a light switch. They would move from monotonous repetition of the words of the Koran into hysteria, wailing and crying out to Allah. At first we tried to sleep through it, and since this was not possible, to plug our ears with pieces of tissue and tie towels around our heads, clamping our hands over our ears. Anything to put a barrier between ourselves and the moronic and ecstatic chanting. Then just as instantaneously they would finish, get up and walk away, talk and laugh with their friends or watch television. These prayers were not acts of spirit in grateful submission and contemplation of God, but rather of personalities massively unresolved. I now began to understand how it was that these men could effect such mercurial personality changes, one minute being affectionate and pleasant and then suddenly aggressive and violent. I could now understand how they confused need with revulsion, and how much they were afraid of what we were. I understood why it was that they had this unacknowledged dislike, or in some cases loathing of themselves.

It was becoming increasingly difficult for us to hold our own minds in balance. On each occasion when these prayers would begin it was as if we were innoculated with their hysteria. As hard as these man prayed I called out to God to shield my own mind from the contamination of this holy insanity. I raged with anger at the pain of listening for long periods as one man after another displayed his sickness in front of me. It was becoming impossible. Both of us were on the edge of screaming. I would much rather be beaten than be subjected to this more traumatic and emotional disturbance.

To combat this onslaught we tried talking in low whispers to one another. The mind needed an exchange with another mind to overcome this oppression. As we tried to engage our minds in something that would release us from the grip of madness, we found ourselves bursting into giggling raptures. Each time these prayers started we would be caught up in a whirlwind of giggling. We were unable to speak for laughter, unable even to look at one another. It was our own hysterical defence, beyond our ability to control. We stuffed pieces of blanket into our mouths or bit tightly on the corner of a book trying to silence ourselves. We were not laughing at these men but protecting our own sanity.

The guards' ecstatic states were not restricted solely to the ritual prayer times. One evening they sat as usual beyond the curtain. The TV was blaring. They were enthusiastically watching the US serial *The A-Team*. Said was in his corner reciting the holy scriptures, then, as we had witnessed so many times before, he began chanting and slowly sliding into self-induced rapture. As we listened, it seemed he was in competition with the television. His prayers got faster, more intense, excited, building up, trying to rise above the gunfire and the screaming cars on the TV. Said wanted the attention of his men. He wanted his great but pathetic holiness to be admired. Then, suddenly, in the midst of his religious metamorphosis he suddenly looked towards Mahmoud and barked out at him to turn off the television. Mahmoud, calm and unawed by Said, answered something that we could vaguely translate as 'Pray if you want to pray . . . God cares nothing about the television.' Mahmoud returned to his viewing and Said to his prayers, at first feebly, but slowly again building to a crescendo. Beginning with deep sobs, he recited the chants hypnotically and he was again transported. Then just as before, he snapped out of his ecstasy. As if he had awoken from a dream and was still half dreaming, he called out to Mahmoud, his voice slow and distant: 'What is the gunfire?' Mahmoud answered uninterestedly '*A-Team.*' Said insisted on making an impression and said he believed it was the Israelis or the forces of Geagea.* He wanted to fight, he declared, he wanted to die for Allah. No-one was impressed. He returned sulkily to his recitation.

One afternoon when the other guards had left Said alone with us, John was dozing, tired from the constant early morning prayers which ripped into our sleep. I lay half awake, trying to enjoy what little sunlight filtered through the guards' side of our room. The sheet that separated us from them was hung just above head height and with the high ceilings of this old Arabic building we could catch some light. Said was moving about restlessly. The radio was on; Said always needed noise, he needed to distract his mind, and this was common to many of our captors. He began talking to himself, speaking words in

* Samir Geagea, leader of Israeli-backed Christian forces in South Lebanon.

English, which he had obviously learned from TV from those violent films. For hours they all watched them in awe-struck wonder. Said spoke: 'You bastard, I kill you . . . you bastard I kill you, bastard, bastard, bastard,' he repeated, trying to imitate the aggressive manner in which he had heard the expression used. Then he was moving about the room again, distracted and restless. As if he was looking for something, anything to occupy him.

My own mind was equally restless, seeking out something on which to concentrate and evade the crushing boredom of the coming hours. The room was flushed with the morning's half-light. Birdsong sparked softly outside. Said and I were caught up in our mutual rapture, drifting heedlessly around one another like fish in a tank. Suddenly the dreaming silence was shattered. Said was weeping great shuddering sobs. This was a different kind of weeping from the automatic religious melancholia of his prayers. He walked around the room crying, the whole room seemed to fill up with his anguish. I felt, as I never had before, great pity for this man and felt if I could I would reach out and touch him. I knew instinctively some of the pain and loss and longing that he suddenly found himself overwhelmed by.

The weeping continued. Said became fleshy and human for me. Here was a man truly stressed. His tears now wrenched a great well-spring of compassion from me. I wanted to nurse and console him. I felt no anger and that defensive laughter which had before cocooned me was no longer in me. I lay on my mattress and looked up over the top of the sheet. Said's shadow, caught in the sunlight, was immense. It flowed up the wall and across the ceiling. He was now chanting, fleeing from his sadness into recitation. His hands were clasped on the top of his head in the gesture of prayer. His body swayed and turned in a slow chanting circle. The room was filled with his eerie shadow and the slow rhythmic utterances choked with sobs. At times his voice broke and he cried out in desperation for Allah. I felt my own tears. I was transformed with a deep and helpless love for him. I had become what he was calling out for.

I woke John. 'Look at this, look at this,' I urged quietly. We both stared at the great moving shadow, fascinated and compelled. After a few minutes, John, exasperated, sighed in disgust and turned away. I remained watching. There was something unbearably beautiful about it. At once terrified and intrigued, my loathing for this man began to fall from me. I no longer thought of him as nothing, and felt guilty for having dismissed him so completely. Said's violence against us was a symptom of his need of us. Here was a man whose mind was forever locked in that desert wilderness that I had known during my worst moments in isolation.

Obo and the Snake

During our captivity we were moved some seventeen times. On many of these occasions we were kept for short periods, sometimes days, sometimes weeks or months in the hills in the south of Lebanon. These places and my time in them all blur together in my memory. To go through them in chronological sequence would be as boring for me as it would be for the reader. It was all monstrous repetition. I have tried therefore to encapsulate many of these moves in one, so that I may miss nothing essential.

We never knew when we were going to be moved until the occasion came. We would hear lots of noise and talking in the early hours. If it was before the morning call to prayer we would know that something was about to happen and that we were to be moved. I remember how stressful it was even though we knew what was likely to happen, that it simply meant a move to another location. We became agitated, upset, nervous, I suppose in the way a captured animal does when its daily routine of feeding and sleeping and walking around its cage is changed, and it becomes aggressive. So it was with us.

The routine was always the same. They came into the room to wake you though you were already awake and pulled the blankets away. They would bark 'Up, up . . . get up.' You would stand while the chains were removed from your hands and feet. Then you would be walked to the middle of the floor and there pushed down, told to 'Kneel, kneel,' and like obedient performers in a time-worn ritual, you would obey. Your heads would be hooded and bound round with thick broad packing tape; an aperture was left only at the nose. You were always gagged, so that you could neither speak nor shout out. After this your wrists were chained closely to your ankles: the left wrist to the left foot and the right hand to the right foot.

In this bowed and bent position the muscles soon began to ache and breathing became laboured. You sat through this for some minutes, wanting them to hurry. With a kind of careless arrogance you would be lifted into a large sack. It was pulled up over the head and the top firmly tied off. In this close confinement the air and heat were thick. The body raged into sweat, the tight constriction of the tape forcing the body's heat back onto itself.

With a sudden jerk, the sack would be hoisted onto the back of one or two of the guards. The chains about your wrists and ankles cut viciously into the bones. Your wrists would begin to throb with a painful drum beat, making the hands feel like they were on fire, then numbed and cold. Your feet would sting with terrible pinpricks as the circulation was severed. You would try to relieve the pain but each infinitesimal movement sent it shooting to your neck or shoulder or some muscle contorted in trying to relieve the stress in other parts. Imagine a child trying to escape from the ever tightening carcass of a dried-up womb. The body screamed in unrelieved agony.

Outside this hot enclosure 'porters' grunted and swore. Your body banged off the walls as they descended darkened stairways. You knew your weight was too much for them. You expected to be dropped and to feel the cold sharp edge of stone snap a bone or wrench your arm out of its shoulder socket. Your bound hands could not shield your head. You awaited that crashing thud that would make you insensible to the raging ache. You wanted the relief yet feared the pain.

It ended as it always did with your corpse being slung awkwardly into the boot of some vehicle. The relief of resting against something fixed was short-lived. You twisted and turned in tiny movements to find some comfort. It was futile. The vehicle moved off and you would be half smothered for the duration of the journey. The torment began again as you were carried upstairs to your new prison apartment.

Many of the journeys were like this but we did not often end up in the relative luxury of an apartment. Sometimes we found ourselves spending weeks or months in the winter in a ramshackle farm outhouse in those south Lebanese hills. Here the snow and rain and icy wind held us in numb subjection. The cold of the chain burned against foot and wrist like dry ice. We spent weeks permanently buried under five or six blankets.

We had devised a way of playing poker with our dominoes, always our dominoes came with us. We would lie under our mountain of blankets huddled close together to hold in our body heat and share it, if we could, between ourselves. Only the fingers of one hand were exposed as we fumbled delicately in the freezing air with our new game. Our bets became outrageous. We gambled a wealth we would never possess but the mathematics of it was a way of blanking out our eskimo existence.

Our abuse of one another was as vociferous as ever. 'You fat-assed fucker, McCarthy, you are a rotten snake, you lost the last five games yesterday, you owe me five thousand,' to which John would reply 'You must be soft in the head like all those Irish that you come from,' and I would bounce back 'Soft! . . . Wait till I tell you, fella, just call me Obo hard as nails.' The word 'Obo' fascinated John, he had never heard the word nor did he know the product: Obo, masonry nails, nails for driving into walls. John loved the sound of the word. 'Obo.' Often thenceforth John would call me Obo and I acted out the caricature that the name represented to him. I in return addressed him, hissing out the word 'Snake' and he would in his turn try all sorts of duplicity and cheating. So the game went on. The days of Obo and The Snake. We were Butch Cassidy and the Sundance Kid. This new name I had acquired made me readjust my game of dominoes. I would attempt to start and finish the game with the same double, as the word Obo begins and ends with an 'o'. When I had achieved this I would bounce up and declare an Obo victory, and John would hiss back 'Obo my bollocks!'

Our conversation in this place we mockingly called the pig-sty was not about our past but more and more we turned with enthusiastic excitement to discuss our future, the places we would go, the things we would do. We lay all day shrouded in blankets with a vast vision of our future. We would not let it go.

These hill hide-outs were so far removed from any town or village that the smallest luxuries such as soap, toothpaste or a toothbrush were forgotten. Our plastic cutlery when it broke was never replaced. We ate with filthy fingers, enjoying the pleasure of the warm food on our hands. Our clothes became filthy. The cold spring water that was brought to us each day for washing was useless. We retreated into the comfort of our own dirt. To stand shivering in that freezing water was an endurance easily foregone.

Every few days they would bring a one-bar electric fire and leave it with us for perhaps an hour. We washed and dried what underwear we could but most of the time was spent drying tissues for reuse. How many times I blew my nose into the dried residue of yesterday's cold I did not know nor did I care. The guards spoke little to us. They did not want to leave the warmth of their fire.

Many times when we were held in the hills Frank Reid was near us. We often heard him being punched and kicked. When one is held alone so long in such awful conditions it is easy to succumb to fear. The mind's flight from fear becomes a refuge of sorts. But the guards saw only his fear. It pleased the weakest of them to abuse him. Their own fear was in those blows. We knew it and were thus protected from it. If they ever tried to be aggressive, we would resist. Sometimes in silence, sometimes with a joke or laughter. They were easily disarmed. They were forced back into their own fear, unable to exploit ours because we would not expose it. Our world was separate from theirs. We had become fierce in our own self-reliance, but they needed our fear to become the men they wanted to be. We would not give it. Nor did they know how to extract it. They were the prisoners of our resistance.

Many of these moves up into the hills were precipitated by the internecine wars that were a constant feature of Lebanese politics. As we knew, having travelled and stayed in many parts of that small country, nowhere in Lebanon is at peace. We spoke frequently about the guards and their peculiar characteristics. We had come to know them extremely well. Even blindfolded, you can observe much of a man. The brutal way in which they moved us was totally unnecessary. Why they couldn't simply walk us down those stairs in the darkness before dawn, slip us into the boot of a car and drive us to wherever they wanted to go was a question we often asked ourselves. The need for hoods and for chains and that bone-wrenching carriage in that smelly hot sack was an illustration of these men's need to see themselves as warriors in the cause of Islam.

I remember telling John how on an early afternoon during my short stay in Beirut I had been walking along the back streets of the area known as Hamra. It was a poor area but close enough to the busy commercial centre to make its own living. As I walked along the street that afternoon with a colleague from the University we observed a small butcher's shop. It was hardly a shop: more a recess with a table inside for the pieces of cut-up carcass and another table outside with a gallows-like fixture on the wall above it. As we walked past, the butcher was hanging a live goat, its hind feet tethered and hooked over that gallows spike. It hung head down, quiet, unable to move, and beside it, tethered to a drainpipe, was a sheep, which sat quietly looking around it undisturbed and unworried. The butcher with a sharp knife banged home a vicious blow that punctured the jugular vein of the hanging goat. Blood spurted onto the street and all over the cobblestones, into the roadside drain and off into the sewer system. The butcher nonchantly proceeded to gut the animal. Its innards fell at his feet. The animal was still alive. We noticed how the butcher saw us stop and watch him for a few minutes. He smiled, whether it was because he saw us looking at him as if admiring him or whether it was his pleasure in his work, I could not be sure. I was at once captivated and repulsed by the viciousness of it. He calmly continued his work, looking constantly at us and not at his probing hands and lacerating knife entering into the still-living body of the animal.

My friend tapped my elbow 'Come on, Brian, lets get out of this place.' I looked at the sheep who sat waiting. It was so calm and placid. I knew this animal was next to be slaughtered, and yet it was totally unconcerned. I looked again at the butcher and he now seemed to me as dazed and as unconcerned as the sheep. The whole scene became for me a metaphor for the city itself, its bloody and continuous slaughter that no-one seemed to care about. It had accepted that slaughter into itself. Even the dying themselves turned blind and nonchalant eyes to it. The city was falling down around them. Those Lebanese I knew spoke often of the war and ended their comments with a shrug of the shoulders: 'Welcome to Lebanon.' The phrase echoed with acceptance and resignation.

The feuding in Beirut since 1976 had given the men that held us an identity beyond the political reason for our kidnapping. They had a purpose, they had a job to do. They were made meaningful. Yet on those occasions when we engaged in conversation about the politics of Lebanon and what they themselves were doing they would shy away, as if answers had not been worked out. They were merely the receivers of orders and if their chief asked them to march into a minefield they would do it, like sheep, like that waiting sheep, dazed and uncaring.

We talked obsessively about the food we received while we were kept in the hills, away from the villages. The food was not always good. It sufficed, but on other occasions we would get those cloyingly sweet pastries, or at the other extreme, pungent and spicy meat. It seems to me still that what we eat as much as how we eat it speaks volumes about our personalities. These men loved their spicy meats and equally adored their viciously sugary pastries. Their likes and their loves sat at either end of one extreme. There was no middle ground. One moment they could be charming, friendly, and within an instant became something that was other than human.

We had long philosophical debates. I would argue that 'anything one human being perpetrates against another cannot by its own logic be called inhuman. What is inhuman if that act is carried out by a human being?' We discussed such questions seriously, picking up our conversation days after we thought we had ended it. In our musings we were examining ourselves, our own responses, the moral identity that we thought defined us and perhaps also the changes, doubts and desires that we felt growing in us. Our world was not the mono-chrome morality which defined and limited theirs. Even in these most deprived conditions we found within ourselves and within those shared discussions a more valuable and richer world than we had conceived of before. We were beginning to learn our freedom, the way Rousseau spoke of it. Captivity had re-created freedom for us. Not a freedom outside us to be hungered after, but another kind of freedom which we found to our surprise and relish within ourselves.

The endless moving had worn us down. It was not the stress of the actual move itself but the dread of where we would arrive. Some of them, such as 'the pig sty', were places where, we both agreed, we would not keep our pet dogs. We frequently expressed our anger at this kind of accommodation to the guards. We would tell them 'I would not keep an animal in this place.' They would simply shrug; they did not have to stay in it. They only brought the food to us, the animals. With each move we expected to descend lower and began to expect less.

On one of these moves we did not have to undergo that awful chaining of wrist to ankle and the hooding but were simply gagged and our hands tied, walked out to a car, quickly put into a boot and driven off. Some fifteen minutes later, we stopped and were taken from the car. We were obviously still in the countryside, the silence was complete. Quickly we were rushed through a door. There was a smell of animals, sheep bleating nearby. Then upstairs again, and we expected the worst as we entered a room, hands guiding us from behind. We were pushed into what seemed another small room. We heard the guards outside the room talk and heard what we assumed were our blankets, bedclothes and mattresses being brought in. We were lifted again, walked out of that small room. We were shoved into

another room and heard a door close. We lifted the blindfolds and as
we had suspected, we found ourselves in a small room, smaller than
the prisons we had been in. But it was covered with wonderful tiles
with vine leaves and bunches of grapes embossed on them. In one
corner was a hot and cold water tap which didn't work. High up on
the wall, too high to see out, was a tiny window perhaps six inches
square. The door to our new prison was a brown plastic folding door.
For the first few days that we remained here, we were not chained. We
were excited as always; this was an apartment, and we were only one
floor up. The door had no lock. Every apartment we were held in
inspired us with schemes of escape. We half believed in them. Here we
began to believe that escape was really possible.

After three days the guards came back with electric drills, strong
bolts, and lengths of chain. Nothing had changed after all. But we
were still exuberant, we thought that it might still be possible, that we
only needed time. We didn't know yet where we were but could
guess. The knowledge we would require to build a plan and execute it
would come to us somehow. With us back in chains, the door that had
been closed since our arrival was now left open. We could look out
from our tiny little washroom into an elaborate kitchen, covered with
the most expensive tiles, both on the floors and on the walls. This was
obviously the home of someone wealthy. It was only part complete:
doors stood in the kitchen waiting to be hung. Immediately outside
our room and to the right of our open door there was a large panel
door, inset with opaque mottled glass.

The chains on our feet meant nothing now. We were delirious. Our
folding door was open every day, and every morning the sun came
blazing in to us. The glass itself seemed to turn a bright glowing silver
with the light of the sun and even through our blindfolds that
dazzling, blinding, silvered pane of glass was a joy and we drank our
fill of it in silence for hours, saying occasionally 'Jesus, light after all
these years . . . it's fucking sunlight out there.'

Several new guards exchanged a rota with some of the men who had
been with us from the beginning. Abed was here, the Abed who had
enjoyed so much his nightly visits with his Kalashnikov. Saafi was
here, one of the original Brothers Kalashnikov. Two new guards were
here, both of them extremely polite, very reverent. When we asked
them questions about the war between Iran and Iraq, which we knew
had something to do with our own captivity, they fell silent. They
pretended to know nothing.

Each morning, the guards came, unlocked our feet and walked us blindfolded across that large kitchen room, through a doorway into a kind of hallway and then we were turned right and walked some ten paces into a bathroom. The door closed and we were left to do what we had to do. The mirror above the washbasin had been removed. The suite in the bathroom was green and the walls and floor tiled in a complementary colour. There was a window here also, high up in the wall. Unlike the other windows it was not shut, but it had some paper or cardboard over it.

New toothbrushes and toothpaste were brought to us. We were given clean towels and new shorts and T-shirts. We were delighted to receive these. The clothes we had been wearing for so many months, sometimes unwashed for weeks, were ragged and torn and had to be held up by our hands or with pieces of string as we walked to the toilet.

Within a week we learned that we were not the only ones being held in this fancy country house. We soon knew that it was again the Americans, Tom Sutherland, Frank Reed and Terry Anderson who were with us. Unfortunately there was no way in which we could communicate with them.

The food had improved. We were occasionally given some meat with our rice, and often we were given fresh fruit. Said was an occasional visitor here, but he sensed that when he spoke with us we were not interested; our curt answers displayed our antagonism. We asked once for books and within days they were brought to us, a huge pile of them. A small television set was also given to us for a few hours in the evening. We knew it was being shared between us and the Americans.

We devoured these books. Most of them were cheap US detective thrillers. Abed, who brought the books to us and exchanged them for those we had finished, would before giving us the book look at the cover and if there was a partially clothed woman on it, he would tear the cover off, then ask us 'Is this book sex?' We would answer cutely 'Don't know, Abed, have to read it first.' He would throw the book at us and walk off. When we weren't reading or watching the hour or two of television that we were permitted, we would be plotting our escape. We had convinced the guards when they gave us the new clothes to let us keep our old ones so that we might wash them and have a change. It was a simple logical request, and they did not refuse.

We heard helicopters flying regularly overhead. We knew we were pretty far south. The only people who would have helicopters in this region were the UN or Israel. We were convinced we were very close to the Israeli–occupied zone. Where precisely we were we didn't know, nor did we care. We were sure that we would be able to get away.

The guards were very heavy sleepers. I used to joke with John that empty minds are hard to wake. On one occasion as I slept and the resonance of their snoring told me how deeply they were held by sleep, I rose, walked the four paces to the far end of our small room, climbed up on the water taps fixed in the wall, opened the tiny six by six window and looked out. All around me was open countryside, to the right was another house. There was no life in it. I looked down and estimated that we were only some eighteen or twenty feet from the ground. Off to the left about half a mile away stretched a patch of scrub land. To the right the landscape rose up to a roadway. I could not see much else but it was enough to fuel the fires of escape.

It was not unusual for some of the guards to unlock John and myself at the same time in the morning before going to the toilet. It meant that we were both off our chains at the same time. We reasoned if there were only two guards and both of us were off our chains it would be worth the risk of attempting to overpower them. We also knew that on occasions, one of the guards would still be asleep, therefore with two of us free and only one guard awake, the escape would be very simple.

During one of Abed's discussions with us as we played dominoes, peering out from under our blindfolds, I saw a small rounded thing in Abed's trouser pocket. 'What is that?' I asked. From his trouser pocket he took a small compass. 'It is for my prayers, it shows me where is east and where is Mecca.' 'May I see it?' I said, holding out my hand. He placed the compass in my hand. I looked and took my bearings and, saying nothing to him, handed it back. He was unaware of the information that he had given to us. He talked boastfully of the Koran and his prayers. Abed loved to brag and from his boasting we could obtain information. The door just outside our room with the glass panel which gave us that glorious light always had the key in the lock. Everything was favouring us. We knew our position in terms of the compass. We knew roughly how many miles we might be from Beirut and we knew the immediate terrain outside the window. We had enough clothes. We were only lacking shoes, and those we were convinced we could take from the guards. We would have to wait until night, then leave through the glass door, drop down onto the ground below, and no one would know until the next evening that we were gone. We would have a full day's start. We decided to try and remain on friendly terms with our captors. We did not want them to become anxious or wary of what we were thinking. We wanted to relax them into carelessness; when they were confident they were weakest. We only needed now to wait until the occasion presented itself to us.

One of the new guards who came to speak with us had good English. He told us about himself. His father was a butcher. The flesh on his bones, the bulk on his forearms confirmed he wasn't lying: he had access to more meat than the other guards. But he would talk on many occasions about his desire to be married. Then surprisingly he said to John 'John, teach me to dance.' In total surprise John laughed. 'What?' he asked. 'Teach me to dance.' We were both laughing now, then John sobering up to the idea answered 'I cannot teach you to dance with chains on my feet.' Bilal, as this lad was called, was quiet for a while then asked 'You explain to me how I am to move.' This was a difficult proposition. Dancing for our generation is a spontaneous response to music, to the emotion that rises in us. We were too young for the era of formal dancing, the waltz and the cha–cha. John tried laughingly to explain. 'There are no movements, you just move with the music; if you take these chains off and bring me some Rolling Stones music maybe I could help you. Why do you want to dance?' he asked curiously. 'For when I am married to dance with my wife at the wedding.' It was simple and honest, and its innocence stopped our laughter.

Bilal persisted with John, several times later asking him to teach him to dance, and John would always answer 'With chains on my feet and with my eyes blindfolded, how can I teach you?' But still he would insist and still the answer was the same. And when he left we would laugh a curious kind of laughter, not at the guard but at our situation. We both imagined John with chains and a blindfold waltzing around the room with this huge kidnapper.

It was not often so playful. The guard Abed had always sensed my antagonism towards him. I remembered the beating he had administered and his pleasure in it. One day he watched me exercising. I would always exercise with a kind of brutality, competing with myself, trying to crush out any sloth or emptiness in my mind. Abed whispered to John 'Your friend very strong.' John quickly answered without thinking 'Yes, very strong, his name is Rocky.' Abed was dumbfounded and I laughed quietly to myself, remembering all those young Arab lads watching *Rambo* and *Rocky*. I knew John had hit a nerve. Abed left. I told John. John laughed and we decided to play the Rocky game with Abed. We could in our own way wreak our vengeance without violence; we could without laying a finger on him terrify him and enjoy it.

Abed carried his information to the guard Saafi, who seemed the oldest. Saafi came one day with the other guards and gave us some fruit. The other guards spoke to John. Saafi's English was very poor indeed. John tapped me on the shoulder and said 'He wants to fight with you.' I turned, amazed, 'He wants what?' 'He wants to fight with you.' 'Who does?' I said, hoping it wasn't the big one whose father was a butcher. 'Saafi.' I sat in silence for a few minutes, then said 'Okay let's go.' I stood up quickly, hoping to frighten them with my enthusiasm and hide my own fear. They laughed nervously and John joined them. 'Come on then.' I bent down and rattled the chain. A large guard came in and unchained my feet. 'Christ,' I said to myself, 'What have I let myself in for?' and I walked out feeling my way into the kitchen. I turned towards the large guard behind, pointed to my blindfold and said 'Take this off,' pretending to be hugely courageous. He laughed quietly. 'Not possible,' he said. I shrugged my shoulders again. 'Okay no problem.' Saafi touched me on the shoulder gently and said 'Jokey, jokey, I joke.' I realized that he was a little more afraid of me than I was of him.

Then suddenly the fever grabbed me, 'Go through with it, Brian, wrestle with him,' and I began. I grabbed the hand that touched me on the shoulder, looking desperately for his feet, but he was behind me quick as a flash and around my neck trying to pull me down. My weight was better than his and my exercising over the past years had benefited me greatly. He could not struggle me down. I turned now knowing where he was and we tumbled and crashed about the room. I was blinded, seeing nothing but his quickly moving feet, and he trying to take hold and trip or pull me down. Finally we crashed to the floor. To my luck and his misfortune I was able to scramble up quicker than him and position myself over him, and then with a stroke of intuition I stopped and said gently 'Okay my friend,' and stood up. He too stood up, nervous, excited, laughing, and I laughed. We walked back to the room together, him tapping me in a comradely way on the shoulder. 'You good, you strong, you very strong,' he was still laughing and inside I was shaking. I went into the room where John sat quiet, and squatted down. Saafi chained my feet delicately and patted my knee before leaving without speaking.

Our relationship with the guards was now good enough for them to give us the keys to open our own locks in the mornings and to lock ourselves up when we came back. It was a golden opportunity. On one occasion I came back from the toilet and fumbling blindly to lock myself in, deliberately looped only the padlock end through one part of the chain. I pressed the lock closed and returned the key. The guard was unaware that I was not locked in. John returned and locked himself in. The guard left. Only hours later did I tell John what I had done. John looked cautious and whispered 'How did you do it?' Equally cautiously I explained. 'Jesus,' he said 'what happens tomorrow morning when they discover it.' 'They won't,' I answered. 'They give us the keys, they don't look.' The next morning, the guards gave me the key and I unlocked my unchained feet. They didn't notice.

The next few days saw us both regularly practising our Houdini stunt. Still no-one noticed. We meticulously went through our plan to get ourselves out of that building. It necessarily meant overpowering the guards, but we were convinced this was not a problem. They would be fast asleep. They would be shocked and terrified to see us standing above them. Our one and only fear was that they would panic and start yelling and that we would not be able to do anything but beat them into silence. The guns we might hold in our hands would be useless to us. Any gunfire would have attracted attention. But we were now ready. There was nothing to hold us here. The next morning we would pretend to lock ourselves up for the last time. We were calm, resolved and confident.

The next morning came and with it came Said. We were distressed but not panicked until Said came to us with the guard who was to walk us to the toilet. He gave some instruction in Arabic. The guard instead of throwing us the key bent down and unlocked us. When we returned Said was waiting. The guard bent down, locked us back again and tested the chains with a strong jerk. Said gave another order and though I did not understand the words I understood its meaning. Never again were we to have the keys.

My devastation was total. Every time we had come near liberation a strange fate had pushed us back. This man Said represented fate and I loathed him. That it had to be him struck me forcibly, that this man so disturbed, so malformed within himself should be the agent of destiny. I was filled with a silent but huge anger at myself, at Said, at the world that had been denied me. Said was, I assume, unaware of what he had prevented.

He squatted down beside John and began talking. I sat in silence. It was the silence I maintained always with him. I knew the strength of this weapon. He spoke with John, common pleasantries. 'How are you, John?' 'Fine,' John responded. 'Everything for you is okay?' Said continued. 'No, I am chained to a wall,' John answered. Said laughed. If one showed any pain or grievance Said laughed. 'It is very bad for you' said Said mockingly. John did not answer. I continued my silent disregard of him. Said tapped John. 'Your friend, why he not speak, he never speak?' John answered 'Ask him, don't ask me!' 'Why you don't speak?' I was silent. 'You hear me, why you don't speak?' and I was silent, all our anger at our foiled escape still being redirected into this silence that I knew was defeating Said. He spoke again to John. 'John, you see, he don't speak, why he don't speak?' John said again 'Do not ask me!'

Said stood up; he began to make jokes. 'I know, he like it here very much, he does not want to go home, he like me to come visit him and give him cigarette. He does not want to go home, he loves Lebanon.' I could resist no longer. I sat up violently, turned to him, my blind eyes staring at him and spat out after an intense silence 'Shut up.' Said leaned into the room. 'What you say, what you say?' Passion was quivering in me. I was afraid of what was about to happen, and yet I wanted it to happen. 'You heard me,' I said. 'You heard me.' The challenge was out. The consequences were to come.

I waited, fearful but filled with desire for this man's brutality. I waited to be dragged out and beaten. I felt joy rise in me at the thought of it and the desire for it. He could do with me what he wanted but I would have the victory. I felt it in my blood's heat.

Perhaps he saw the perfect stillness of the anger in me. Perhaps he saw that I could welcome death just as vehemently as any Muslim warrior. Perhaps he knew that no amount of pain would frighten me for I had gone beyond it. But after a few moments of silence he said calmly 'Do not speak it again.' He walked off. I flung myself back on my mattress exhausted, more tormented than if I had been physically tortured. John sat in silence for what seemed a long time. I lay quiet, the anger slowly dissipating. John's hand touched me on the shoulder, 'Don't worry old son, there'll be another time, there'll be another time.' John sensed more than Said did. He knew the thoughts that were charging through my head.

The next morning Said was back. I sat alone. John had gone to the toilet. Said squatted a few feet from me in the tiled kitchen. From under my blindfold I could see his reflection in the polished mahogany of the doorframe. With an elastic band he was swatting flies on the door and as they fell injured to the floor he would squat over them with his elastic band and say 'Little fly, little fly, you die, little fly, you die, little fly.' He was back playing his cartoon role. I was revolted. Swatting flies, talking to them as they lay crippled and crawling about the floor. In that moment I witnessed all the obsession, fixation, and infantilism that commands the mind of a man as disturbed as Said.

I felt again a kind of pity for him, but I would not let it overwhelm me. I kept it in check. Angrily I wrenched at the chain. Said looked at me. 'Break it, break it . . . you want to break it.' His malignant comments mocked me and I withdrew in silence, and grinned broadly. I felt him sit and watch me. This was another kind of battle. For some reason Blake's aphorism swam into my head: 'The tigers of wrath are wiser than the horses of instruction' and with that thought I silently hummed to myself 'Bring me my bow of burning gold, bring me my arrows of desire', and at the same time pulsating in the back of my head came the words 'Yea, though I walk through the valley of the shadow of death, I will fear no evil'. The tension between us was fiercely charged. Something broke. I heard Said strut off barking orders to the guards in the other room. I never saw or heard him again.

Bastinado

The next few months were a blur of routine. Morning, toilet, return, lock up, read a book if you haven't read it before and if you have, read it again. Talk if you can find something to talk about. The sunlight coming in had lost its magic. We were, after all, constantly blindfolded. It had been this way now for many, many months. We both began to feel a kind of unresolved irritation. We both knew it was caused by the tininess of the space we were in. The brightness of the light reinforced our confinement. Now we thought that those long months in the dark had been less exasperating. In the darkness you can't see the walls. In the darkness the mind can dream, but in light, you see the absolute limitation of your condition and can measure it in inches. After months and months it hammers into the back of your mind and causes pain and distress at the most unlikely moments. We each began to sink back into periods of manic depression. We would recognize them in each other and attempt to pull one another up from their horrid depths. But they would come back again, for longer periods. In these states the mind would fly off leaving us dizzy, trying to find our balance.

Abed had begun his old tricks again, walking us to the toilet with our hands tightly twisted, high up our backs, and a pistol jammed in the side. Our response was always the same: laughter. His reaction was always to inflict more pain. He had become more frightened. My playful wrestle with Saafi and my confrontation with Said must have made him even more wary than he had been before. Daily he abused us and on occasions came into the room to wave his gun and give unnecessary orders. We smiled and complied.

The stress we were undergoing in such a tiny space was making it more difficult for us to contain ourselves. My loathing of Abed would not let me rest. His antagonism fuelled mine and on occasions I would turn to John and say 'I can't take much more of this . . . If that little bastard keeps this up I am going to push him through that fucking window.' John laughed 'Don't do that Brian,' he would continue. 'That's what he's waiting for; don't give him the pleasure; that's what he wants you to do . . . start something, say something, he is looking for an excuse.' 'I know,' I would answer, 'I'm just finding it harder to contain myself.' John, reassuring and comradely, placed his arm around my shoulder 'Don't give in to him Brian, don't give him what he wants.' And I answered 'I know, you blue-blooded bastard, you're always right.'

For a long time now, John and I had played a game. 'The double voice' we called it. When things were going badly or there was something to be angry about I would be the one to be angry and John would come echoing in behind with sweet reason. The guards would be confused, they would understand that we were angry, but also that we weren't angry. They would either leave us in peace or do something about whatever it was that we were complaining about. It worked for a long time. It allowed us to give in to our anger without creating a situation which would rebound badly on us. But this confinement was wearing us down. The anger was now more real. There was less sweet reason to temper our anger. Controlling the game became more and more difficult.

Waking early one morning, always looking to catch that first sunlight come streaming through the glass panel, I lay waiting. John had been dreaming. His dream had made him moan, those fearful moans none of us can control. His feet lashed out and kicked me. I wondered what he was dreaming and let the dream die in him, rather than wake him in the middle of it. He was sleeping peacefully now. I lay and watched the sun begin to stream through the glass. An old Arab saying flooded into my head with that first sunlight, 'Rise early, for the hours before sunrise are taken from paradise.' In the silence of that slow, soft first light, I heard feet approaching me. I lay still and untroubled. It was Abed, I could tell from the footsteps. He stood looking in at me. I was passive, unmoved. I heard him rattle some chains just outside the door. He went off; I sat up now to think and tried to find in my mind a beginning for this day. His feet slowly returned. Abed stood staring at me. I sat soaking in the silence of the light.

He barked an order 'Open the window!' Quietly I said 'You open the window. I do not want it opened.' 'Open the window!' 'Fine,' I said, and got up slowly, walked my four paces to the end of the room, stretched up on my toes, opened the window, walked back, and pulled the covers over me. The morning air even with that first light was always chilly. 'Close the window,' came Abed's voice again. Calmly I said 'You want it open, I have just opened it.' 'Close the window,' he ordered. I got up slowly, walked to the window, closed it and went back to bed thinking that that would be the end of his abuse for the next few hours. But no. 'Open the window!' I answered again passively 'I have just opened the window and I have just closed the window, what do you want? When you make up your mind, do it yourself!' Something was going to happen. Someone would have to give in, but I had done my share of it. I had opened and I had closed this window for no purpose other than to satisfy this man's ego. 'Open the window.' I got up, flinging back the blankets, walked to the window, opened it and went back to bed, pulling the blankets back around me to find some sleep, hoping that he would go away. 'Close the window.' I lay still. 'Close the window.' Abed's voice was urgent. My urgency met his, I thrust back the blankets again, walked slowly to the window, reached my hand up and with every ounce of muscle, power and strength in it flung the window closed. It slammed with a loud bang.

Abed charged into the cell, punching me viciously in the stomach, kicking at my feet. This was it, I had waited, it had come and I could not resist. I reached out. In that tiny cell the closeness of his body allowed me to put him where I wanted him, I thrust him against the wall, my hands about his throat, my eyes blinded more by fury than the towel around them. I began not to squeeze, but to hold him against the wall, so that he might know what it was like to be trapped.

He screamed. In ran Bilal, the big butcher's son, and pulled me from Abed, thrusting me into a corner. I heard Abed run out of the cell, shouting, yelling. Bilal held me down. I was serenely calm. I felt nothing. Abed came charging back and ran into the room as Bilal quickly squeezed past him. He began then to do what he had wanted to do for so long. He had a brush pole and began beating and beating and poking the brush pole into my chest, into my genitals, beating my thighs, my back, my shoulders, my neck, but careful, so careful of my face. Every part of me sang with this dull thud that slapped against my skin. He continued and I could only squat in the corner. John, anxious now, shouted to him to stop, not seeing but knowing what was happening. He shouted out 'Stop it, Abed.' Abed turned and began flailing him about the body and then, turning back on me squatting in the corner, began again, filled with an uncontrollable fury, beating everything in the room. The man was no longer a man but a crazed animal. And so the blows rained down, more hurtful because they were so uncontrolled, more frightening because you never saw them and felt them only after the blows had landed. After several minutes, how many I don't know, time seemed so long, he stopped, exhausted, and ran off shouting.

John and I sat silent, shocked by the assault and desperately worried about one another, but not being able to see the extent to which we had been hurt. Before we could collect our thoughts, Abed returned with Bilal. I was grabbed by the hair, thrown down on my face. A heavy foot stood on my neck. Abed's hands grabbed my wrists, jerked them high up behind my back, laced chains and padlocks round them. Still shouting, he wrenched up my feet and chained my wrists to them. My feet were in the air, the soles pointing upward.

I felt my whole body strain and scream at being held and chained in this position, every muscle of my shoulders, chest and thighs pulling against one another. Then he began; down hard and solid came the brush pole across the soles of my feet, again and again the blows rained down. John cried out 'Stop it, Abed, stop it,' but he could not stop. He squealed something in Arabic and still he flogged me. At first I felt nothing, the shock of what was happening numbed me. This was the ritual Arabic punishment. The blows kept coming down and coming down, my swelling feet only felt the sting of them. That slow soreness began, and again he kept hammering the blows, like a crazed axeman at a log that would not split. He chopped and chopped and beat and flailed against my feet. The pain was excruciating and I believed somehow that he must stop, that he could not continue this, it must end. Still he beat me. For a full fifteen minutes, screaming and beating down. I was consumed by pain. I moaned with each blow. I prayed desperately for it to end but I knew it would not. His excitement was beyond control. At times I thought he was almost singing. His rage was spitting out of him like fireworks as the shaft flailed down.

Somewhere in my head as I prayed and ached and moaned, I heard thcsc words 'Forgive them, for they know not what they do.' It was so with this man. Nothing in him could control himself. He was not even beating me, he was beating something bigger than me. Maybe he was beating himself. And then I heard it.

A noise that I have never heard before, nor since, nor do I ever want to hear it again. I know only that it came from me, yet it did not come from me. It was a cry so awful and so excruciating, which came from some part of me, but was not willed by me. It was a primordial sound, fusing every moment of anguish in me. Where it came from I don't know, only that I was the vehicle through which it passed. That one awful anguished scream. Suddenly it was over. He stopped. It was as if that cry that came through me had silenced him.

Abed knelt down beside me. Taking a fistful of my hair, he jerked my head back off the mattress and spitting into my ear said 'You want to fight, you want to fight, you want to fight.' I could only spit back at him half choking with fear, with rage, 'Kill me, kill me.' Abed stood up, his feet upon my neck. He muttered something in Arabic. I heard Bilal, the boy who wanted to learn to dance, say to him 'Enough . . . enough . . . enough.' Abed kicked me and left.

A long silence. John was choked with pain and with his own horror of what had happened. He couldn't speak. I lay trying to remember every moment of that beating to take hold of it before it took hold of me. 'Jesus, are you okay? Brian, are you okay?' I could feel John's voice trembling with concern. 'Yeah,' was all I could answer. Across the hall Abed was screaming at the Americans. There was silence.

Twenty minutes later, while John and I fumbled to find reassuring, supporting and comforting words, Abed returned. He had with him a television. He set it down in the far corner of the cell, and switched it on; as he walked past John he touched his shoulder. He left. I lay chained with my feet in the air, my arms tearing at the shoulders. 'Brian, they're not going to leave you like this all night?' 'Maybe,' I said, dreading it, dreading it more than anything. I wondered what would happen if they did. It would be impossible to lie like this all night. John tried to watch the film, confused, there were no words.

I lay in silence, wondering how long I could bear this. So many things come out of pain. They become in their own way a fascinating kind of balm. But I knew the mind alone could not overcome the pain of lying stretched like this. I turned to John: 'You're going to have to bring the bottle over and hold me while I have a piss.' 'Sure,' he said. 'I don't know how you're going to do it chained up like that.' 'I need to do it, John, nervous reaction . . . It's either that or flood this mattress and sleep in it all night. I don't want to give that little bastard another excuse. Can you lift me up and point percy at the bottle for me,' I said, searching out a joke. This was a most embarrassing favour that I was asking and John with great tenderness was fully compliant. As he struggled to try to turn and lift me, Abed came back. 'What are you doing?' John, now fiercely defiant, said 'Abed,' his voice was calm but there was a steel in it, 'I need to help him.' John tried to lift me and arrange me. Abed saw that John was not afraid of him and he knew he could not do this again. He came back with a plastic bottle, and removed the chains.

I sat back against the wall, relieved, waiting for the slow pain of the bruises to begin and waiting for that bone soreness to numb me. Abed's voice spoke slowly but urgently to John behind me. 'He made me do it, he made me do it, he bad man, he bad bad man, he made me do it.' He was pleading.

Abed was on the very edge of emotional collapse and exhaustion, just as I was. I felt his tears in the hot sting welling up in my own eyes, but I would not cry. I knew that in that moment he was very close to me in everything he felt and thought. John's voice was now completely calm and authoritative: 'No, Abed, you wanted to do it . . . You planned to do this thing . . . You wanted to do it . . . This man has done nothing, you have done this thing because you wanted to do it.' Abed was silent. John had him, his words held Abed hypnotically and then with concern for me, born out of huge anger and compassion, he administered the *coup de grâce*: 'There was another man in the prison who beat us many times . . . He wanted to do it, just like you, Abed.'

That night for me, there was no supper. I was glad of it. I would not have eaten it. Abed said calmly 'How are you?' I answered 'Fine, I needed the exercise.' John laughed out loud, rejoicing. That night was the longest of my life. I lay awake trying to patch together all the split and splintered pieces of my mind, and get back some semblance of myself. I wondered would I or could I be the same again. This thing was not over because it had ended.

Letter From Home

The next morning was full of surprises. Not least John's first remark to me as he raised his blindfold. 'Oh holy good fuck, your body looks like blackberry and custard pudding . . . How're your feet?' he continued. I answered drily, admiring his remark, 'Well, I'll not be skipping the light fantastic for a while! How are you?' I asked him. 'I'm fine,' he answered, 'I didn't get it as bad as you.' 'Bollocks, you're always trying to be better than everybody else, John.' Our humour was not heroism, quite the reverse. It was a way of putting the previous night at a distance from us, screened behind humour and affection, so we could take control of it before it took control of us. The last thing we wanted to think about was a repetition of this incident.

Abed came with breakfast. 'How are you?' he asked. 'I'm fine . . . I just won't be running in this year's marathon,' I answered, keeping up the quips and keeping him and the night before away from me. The humour was lost on him. John's laughter at my remark was perhaps enough to silence him. After a few moments he asked 'Can I do anything for you?' I said 'Yes, I want a bath . . . I need to prevent these bruises from getting worse.' He agreed. I could not believe he was so compliant: if I had asked him to take me for a ride on a motorbike he would have done so. I don't know to what extent he felt guilt or if he had been ordered by his chiefs to accommodate me, to get me medicines, to calm me. I had heard long conversations on the two-way radio in the night.

I walked slowly to the toilet. My feet like huge, heavy sponges. There was little pain, for I tried to walk on the sides of my feet. The swelling shielded me from the real pain. I took a long luxurious bath and felt I had merited it. The hot water lapping my body made me want to vomit; I couldn't, though I felt I needed to. I felt nervous and emotional confusion rather than any real illness. I hobbled back from the bathroom and sat down on the bed. Abed wanted to show John the bruises on his neck. He wanted to prove to John he had an excuse. John did not care to look. 'What can I do for these marks?' he asked. 'Bathe them as Brian has done,' John said.

I ate little for the next few days, not because I was not hungry, but my mind was preoccupied with other things and hunger didn't bother me. I thought of Abed's words 'He made me do it', and thought perhaps that I had. Maybe my aggression was arrogance. I felt no pride. I felt a huge unspeakable guilt for my friend John. He had been beaten for my arrogance, for my cocky stubbornness, for my insistence on not being humiliated, for all my absurd antics; he had suffered, and suffered more perhaps than I had. Sitting only inches away listening to my screams and being so powerless, unable to do anything. He endured every blow that I received. What right had I to cause such pain to the person who after all was my life support? I also felt another layer of guilt that I had failed to do more than grab Abed and throw him against a wall, holding him around the neck. My sense of myself was withering rapidly; I found it hard to hold it in check. These thoughts tossed and tumbled through my head for days.

They were long days for John as I spoke little. He read, knowing what I was going through, and knowing that he would be powerless to help. Then after a few days he tenderly put his hand around my shoulder and said quietly 'Well, you did it anyway, didn't you? It's over and you did it.' This comfort was more than I could bear. I didn't know if he knew what I was thinking, but I am sure he sensed it. I turned to him and in the only way I could, wanting desperately to apologize to him for what he had had to suffer, I said 'It's pretty bad when you have to suffer for my Irishness, being the shilling-taker you are.' He did not laugh, but he understood. He smiled, and knew that I was trying to reach out to him, to be forgiven for what I had done in seeking only to satisfy myself.

The next weeks were uneventful. The old routine established itself again. My bruises disappeared, the pain went away, only the self-reflective anguish remained. We all have to deal with these things on our own.

Some weeks after the beating, one of the chiefs came to visit. He said nothing for some minutes and merely looked at me. Then he quietly said 'If you do bad things, you will be treated badly.'

Anger roared up in me and I caught it by the throat, choked it and held it back. I said nothing, I merely turned and stared at him with my blind eyes as I had at Said, then turned away. He waited for me to speak. I would not. He squatted down beside me. 'How are you, my friend?' A few more moments of silence, then he called something to the guards. Three of them came. A piece of paper was put into my hands. 'It is a letter from your family,' he said. I felt the newsprint and knew it to be a cutting from a newspaper. I lifted my blindfold. I held the letter addressed to 'the Irish Hostage', choking back this time not anger but the hurt that was welling up. I read the letter in silence, then passed it to John. John read it quickly, then passed it back to me to read again. Saafi, my wrestling partner, was behind me. The letter was written in English and beside it was the Arabic translation. He read the Arabic pronouncing the names of my sisters and mother.

The letter repeated many phrases and paragraphs that I had put in that first and only letter I had written some six months before when we were interrogated. It was obvious to me that the letter I had given to my captors had gone somewhere, perhaps not to my family, but certainly the repetition of key words and phrases was a sign to me that someone had received it and a signal that something might be happening. I talked with John about this after the guards and their chief had gone, repeating to him the phrases in the letter that I had used in my own. There were names of friends and acquaintances in this letter that only friends or family or someone who had been meeting with my family would know about. To this day both the British and the Irish governments deny they were given any letter and that the repetition of those phrases in the letter I received on that 29th of August was a pure coincidence. This repetition hinted very strongly that either the British or the Irish government had made contact with our captors. This both governments strongly deny.*

The letter, whoever it came from, was mannah from heaven. Whatever bruises or pain I felt were extinguished instantly.

For many days we both lived off that letter. The guards had taken it with them but I remembered every word and every phrase and still to this day remember most of it. We talked for hours of what it could mean; who could have received it, who could have published it in the newspaper, and what might this mean in terms of negotiation?

The guards were very relaxed with us now. They would often come into our tiny room and sit behind us and watch TV. I remember laughing heartily at my wrestling companion who sat behind me and cracked jokes at the American movies. On other occasions he would

---

* Since my return home, my family and friends have confirmed that they received no letter from me at any time.

sit behind me crunching and crunching on an apple. The noise of it and the smack and the crunch as he devoured it drove me almost to distraction and I could only calm myself by laughing. On other occasions, though they loved to watch these movies, whenever music played, particularly Western rock music, Saafi would rock back and forward as I myself had done long ago when I was locked up alone, and sing Muslim hymns or war-songs to drown out the noise of the pop music. I remembered that mystical music I heard in my cell and saw a shadow of myself behind me, as Saafi tried to block out the soundtrack to the movie. It was genuinely painful for him.

Saafi had little English, yet he had a quality the others lacked: he had a sense of humour. He cracked jokes in Arabic we couldn't understand but the sense of them was obvious. These were Saafi's gifts. Both John and I liked him. Saafi had changed since the days when we knew him as one of the Brothers Kalashnikov, when he had shot into the shower room. Ever since, and perhaps because of our wrestling bout, there was a bond between us, a mutual liking, though one would hardly call it respect. Saafi also exhibited guilt when we complained of our chains. He would say 'It is same for us . . . We can go nowhere, we can do nothing . . . Prisoners here.' It was a feeble excuse, but the tenderness and the honesty behind it touched us.

We remained in this place near the Israeli-occupied zone for approximately nine months and experienced extreme conditions, which we somehow managed to survive.

Both John and I had suffered bouts of illness throughout our period of captivity. We simply called it 'Beirut Belly' and it was usually a dose of bad stomach pain followed by long bouts of diarrhoea. We had become habituated to it and knew that it would pass in about a week. On many occasions it was simply that the plates on which we were served our meals were not washed. One day's food was piled on top of another's. In the heat this was sure to cause severe stomach problems.

One afternoon, I sat talking with John about a book we had both just read and how it could be improved and what parts of it we thought were of some merit. We had both become quite the literary scholars. In the middle of the conversation I felt everything drain from me instantaneously. I thought it just a spasm that would pass, but I did not recognize the symptom from any previous attack. This sudden onslaught of weakness was new. For the rest of the day I could not eat and night brought the full evidence of what the next two weeks were to be like.

As I settled down for sleep, the cramps knotting in my stomach, my body sweating, I could feel the sweat running into my eyes. There was no reason why, it was not hot, yet my body was on fire and my stomach felt as if it was being twisted and then wrung through a mangle. I lay down hoping to find the sleep of oblivion which we often sought when the situation exceeded our ability to control it, but sleep would not come. Instead I felt as if my bowels, my intestines and all my organs were screaming to get out of me. Suddenly I needed to shit. There was no time to call a guard, the urge was desperate and I could not hold it in. I dived up, fumbled in the darkness to find a plastic bag, ripped down the shorts from my loins and held the bag at my backside. I felt the whole of me pour out, hot and streaming. It seemed to go on for ages and finally in exhaustion I lay down, tying the neck of the bag, which now reeked, and hoped John would not awake with the odour of it. That night I shat in a plastic bag nine times. I sweated like a horse after a race.

When John awoke I was urgently apologetic, the smell in this tiny room was beyond endurance. 'John, I was very sick last night, I'm sorry about the smell.' 'I know . . . I heard you and I smelt you.' We both tried to laugh. No sooner had we begun laughing than I desperately needed the bag again. I leapt up from the bed and unashamedly bared myself and shat into the bag no more than three feet from his face. 'God, you are in a bad way,' he said. When the guards came to bring us breakfast, I could not eat. John told them I was very ill in the night and had to go to the toilet many times, they must bring medicine. They only said, as usual, 'Bukkra,' and left.

For several days I could not eat and all day and all through the night I filled my plastic bag. They would not take me to the toilet and I would not try asking after the first day. I needed to go so often. The pain was continuous and the sweating relentless. There was nothing to excrete, yet my bowels screamed to be relieved. In all that heaving and pushing and forcing and wrenching of my stomach nothing but small squirts of white mucusy substance left me. Even when the guards came to make their daily prayers to Allah with their heads bowed eastwards towards Mecca, I would be jumping up, swiftly pulling my shorts down about my ankles and heaving this sickness from me. At first they were not pleased, even angry. And later they realized that I truly was ill. Again the chief was brought.

I had fasted for seven days, and had slept very little, lying awake in the night praying for relief from this agony. Jumping up every ten minutes and heaving excruciatingly. Nothing would come. They took me off my chains and made me walk for the chief. With the lack of food and the exhaustion from not sleeping and the sheer physical effort of constantly trying to relieve myself, I was unable to walk. My head was dizzy and I swayed and rocked unsteadily. I was exhausted after a few paces. They quickly brought me back and locked me to my wall again. I explained my symptoms slowly, wearily. He nodded. He told me he would speak with a doctor. He would return with medication. I didn't believe him. I had come to know that one would have to be almost dead before any medication would be brought and I also knew that others had been left to die.

For almost two weeks I could not eat and suffered the pain and indignity of the plastic bag and living through the stink of it until the morning, when I would take it to the toilet, wash it and return with it. John suffered too, knowing my pain and my total exhaustion. I raged at God for not ending this suffering. I could not endure this constant emptying of myself into a bag, followed by vomiting. I drank, and it came through my bowels. I thought my urine had redirected itself. I had neither the energy nor the will to make that quick dive to the corner and get my shorts around my ankles and place that bag strategically.

On many occasions it came out of me before I could reach the bag. When I did try to eat, the solid food ran from me like hot chocolate. I could not reach the bag in time. The mess ran from me and over me and onto my mattress. Lying exhausted, with an agonized embarrassment I watched my friend clean the mess off me without complaint. He was a very proper nurse, diligent in his work and tender in his passion, never once complaining of the filth he had to dip his hands into and never once complaining of being constantly wakened in the night by my wretching and by my bowels exploding.

I often thought how having to live beside a man so ill and watch his illness and his helplessness is almost as bad for those who watch as those who suffer. John's crack buoyed me up: 'We could sell your arse to a medical experimentation centre when we get out of here.' It was the longest illness I had ever known. Weight fell from me. My legs were like needles; all the muscle tone that I had spent so long building up was gone.

John's unremitting ministrations revealed another side of him to me. The buffoon, the fool, the comic was a man of vast tenderness, a man of compassion. His buffoonery hid this tender part of himself that he would not normally display. I wondered if my stubbornness had forced him to emulate me, obscuring this much greater strength which his tenderness revealed. I was indebted to him. His very presence, apart from his help, meant more to me than all my beliefs about who I was throughout these two weeks of constant pain, filled with hours aching and praying for an end. I wondered frequently how much of oneself does one give away or can one give away even to a suffering companion. During one of those long afternoons I lay, pain twisting and turning in my gut. I said nothing and hoped John would continue reading his book. I lay trying to sleep, to relieve this pain, but still it twisted and knotted. Through the mangle I went, and was stretched and pulled. I believed John thought I was sleeping, then I felt his hand lie gently on my stomach, and it remained there. He was praying. I was overcome. I was lost for words again. I wanted to join him in prayer, I wanted to thank him for this huge and tender gesture. It revealed more courage than my battling with the guards.

This new revelation of John's inner strength made me question myself and my actions. For days I remained troubled. Was my will to resist merely selfish, an arrogant self-indulgence? I spent hours in long silent dialogues with myself, seeking out a resolution. I had wanted to push Abed as far as I could. Having pushed him so far he would push me over the edge. I would have the ultimate victory in my own self-destruction. I had been along the road of hunger strike before. It still intrigued and drew me. The sense of power, illumination and self-possession which the hunger striker experiences were weapons that these men barely understood.

It was Easter time. We sat watching television. The Christian Maronite faith in Lebanon celebrated Easter with a devout intensity. We watched hours and hours of religious services all conducted in Arabic. The passion and the trance on the faces of the communicants held me. What was this fascination with death, a fascination that repeated itself in the aspirations and pathological thinking of our Muslim captors? Here was a world and a people trapped in death's shadow. The eclipse of the sun at the moment of crucifixion had not passed for them. My own thoughts of death were the reverse of gloomy. It was dazzling and light-filled. Death was only a moment of life bursting into life.

Was I becoming heady with such thoughts? Had my egotistical obsession with death broken the bonds of my humanity? Was I only a mirror image of the strange psychopathology of my captors? These questions troubled me. I was irresolute, but not unresolved. I needed to commit and focus my inner understanding and strength outside myself. My relationship with and responsibility to John was part of my resolution. I could not make any choice which betrayed that responsibility to him.

John sat behind me silently watching a programme about a hospital run by nuns for the mentally handicapped. It was one of the religious programmes that filled Easter week on TV. The answer flashed up in front of my eyes. In the television film a nun was attending one of the patients, a full-grown man whose mental retardation was so severe he had spent his whole life in a cot-like bed. His frail skeletal body was ageless. He lay naked and unmoving, his dark hollow body in stark contrast to the nun's white habit. I watched her as she patted and pawed him all over. Her touch was not the gentle pat of affection. She seemed to be slapping him. Her blows were a brutal compassion. I understood then that she was trying to break through the useless withered shell of his body to touch his semicomatose mind and give him a sense of himself and the otherness of the world around him.

I watched entranced. I was a secret communicant again. The eyes of the paralytic mesmerized me. They stared at the nun with such questioning intensity. They were asking 'What are you doing? What do you want?' Those eyes, so big and bright in that dark face, were staring right through the nun and beyond her. In that instant I knew the nun's need of this pathetic creature was greater than his of her. The intensity of his eyes watching her told me that somehow he knew it too. They were creatures in symbiotic relationship. Each was meaningless and lifeless without the other. Something erupted within me. I was filled with absolute assurance, a resolution of confusions beyond my immediate dilemmas. I gasped for breath. I sat staring at the TV, seeing nothing, feeling the shock recede. I was dimly perceiving a new world of meaning.

The Hostages
A Song for Elton John

Tara Tara Tara

They have taken the heroes from Tara
    And tucked them away in the Tain
There are whins of the Rath of the Synods
    And the Kings are in Brugh na Boyne

Tara Tara Tara

The shackles are rusted and broken.
    The hostages are gone.
They slept in the dark at Tara
    And woke in Lebanon.

Tara Tara Tara

The heroes have risen from Nemnagh.
    The kings are at the gate.
They have sounded the horn for McCarthy
    And Sutherland and Waite.

Tara Tara Tara

And here is the Mound of the Hostages.
    This is the Mound of the hostages.
Where have they hidden the hostages
    Who wore the chains of Kings?

In the dark they are speaking in whispers.
    They are fettered hand and foot.
But in front of the Mound there is open ground
    From Tara to Beirut.

Tara Tara Tara
Tara Tara Tara

Conor S. Carson
August 1990

Into the Bread Basket

I am standing in the centre of a room. Men are talking around me.
An old towel is draped over my face. On my mouth they tie a gag
tightly. The cloth covering my face and head is now taped over
with thick bands of scotch tape. A slit at my nose allows me to
breathe. A man now is at my feet. He pushes my ankles together
and begins taping up my legs. The thick bands of scotch tape are
tighter than any rope. The crackling tape snakes up my legs. My
hands are held firmly by my side. Over my loins the snaking tape
winds itself and entraps me. I am being embalmed and mummified. I feel my senses falling apart, nervous tension runs in and out
and over me like a crackling electric current. And still the tape
wraps around me, over my chest now, pinning my upper arms
tight into me. I am suffocating.

I know what this means. I am going back to the coffin. I am going
on that awful journey. I try to think of something else. The tight
confinement of the tape around my chest and shoulders will not
let my mind escape contemplation of what is to come. Around me
are my guards, noisy, I think of the conversation of bees. This is
babble, whispering and hissing, 'Do nothing . . . I kill you.'

I am the chrysalis of a butterfly and I cannot break out of this
larval state. Around me these men walk pulling, tugging,
making tighter the sticky tape. My mind is filled with the dread of
the coffin and the journey. I stand still trying to calm myself from
the riot that is bursting out within my senses. A voice at my ear
says 'No noise, no speak.' I stand unable to respond to this
idiotic instruction. How can I say anything. I am already a
complete mummy. No part of me can move, only my toes are
exposed and I wriggle them forcefully as if letting loose all the
fear that is slowly welling up inside me. I feel myself trembling
within this mummified corpse of myself and think if I fall, I will
fall like a felled tree. I hear behind me my friend being similarly

packaged. A thought flits through my head: 'Why don't they just stick a stamp on us and post us to where we're about to go?'

We are lifted and carried in the arms of our captors to that unholy confinement in the underfloor of the lorry that is to deliver us somewhere else. The increasing heat makes me feel like a fat slug, a worm encased in stickiness. They slide me brutishly into this oven. Beside me I feel my friend being thrown down. There is silence and darkness and airlessness. We cannot reach out to touch and reassure. This is the ultimate emptiness.

We lie on our backs and try to blank out what is happening. Trying with our minds to push away the turmoil that is bubbling up like hot poisonous lava to suffocate us. Amazingly one of the guards crawls in and lies half between us and half on top of us. The doors bang, the engine roars and in this horrific constraint we travel for six hours.

At first I try to sing to myself. But the words will not squeeze out the panic beginning to bite great lumps out of me. The diesel fumes and the heat and the bumping of my head and body as the lorry careers across the broken road begin to overwhelm me. The suffocating heat of the air entering my nostrils is a fire inside my skull. The scotch tape will not let my flesh breathe. Perspiration slithers out of me, I am cooking in my own fat, like a basted bird. The guard places his gun on my face. I can't expand my chest to take in a breath of the reeking diesel-filled air. My heart is about to burst out of my skin. I am panting like a woman in labour. Prayer is hopeless, the mind is inundated with nightmare images. No thought can complete itself before it is consumed by another and another. I struggle to free my hands and toss my head to release the gag. I need my own noise to return me to myself. I hiss, my mouth now free 'Mazin, you poisonous little bastard I am going to kill you . . . You hear, I am going to kill you.'

The guard's gun jams into my face again. I gulp for air and blast him with the violence of my tongue 'I am going to rip off your head with my bare hands and shove it up your arse.' Mazin, lying on top of us, realizes I am suffocating. He fumbles uselessly to release the tape from my chest. 'Mazin, I am going to eat you . . . I am going to eat your living flesh, then spit it out and walk on it . . . Mazin, I am going to eat you,' I snarl at him.

Now my mind has flown full flight from me. I forget about the man lying on me, crushing out the air from me. For hours the poison pours out of me. I roar for life and scream for death with the same breath. Laughter, my constant saviour, is transformed into a maniacal rage.

Mazin crawls on top of me. His lips are at my chest, then on my face. The stench of his garlic breath is in my mouth. I feel his thin lips on mine. I return to myself, pulling my face viciously from him. 'You little gutless, insignificant piece of offal . . . I am going to eat you raw,' I hiss and spit at him. Mazin's kiss isn't the kiss of a lecher, he is trying to calm me, in the only way he knows, for he is in this black confinement sweating with fear at the rage mumbling beside him. It is a kind of lover's kiss for it seeks to ease me. His hands are pulling hard at the tapes on my chest, letting my lungs loose to gasp in the air that is forbidden me.

The hours go on in this black airless hole. I won't be silenced. I try to fill this emptiness with all of me. I roar into what little air is around me. My dark lover's calming kisses are as meaningless to me as he is. I consign him to oblivion.

All those long, crushing, grinding hours this maniacal outburst continues. It is the only part of me alive during that hellish descent. I can't let go of it. I stare into the darkness within me and see its dark eye stare back. I feel that to give in to the darkness inside us is to live forever in the shadows, and I am not a shadow, I am a man. That six-hour journey from south Lebanon up into the Lebanese hills and down into the Bekaa valley is an eternity. How many deaths a man may die, he alone can know.

Beside me and half buried by the guard, my companion lies silent, a living corpse. 'Rage, John, rage . . . Rage . . . Rage, John, rage.' I chant out these words hoping that the noise I am making may enter into his own madness and somehow communicate life to him.

This journey ends like all journeys. That the human mind can travel into those dark regions and return exhausted but intact is more a miracle than that word can ever convey.

The doors bang open. The onrush of air, clean and cool, is an anointment.

It was some ten minutes before the guards pulled me like a dead fish from that underfloor coffin. I was carried into a room and laid on the floor. I sensed the guards standing above me, staring. I wondered what were they looking at, what were they thinking, why they didn't take these mummy's bandages off my body. Suddenly a knife was hacking at me from my chest to my groin. Carelessly cutting through the tapes that contained me. The knife near my genitals filled me with an instant of fear. To go through all that and have this ignoramus castrate me struck me for a second as frighteningly funny, but its comical aspect was the light edge of hysteria. The gag was ripped from my mouth and I lay drinking in great drafts of air. My body spasmed, the nerves refinding themselves. A calm voice beside me asked 'You want anything?' I answered: 'Get him out, get him out, get John out.'

I sat in my blindfolded darkness, gulping water as the operation was repeated for John. After some fifteen minutes, slowly coming back to ourselves and sharing words of reassurance, we were walked across the room into which we had been delivered. Bricks were taken from a wall and tiles lifted from the floor. Beneath us was yet another hole into which we were to descend. This time there were rough concrete steps. We were guided down some twelve steps and then immediately in front of us was a large iron door. Keys turned in a huge padlock. We entered, a hand guiding us from behind. We walked across a room and were gently pushed onto a mattress on the floor. The door banged closed.

As always John and I cautiously lifted our blindfolds. There was light in the room, quickly we pulled the blindfold up to our foreheads. In front of us, chained to the wall a few feet away, sat our American companions. For a few moments we stared at each other in silence. I looked at each of the men who for so long I had only seen above the bridge of a nose, and took in the full face, bearded and unkempt. I remembered how in those silent conversations shaping words in the air I had so desperately wanted to reach out and touch these men.

The Bekaa valley is a huge lush valley through which one must pass to enter Syria. It is renowned for the ruined temple of Baal, a pre-Christian deity. The Romans, when they entered this area, unlike Lebanon's most recent invaders, did not seek to destroy the civilization that existed there but merely to conquer and control it. The fertile land and the seasonable climate allowed rich harvests to grow here. The Romans grew grain to sustain the population and their own occupying armies. Much of the other produce found its way back to Italy. It was known to the Roman conquerors as the bread basket of the region. The ruins of the temple at Baalbeck are still standing. But the tourists from Europe, the archaeologists and students of history have long since left. It is no place for a Westerner, no matter how passive or academic he may be. The valley itself shelters many different factions. The Syrian army makes frequent excursions into it, and factions of the PLO maintain their headquarters in the valley. A contingent of the Iranian Revolutionary Guards had set up quarters in an army barracks evacuated by the Lebanese army many years ago. Strange to think that Kahlil Gibran, Lebanon's famous poet and mystic philosopher, used to wander these hills.

Five men in this underground room somewhere near Baalbek sat looking at one another, unaware at the time that our presence here added to the notoriety of the valley. Our exchange of greetings was not the exuberant welcome between comrades-in-arms or even between prisoners suffering under the same system, reunited after separation. We looked at one another, embarrassed and shy, curious and I think a little bit frightened. It had been years since either John or I had been in a room with other men with whom we could talk. The Americans' initial hesitancy spoke, I suppose, of the same inhibitions. Terry Anderson was first to break the ice and introduce himself. 'I'm Anderson . . . you must be McCarthy.' John shook hands, and I followed, then Tom Sutherland introduced himself. Frank Reed sat back, silent. He did not seem to want to come forward. Terry said 'This is Frank Reed . . . He's been with us for some time now.' Frank edged forward on his mattress and shook hands with both of us. Unlike us Frank kept his blindfold shielding his eyes, and on his head he wore a towel. I wondered why, but said nothing.

Initially we spoke of the horrors of the journey that brought us all here. The Americans had been carried separately by the same method. They were amazed that both John and I and a guard should have travelled so long under such conditions. We all agreed that it was an unbearable experience and none of us wanted to repeat it. In the next few days we shared what news we had collected at the different locations and from the different guards who had held us. Criss-crossing with this exchange of recently acquired information each man in his turn talked about his own abduction and the conditions in which he had been held.

Terry Anderson told how for the first few weeks he had been chained by both wrists and both ankles to a mattressless bed. It was extremely uncomfortable. The guards seemed not to care when he complained. Often in the night, chained on the bare springs of a bedstead, blindfolded, he would be visited by the guards and some would poke their guns at him and others stroke his chin with a handgun and whisper threats, laughing teasingly. Others would stand on his naked body and jump up and down. There was another whose perversion was of a different kind, for his mind was full of childish horror: at night he would sit stroking Anderson's face with his gun and say 'I am Dracula, tonight I kill you.' At first, said Anderson, the humour was not lost on him, but as the nights went on this man's visits and his childish abuse became sickening.

Anderson was known by his captors to have once been a sergeant in the American Marines. Hence the prolonged period in chains. He told us how one of the chiefs of the organization, who we all came to know as the Haj, had come to visit him and warned him with slow and serious deliberation that if he tried to escape he would not be shot or killed but he would suffer great pain for many, many days. It was simple and direct and he meant it. Anderson spent only a short period on his own and then was put into the company of the American hostages Jacobsen, Jenko and Weir, all of whom had since been released.

Sutherland's story was different, for he had spent only a matter of days on his own before being united with the other Americans. He spoke about his abduction and those first months of his captivity in a different voice.

He spoke slowly and softly, sometimes faltering at the memory of his early experience. Even with the companionship of his American friends, he had felt himself completely devastated. For months his mind was in such turmoil that he could not relate to the people around him. He found their simple questions confusing and could not indulge in any conversation with them. He felt so worthless that he sat for many hours every day in these first months in uncommunicative silence. Tom's face as he spoke showed he was still deeply troubled by his experience. We listened in silence. For each of us knew what he was talking about.

When we related our own stories I spoke directly to Tom. The others listened but I wanted to speak to him. I wanted to reassure him that what he had felt and might still feel was common to all of us. All of us were subject to that debilitating loneliness. All of us felt impotent before it. I spoke of some of my own experiences and feelings. However something in me warned me to be careful. It was not time yet to give oneself wholly. For we were still feeling one another out, taking the measure of each other to discover how much we should withhold.

Tom had been physically abused, sometimes badly. As we already knew, the guards considered him a spy. A man less likely to be anything of the kind I could not imagine. As the weeks and months went on I thought to myself how often that word 'spy' was in the mouths of our jailors. Spies are men more used than they are capable of using others. Tom's honesty, his openness, his innocence and occasional naivety would make him a sound target for those agencies which work in darkness. But Tom had no capacity to be involved in that murky underworld.

Frank spoke little of his experience. He told the story of his abduction in detail. But something in him prevented him from revealing his feelings about what was happening to him or how he had come to deal with it. We didn't question him about intimate things. One learns in such situations to receive, with thanks, only what is given. To drag a man into talking of something he has neither the desire nor the ability to discuss is a kind of selfish brutality. Each gives according to his abilities. The appropriateness of what he gives is not a subject of moral evaluation. In this hole in the ground, all of us were equal, none was better than another. Our captivity was the great leveller by which position, status, intellect or ability ceased to be self-possessions. They became the common goods of all.

Having told his story, John was curiously quiet for the first couple of weeks. Gone was that outgoing exuberance. He was not withdrawn, but retiring and observant. I sensed his reticence and in those early conversations would try to draw him in with a joke or abusingly accuse him of something. He would retort with some equally abusive crack, but he was not ready to go beyond this, to be fully committed. But as time went on, and we became more confident, we all began to interact more directly. We began to explore each other with more openness. There was increasingly less need for retreat into silence and observation.

The room that was now our prison was approximately eighteen to twenty feet long by perhaps thirteen feet wide. There were no windows underground. In one corner our toilet and shower room stood, a brick-built oblong with a door, the usual hole in the floor and a shower head. The rough concrete surface was covered with a torn blue rubber-backed carpet. In the corner opposite our toilet a drainpipe ran up through the roof and into the daylight. From this we received our fresh air. One small fan at the aperture of this drainpipe-like air vent drew in the air and another small fan near the door of our cell blew it out. In the opposite corner from the air vent a closed-circuit camera was mounted.

Each morning after breakfast the three Americans would be

unleashed from their chains to wash and take twenty minutes' exercise. After them, John and I would fulfill our routine. All of us except Frank took the opportunity to exercise, but he sat quiet and preoccupied behind his blindfold. Frank never revealed his eyes to us. He would always sit in the years ahead, on the occasions when we were with him, with his blindfold on. It was for him like a child's security blanket. Behind it he was safe, he could not be seen; behind it he travelled in his own space and time, occasionally returning to us to join in conversation. Frank rarely entered into a conversation spontaneously. Only when a question was put to him directly would he answer. Always his response was short. Sometimes his answers when they were of any length seemed unrelated to the subject we had been discussing. Often he went off on odd tangents, confusing us.

On other occasions we might be discussing some point at great length or in great depth. Suddenly Frank would interject, angrily contesting some statement or some statistic that his fellow Americans had contributed to the conversation. He would be adamant that they were wrong. I later became aware that Frank's sudden interjections, sometimes full of bitterness, were not made because he disputed the claims of Tom or Terry but rather because he disliked them. Here was a man chained between two of his fellow countrymen and he chose to hide himself from them. There was something in Frank's interruptions that spoke more of envy than of disputation.

He had been through a lot. He had been beaten frequently and was still being abused by the guards. He had suffered long periods of isolation. Such isolation drives men deep into themselves. Finding only what is within us to entertain us, to guide us out of the periods of madness, we are forced to drive ourselves beyond our capacity. We were all bruised by our own perceived inadequacy. We became self-loathing creatures, unable to bear ourselves, and we chose to off-load this burden onto others, someone we admired, perhaps even someone we loved. All of us had to struggle with this inward—turning anger and seek to take control of it and to understand it. When we were held against our will, when the only human beings who entered into our tiny self-contained world beat us and abused us; when they spat on us and kicked us; when they tortured and humiliated us; when they laughed at us and treated us as less than animals, then that awful self-loathing could imprint itself permanently. No human being can abide such absolute self-loathing. He must as we all must seek to escape. But when the walls around you are impenetrable and the guards who hold you too numerous and too strong then you can be tempted to seek another route, half-unknowing, that of inner flight.

Sometimes that flight takes on its own perversity. We seek to escape by seeing in others the ugliness that is in ourselves. Frank's outbursts were really moments of affection and admiration for these men. But he had lost his way for too long; he had been exposed to too much brutality. The ability to express love, affection, desire and warmth was sometimes diverted or twisted from him, but only momentarily.

Like all men, Frank had many sides to his personality. Sometimes, tired by his self–possession, another Frank would emerge into our prison and I would listen with rapturous delight to stories so funny, so rich that I wanted to reach out and hug this man, so deeply hurt yet so deeply human. 'Frankie the Shoe''s stories of the street life of Boston and the vivid characters that lived in them had us laughing recklessly for hours.

The Tollund Men

The French word 'oubliette' means a place underground where prisoners are kept until they are forgotten. Those who resided in our oubliette will not easily forget it, even if in time the world shall forget. Here in this netherworld were living men. Each suffered his own torments and his own personal hell. But we learnt to talk confessionally to each other about our feelings and of our desire and of our experience, without hiding or turning away. As we suffered with a friend his deep moments of loneliness and grief, that awful renunciation of life itself, we each of us acquired, almost instinctually, a deeper and richer capacity for joy, for humour, for laughter. When you have so little you find joy in insignificant things.

John and I were back at our antics. Our exercising periods were less exercises than dances of delirium around our confinement. Again the insatiable hurling of dog's abuse at one another, and laughter bursting forth, cradling us in its outrageous obscenity. At first the Americans looked at us in disbelief, unsure whether our seemingly malicious and deliberate abuse of one another was real or not. An Irishman and an Englishman so far apart in background should obviously be at one another's throats. We played out the game oblivious of them, each of us silently acknowledging that we were the entertainment in this place. We were performing for them. And their amazement and confusion entertained us. But as they came to understand and be delighted by our buffoonery, they themselves became intimate participants in the game.

Tom Sutherland began telling jokes. His eyes filled with tears and, giggling hysterically, he infected us all. And no matter what the punchline of the joke, which usually fell flat, the sight of this man uncontrollably laughing at his own joke reduced us to a quivering mass. Even Tom's half-confessional, half-delirious tales of his adolescent love life thrust him again and again into those tear-filled raptures.

Terry, though enjoying the comic atmosphere, would not allow himself to be overcome by it. He was a man of vast intellect. It needed feeding. He was ravenous. He could not do without deep, complex conversations. Everywhere he went he insisted that his Bibles be brought to him. He always had two or three. He had become an authority on the history of the Scriptures. Though not a deeply religious man, he found himself now profoundly sensitized to needs within himself. I always felt that beneath that bluff and hard-nosed journalist there was a very tender and compassionate man. Terry, too, had reached inside, had seen things we all would prefer not to see. But being the man he was, rather than run or hide away, he chose to remake himself out of the self-revelation that his incarceration had thrust upon him. He spoke deeply and passionately about his family, as did we all. But now he found in himself other qualities that had long lain redundant or undiscovered.

I am still and always will be amazed at the qualities men find in themselves when they have only themselves in which to find a source of life. I had seen John McCarthy turn from someone who was frightened, as we all were, into someone who was unafraid and totally committed to life. He found and gave a sense of delight to all of us. But beyond this I had seen him become confident and challenging to those who were holding us. And underlying this he was a man who remained deeply sensitive.

In that long time of captivity I had also come to know all the many people that were in me. Here again, I saw the same: many different qualities in each man and each of them looking and seeking for expression. Though we were all different, our shared suffering had made of us a collective community. We sought to complement each other, to understand the different aspects of each others' personalities and meet with them meaningfully. By so doing we were always aware of each others' mood swings and frustrations.

At the beginning as John and I recommenced our affectionate and playful lunacy I thought I saw in the faces of some of the others a kind of jealousy or envy. And I could well understand it. For so long these Americans had sustained themselves with debate and conversation, a competitive extracting from one another of each others' intelligence or interests. They seemed not to have, or to have lost any capacity for playfulness, for laughter. But as I came to know each of them in the confines of this room, I began to reunderstand that each man's humanity and capacity to love expresses itself in different forms. In those sharing moments I discovered qualities that were lacking in myself.

Sometimes we create too finely, too exclusively, and think our own world best of all. This theme was a frequent topic of discussion between us. We each had a vision of our own Utopia, but being so far removed from the world we had the time and opportunity to examine it in great depth. Each of these separate, self-chosen, self-constructed worlds we laid upon the table, that each might see and evaluate and question. I don't remember a bitter row, I can hardly ever remember anyone turning aside from his comrade, though those debates went on long into the night and re-emerged perhaps days or weeks later. Someone had forgotten to make a point, a new observation occurred to someone and he would bring it back to the table to be resolved.

The squabbling, when it did come, came over insignificant things. Always it is the case that when the mind is empty or tired or when like a child we need to be fed, we cry out in tantrums. Some men needed to be proved right to gain a small victory over their neighbour. It was a means of restoring identity. We all needed these things and we sometimes turned squabbling like hungry birds fighting over crumbs. At other times we realized the pettiness and futility and turned away embarrassed. Offence would be taken at insignificant and undeliberate abuse. For days a man might sit in silence, considering his dignity vastly insulted. At other times the dispute would be respectful but forceful. There would be no compromise. From all this John and I eventually turned away. We would no longer be participants. Our silence drew the disputants to us. They sought allies for their individual cause, but we would not be arbiters or referees. In the end these minor skirmishes ended silently and on most occasions amicably, though the return to friendship sometimes took a few days. When one is constantly subject to a heightened reality, all things are disproportionate.

I have watched a man lie still for days, his body a living corpse. His face stares back, a pallid mask of the man he was. Nothing will arouse him from his torpor. We are wordless and angry at the constant sight of his silent corpse. We push down our anger, looking to one another to see which of us might have the energy to go in and find this man and bring him home to us. Our empty faces and our shrugging shoulders display our own fearful anxiety.

I speak to him as if nothing strange is happening and the day is like all the others. 'Tell me about bees,' I suddenly say without knowing where the thought came from, only that I am now at this instant interested in bees. There is no reply. I speak again to him but know that I am talking to myself, and start pulling from the air of my imagination some facts that I know about bees. I talk about them and ask odd questions that occur to me. Nothing, no response. It's time to find another key. I begin talking about cheese-making. I have always wanted to know how to make cheese, but the subject is boring and my knowledge limited.

I jump from one thing to another desperately tying together disparate ends to find a way in. 'You know what I am going to do when I get out of here? . . . There is an island just off the North Antrim coast called Rathlin Island. It's a place where in the fourteenth century Robert the Bruce went to hide out from the English armies. It's the place where he saw the spider. Rathlin Island is sometimes called the disputed island because the Scots claim it and the Irish claim it and the Brits claim it because they claim a part of Ireland. But as far as I know, and it's only a small island, nobody has ever found the fucking cave where the spider went swinging back and forward, back and forward, back and forward. I think if I get out of here I am going to hunt all over it till I find the cave and if I don't find one big enough I am going to see somebody with a lot of explosives and blow a bloody great big hole in the side of a hill somewhere and call it the Robert the Bruce Cave, and then what I am going to do is I am going to fill the fucking island full of goats and then I'm going to . . . No, I'm not going to fill the island full of goats, that's ridiculous, 'cause everybody knows about goat's milk cheese and everybody knows about sheep's milk cheese . . . What I think I'll do is, I'll get a load of pigs, they're cheap, and I'll milk the pigs . . . When I've made all the milk into cheese I'll put the cheese in this cave and I'll call it Robert the Bruce Cheese and make a killing because with everybody disputing who owns this island how can anybody tax me when I start selling the stuff, and nobody will ever have eaten cheese like it before because there is nobody who eats pig's milk cheese.'

My own lunacy is beginning to intoxicate me. I am sitting close to the dreaming man. I look quickly at him and see what I haven't seen for days. His eye brightening. Pretending not to notice I carry on ad-libbing. 'I'll have to make this cheese look different . . . You know, all cheeses look the same but this being a special Robert the Bruce cheese made on this island, which has never been known before and stored in these caves . . . I think the French store their cheese in caves but how did it get that funny colour in it . . . You know you get this smelly-sock cheese and it's all marbled with blue, well my Robert the Bruce cheese is going to be mottled green 'cause its obviously going to be Irish cheese . . . Now how the hell do you get all that green mottling in it? . . . Do you inject some sort of bacteria, or maybe I could get a lot of shamrocks and stick them in it and maybe the bacteria from them would turn it green or something, but then nobody will eat green cheese so I just have to get it mottled the way Danish Blue is. Look at the Danes, they just spread a whole lot of blue ink over their cheese and everybody is buying it.'

Laughter beginning to ripple up. Again I continue 'What are you all laughing at? . . . I'm deadly serious, this thing could work, think of it . . . you could make a fortune . . . Pig's milk cheese, stick Robert the Bruce on it, go to this island, blow a big hole in the wall, who is going to know? Who is going to know if that is Robert the Bruce cheese or not, you get a lot of spiders from somewhere and hang them all over the place; that's your evidence and then how do you get this green stuff into it?' In the middle of the laughter, even the 'dead man' begins to come to life. Suddenly his voice says nonchalantly 'You need to bury some copper wires in it, Brian, and after a time pull the wires out, it leaves a green mark throughout the cheese.' 'Fuck me, how did you know that?'

A man emerges back into life, not because of anything I have said, but the lunacy and the laughter that is at the heart of our life beckon him back and he cannot resist it. There are many things a man can resist – pain, torture, loss of loved ones – but laughter ultimately he cannot resist.

We moved in and out of these moments of intimacy and compassion, of sharing and of rejection, at times when turmoil turned us inward to deal with what troubled or confused us. I sat back to watch and attempt to comprehend. I remembered Terry Anderson's words in that prison where we were all held, sometimes separately, sometimes one or two of us together. 'Why me, Lord? . . . Why me?' He would half remonstrate and half joke with God and even here he echoed those words, always in jest. 'Why me Lord? Why me?' I tried to learn from these men, from their thoughts, their confessions, their behaviour, something that might answer Anderson's question for all of us.

I remembered a story I had read when I was young, Thornton Wilder's *Bridge of San Luis Rey*. The story is located in South America. It tells of an incident that is supposed to have really happened. An unrelated group of people is crossing a rope and wood bridge stretching over the river and gorge called St Luis Rey. Amongst them is an old aristocratic lady, a few children, a youth and an old man. As they attempt to cross the bridge it snaps and breaks and they tumble to their deaths. The incident was insignificant in world history. But a Spanish Jesuit priest sought to understand the significance of why all these people, having no relation to one another, should be killed, by an 'act of God'. He researched diligently into the backgrounds and relationships of each of these people who had died, trying to find a connecting thread and from that connection to perhaps clearly understand the will and purpose of God, believing that if he could decipher such a meaning then not only might he prove God's purpose but make God more real to himself. Seeking to find proof of God's purposefulness in this incident was indeed a daunting task and one that only the priestly mind could conceive.

The author uses the device of collecting the priest's researches and sought in an imaginative reproduction of this story, and of the lives of the dead people, not to answer the questions that the priest had sought to answer but to provide an imaginative landscape for the reader. The book was not simply a story but an exploration.

Perhaps self-interestedly I tried to apply the theses of the priest and of the novelist to our own situation. We were all from diverse backgrounds. Each of us had different life experiences and a different complex of needs and aspirations. There was nothing in our life histories that should have brought us together. We were all in our own way innocently walking over a bridge that had collapsed and we had all tumbled down here into this hole in the ground and found ourselves together. Why? Why were we picked specially to be here? The interrogator's words so many years before – 'God is testing you' – were not sufficient for me. I rejected them for there were others with me who thought differently. What was there beyond the pathetic politics of the struggle outside our jail that had brought us to this? We had each of us revealed as we talked through the long hours of many mornings something about forces greater than ourselves, our minds having been pushed through all sorts of dark mysterious places. We had all had moments of religious mania and hard times of deep contemplation. Whether it was a paranoia of isolation or whether it was some rage as great as the religious fervour of our captors, we were as yet still unclear. In my observations of and conversations with these men, I found that like the group in Wilder's book there was a single common denominator that bound us together. We each had turned inward intensely. In searching through the complex panorama of our past, one thing emerged again and again: our relationship to and understanding and experience of love underlay everything else.

In his story Wilder hints that the lives of his characters were somehow lacking in love: either they had never known it, or they had passed through it into a condition of life devoid of love. Some of them, the children who died, had not yet experienced it. The priestly researcher would have concluded that their death was a sure sign of the love of God coming to take them into his passionate embrace. Wilder allows the reader to question this. The men I watched silently, or talked and argued with, these men with whom I laughed and played, were for me the five people on that bridge over the St Luis Rey. We each of us had fallen down into meaning, if we cared to seek it out, and to climb with it out of that awful chasm into which we had been toppled. The experience of love was the stepladder up which we could climb.

Between the time we had left the Israeli–occupied zone and our arrival at Baalbek we had spent some months in an apartment in the southern suburbs of Beirut. We knew that Frank and a Frenchman were being held in a room adjacent to ours. We could not communicate with them. The Americans now told us that they had each been held with a French citizen during those months. Indeed before our arrival here Tom Sutherland had occupied this very room with Marcel Carton. He had previously been locked up with Jean-Paul Kaufmann. Tom's excellent French allowed him to glean much information from them. Carton was an elderly man who had lived for many years in Lebanon and spoke good Arabic. His facility gave him immediate and intimate access to the guards' conversations. 'Every day, tout les heures, they speak only of sex always, always sex, sex, sex and Allah. Always it is the same. It is the minds of boys in the bodies of men.' They spoke frequently about AIDS and the sexual perversion of the American imperialists. This struck a chord in my memory. I recalled how on many occasions when we were ill and required medication the guards would spit at us 'You AIDS, you AIDS.' Even in the minds of our captors love or its perversion was the prime mover.

For our captors homosexuality was a vice exclusive to the West and it was the wrath of Allah's judgement that we should be poisoned with AIDS. 'Woman is for man,' a guard would remonstrate excitedly. I remembered the line from the Koran. 'Women are as your field, go into them.' Carton had also observed to Tom that in their discussions of Allah and the Koran half of them could not read the classical Arabic in which the Koran was composed. They were therefore not so much receivers of the word as followers of the instructions of their immediate religious superiors.

I listened as Tom related his stories about what he had learned from Carton and Kaufmann. I was reminded again that our captors' obsessions with God and sex were not about religion or morality. They were ciphers for their own powerlessness: an impotence that they experienced unconsciously at a deeply personal level and also in the world of politics.

Tom also told us how at the beginning of their captivity the French had been treated with courtesy. They were allowed to cook their own food occasionally and to make coffee. However, as the duration of their confinement increased many of these prerogatives were taken from them. The French, Tom had gathered, had had a bad time not so much from the guards, but from each other. Apparently there was much bitterness and division. Only Jean-Paul Kaufmann held himself above this.

Tom and Terry spoke occasionally of their own early period of captivity with those other Americans who had been released years ago. There was occasional rivalry there too.

We were not always engaged in such deep conversations. We resorted as we had done so many times before to games. Terry Anderson had a meticulous mind and excellent recall. With a piece of cardboard carton and a pen scrounged from the guards he constructed a precise replica of a Monopoly board. On scraps of paper, usually the backs of cigarette packets, we made our Community Chest and Chance cards. Old pieces of newspaper, or tissue or cigarette packs became money. We played for hours. The playing of games is anathema to the fundamentalist mind, which believes it should have no preoccupation but God. Our God, we quietly acknowledged, existed in each other and it was to please each other and ourselves that we played our games, with the omnipresent eye of the camera watching us. A deck of cards and a chess set were also constructed over a period of weeks.

These games were a revelation. The way men play them, the games they choose not to play and how they handle victory or defeat define much about their character. Some men would not play for they could not bear to lose. Others played for the game itself, which engendered a kind of comedy that was inspiring for all of us. At other times the game played seriously was a way to feed a hungry or exhausted mind. Without games perhaps we would not have been able to bear one another as long as we did.

But our playroom was not always filled with laughter. I remember late in the evening, lying in the candlelight looking around at my sleeping friends. My eyes rested on Anderson. He was lying awake. On a small stone shelf above his mattress, he had rested a tiny newspaper photo of his daughter, Salomé. She was born after he had been kidnapped. In the five years since he had disappeared he had seen only three photos of her. I watched him as he lay awake, his eyes and mind fixed on the yellowing crumpled newspaper photo. What was in his thoughts or in his heart? Terry chose to keep these things to himself. Maybe they formed for him the private treasure house that no-one needs to share.

Christmas came again.

For us it was not a time of festivity. It merely marked another year on the calendar of our captivity. In the months before Christmas we had been shown one or two video films a week. Only Frank, hidden behind his blindfold, refused to watch them. They were the usual low budget war movies or shoddily made Kung-Fu karate films. We watched an old version, I think the original one, of *The Dirty Dozen*. Telly Savalas played one of the leading roles, a bald, fat, aggressive killer. Our captors believed that these films were true records of the Second World War. Saafi, my wrestling companion, sat behind me as we watched. He cracked his usual jokes at each killing sequence, 'Not bad two dollar tomorrow'. Full of serious intent he tapped both John and me on the shoulder, and pointing to the image of Telly Savalas he asked in all innocence: 'He Churchill, yes?' Laughter erupted from us. It was as if God himself had cracked this joke. Telly Savalas's malign face sucked at its cigar and stared back at us from the TV.

Christmas Eve found us contemplating what delights they might bring us to eat. Usually we were guaranteed one slice of cake each. Upstairs the television was blaring. We could hear the film that was being shown. It was the story of the killing of the Israeli athletes at the Munich Olympics. We talked or read while we waited for the guards to come and unlock us for the morning toilet. I was humming the tune of 'The Little Drummer Boy' quietly to myself. Above us the film roared to its conclusion. The silence from the television room was followed by footsteps descending to our crypt. A key turned in the lock and the guards Ali and Bilal entered. They paused for some moments, then unexpectedly came first to John and myself. Normally the Americans were released first. Ali had been with us for some months and had also been at some of the other jails in which we were held. He was devout, a zealot. I knew he would have been enjoying what he saw on television. I sat waiting as I normally did, my back to the wall, my knees pulled up towards my chest.

Ali leaned over me. Normally he squatted down to unlock the padlock and chain and I waited calmly for the usual routine. Suddenly he yanked fiercely at the chain, pulling my feet from under me, my head whiplashing back and banging against the wall. I knew instantly what this meant. Ali was drunk with the movie he had just seen. He wanted to replay it here in this place. 'Don't do that again,' I hissed at him. My neck was bulging with anger. The words snarled out of me. Ali hesitated then with double force yanked once more at the chains on my feet. Again my head banged off the wall. Anger suffused me. I jumped to my feet. Not to attack but to make myself ready for what I knew was about to happen.

Ali ran from the room shouting and screaming. He disappeared into the silence upstairs. I knew the camera in the corner would be watching. Slowly I sank back to my squatting position. I felt that as I had not been attacked immediately, Ali would simply bring down a senior officer and I would be questioned. In the silence I felt the expectant fear of my friends. No-one knew what to say and as I said nothing, they sat silent. I heard the footsteps returning. The quiet about me seemed to calm and steel me. Ali ran quickly across the room to where I sat. Without warning, I felt it again, the dull thumping thud of the butt of a Kalashnikov banging into my shoulder, my arms, my chest. The man was kicking me and grinding the gun butt into my thighs. Crashing it against my knees, screaming something in Arabic, no doubt some street abuse. The gun continued to smash down. I had had this before and I could only grunt as each blow landed on me unexpectedly. My mind tight now, not caring. I was bored with it. I only wanted it to be finished and over and the foul presence of this man gone from me.

My friends sat in helpless silence, feeling pain with every blow. My mind reached out to them.

In a fit of beating and kicking, of spitting and screaming, the hysteria washed over Ali. Exhausted, he knelt down beside me, pushing and grinding the gun hard into my face. 'Tomorrow for you I am returning.' In the background I heard Bilal's forced laugh. I was angry with him. I had liked this young man. He used to sit with us mimicking the song of the birds that lived around his farm.

They left and the door locked. Slowly, simultaneously we each pulled the blindfolds to our foreheads. Anderson was the first to speak. 'Are you okay?' 'Yes, I'm a bit shook, but I'm getting awful fucking tired of this.' 'What happened?' Anderson asked. I explained. Each was silent for a while. Sutherland asked: 'You know he is coming back again tomorrow?' 'Fuck him.' Anderson walked towards me as far as his chain would allow. Tom Sutherland and John were closer to me and stood beside me examining the bruises. I stared with menacing vengeance towards the camera. Then quickly changed my expression. I smiled. Not the smile of a valiant hero but someone who was smiling at themselves. Ali's blows fortified me. Without knowing he had strengthened my resolve.

For the rest of that day, there was much discussion about what we should do. The ultimate sanction was to refuse to eat, but how long would our guards tolerate that without beating us into submission? Yet there was a need in all of us to do something. To sit quietly and accept this animal humiliation was not worthy of any of us. All of us were aware that we had also to accept that we were powerless and anything that we might do they could do ten times worse.

The day passed into evening. Each of us said what we should do. It was a way of protecting ourselves from our utter hopelessness and futility. Each of us had to believe we could do something.

The next morning we each refused to eat. It was not a group decision, an ordered and collective response, though we had discussed it long into the early hours of the morning. It was only good to take this decision if we had a strategy we could follow through. By the morning this was not resolved, only that none of us could eat. We had to make some kind of gesture.

The guards had anticipated this and were prepared. They left the cell and after about half an hour returned with one of the junior officers. He went immediately to Terry Anderson. 'Why don't you eat?' he asked. Terry was silent. 'Why?' he asked. Terry calmly said 'I don't want it.' It was obvious to our guards that it was more than a matter of not wanting food, and they were becoming angry.

Terry was unlocked and taken hurriedly from the cell. We heard his steps as he went up the stairs and crossed through our guards' toilet and into their room. We looked at each other in silence. We heard the mumbled voices above us but could not make out what was being said. A long pause, then a gunshot. We smiled at one another. We knew this game. With the gunshot a voice let out a long moan. It's pathetic, I thought. The guards returned, went to Tom and John and spoke with them. Their intention was obvious, to frighten each of us into submission and into eating. None of us would indulge in this childish game. Fifteen minutes later Terry returned and was locked back into his chains. Terry told us they had simply asked him what had happened and that if we did not eat there would be much trouble for all of us. I sat in silence and watched the faces around me and then said 'Yes, they can make trouble for each of us, so each man decide only for himself, this cannot be a group thing, it puts too much pressure on everyone. Ultimately what you do you do alone because only that way will you be able to go through with what you choose, resting on no-one's support.' For the rest of that day we did not eat. We were each prepared to continue our strike on the following day.

The next day the guard Mahmoud entered our room. He too went straight to Terry. 'What is your problem?' he asked. His voice was firm but not unfriendly, and we had come to like this man. He had not been involved in any of the brutality. And we could have a conversation with him, where he would as a kindness venture information he was not permitted by his chiefs to give. Terry's angry response could not be contained. 'I don't have a problem, you have a problem . . . Look at Brian, ask him what the problem is . . . We are not animals in here, but you've got an animal! Get him out of here and keep him out of here.' I was surprised at the vehemence of Terry's words. Mahmoud came immediately over to me. The two days had brought the bruising out on my body. I looked a bit like a dapple cow or a Dalmatian. 'Who done this?' he asked. I quietly answered 'You know.' There was silence between us. His hands felt over my body, turning me around to look at where the bruises had come up. 'What happened here?' he asked. I explained quietly. I knew this man was listening not to my words but to how I was saying them. He was trying to interpret how I was feeling. Mahmoud rose, spoke some words with John and Tom, and they reiterated my story. He came back, and squatting in front of me, said solemnly and aloud for each to hear 'I will speak with my chief, perhaps this man will be punished.'

That evening we were informed Ali would not be returning. It was enough. There were worthier things to die for.

No-one watched whether I ate or not when lunch arrived. My friends did not want to be voyeurs of my suffering. And I had calmly resolved to myself that to continue to refuse to eat would be an imposition on them. If I continued with this thing, I would be setting precedents that some of them would be obliged to follow, if something similar happened to them. Could I be so self-interested that I didn't care for them? I had no choice. I lifted the food to my mouth but I could taste nothing.

There were many other incidents in this hole in the ground. But each of them was an affirmation of human capacity to overcome despair. I could write at length and try to reveal each of those situations, some hilariously funny, some pathetic, others undignifying and ignoble, but that is not my purpose. For each of these incidents revealed what each and all of us are. We are all made of many parts; no man is singular in the way he lives his life. He only lives it fully in relation to others.

The Corn Crake
(For John McCarthy)

Somewhere in Fermanagh it still survives
In the gentle grass, the corn crake,
Thrashing through the field as happy as Larry,
Its piteous cry its beautiful song.

One summer we were plagued by a corn crake,
Cracking its lullaby – harsh was the night.
Next door 'Pat the Twin' roared in unison,
The whole of Marion Park cursed the bird.

What would I give to hear its song now?
Value what you have, lest it's lost.
Guardians of the air, birds of the earth,
If there be paradise, they live there.

They have seen the world. This solitary cell.
As they fly, in chains, can you hear
The corn crake surviving, singing in Fermanagh,
Remember me, remember me, remember me.

Remember

Frank McGuinness

Back to Beirut

Conditions in our cellar underneath Baalbek had been much alleviated towards the end of the Iran/Iraq war. In June 1988, the guards brought us the first copies of *Time* and *Newsweek* that I had seen since the early weeks of my captivity. We had not seen any newspapers for some three years. Our captors were careful to censor these magazines. Any articles referring to the situation in the Middle East, particularly the war, were torn out. Any articles referring to ourselves or the situation in Lebanon were also censored. But our captors' strategy was a hopeless one. By simply reading the contents page of one issue and then reading the letters page in the following week's edition we were reasonably informed about what they had prevented us from reading. For the four or five weeks in which we received these magazines we devoured and discussed them at great length.

The ending of the first Gulf war and the fact that we were given these magazines assured us that something would happen in the very near future concerning our release. We asked for a radio and much to our surprise we were given a small portable. We listened avidly to the local news and French news from Monte Carlo. Only Frank remained uninterested in this new situation. He rarely listened to the news and never bothered with the magazines. Our conversation about what we read seemed to supply him with as much news as he required.

More importantly for me, these magazines brought more than printed news. They were filled with coloured photographs. It was the first time we had something other than the four bare walls and ourselves to look at. I looked at these magazines and read them with the kind of fascination a child has for his comic book. I still remember a large full-page ad for Singapore Airlines that depicted the faces of three air hostesses. They were extremely beautiful. On many occasions I sat in a stupefied torpor looking at the faces and into the dark oval eyes of these creatures. The holiday ads for the Far East and India transported me. The shapes and styles of the latest motor cars

and the new incomprehensible world of computers fascinated and
sometimes frightened us.

We read with some anxiety about the *Vincennes** incident. It was not
the fact of the tragedy itself, but rather the genocidal potential of this
new military technology that frightened us. We had no fear now for
our own lives. The end of the Iran/Iraq war augmented our value at
the negotiating table. We were confident that our release could only
take a matter of months after the settlement of the conflict. The more
relaxed attitude of the guards reinforced this view. For some of us
hope of freedom brought its own anxiety. The dread of being so near
and being let down again was a terrifying one. Once before, the
Americans had been assured of their release. They had been given new
clothes and shoes and were about to walk through the door to
freedom, but after a few hours, the guards came and removed the
clothes and shoes.

Whenever anyone had doubts we would gather around him, cajole
and convince him that such doubts were groundless. It was a time
when one had to be calm, patient and to believe in something we had
neither the courage nor the energy to believe. It was agonizing to be
standing at a doorway waiting for it to open telling yourself that it will
open and you will walk through. Impatience is the brother to panic.

After some five or six weeks our deliveries of *Time* and *Newsweek*
suddenly stopped. The radio was taken from us. No explanation was
given. We did not press the matter. We had stored enough information to keep our imagination and our critical faculties well-oiled and
working. Tom was greatly depressed by the loss of the radio. That
contact with the real world was a great boost to him. The last item of
news we heard on the radio before it was taken away was that Islamic
Jihad had threatened the lives of the American hostages unless some of
their demands were met. The following day when the guards came to
unchain us, Terry Anderson quipped 'Those who are about to die
salute you.'

Frank Reed was the first to leave. One of the chiefs confirmed that he
was going home. They asked Frank his shoe size and measured him
for trousers. None of us believed that he would really be set free.
There was something not quite right about the situation. None of us

* The American naval vessel *Vincennes* shot down an Iranian passenger aircraft in July
1988, killing all 290 people on board.

would hint to Frank that these men were lying. Frank made no comment on what he had been told. A few days later he left us.

We were anxious for Frank because of what we had heard on the radio, but we were sure if our kidnappers were intent on carrying out their threat they would have taken more than one American, and they would probably have asked the Americans to make a video broadcast. We decided to play up our anxiety about Frank with the guards to get back our radio. When we challenged them about the radio and Frank's safety they became extremely anxious themselves. They were worried that if we believed Frank had been executed we would cause trouble for them. We had little to lose if we were going to be taken one by one and summarily shot. To placate us they returned the radio for a day. We listened to all the news reports, sure in ourselves that Frank had not been released. The news that we heard confirmed our suspicions. In the morning the radio was removed from us.

A few weeks after Frank left, Terry Anderson was taken away. This time there was no warning, and no suggestion that he was being released. No-one came to measure him for clothes or ask his shoe size. The guards simply came into the room, unlocked him and said 'Terry come.' Terry went with them and never returned. Tom, John and I discussed the significance of this but could come to no agreed conclusion.

Tom talked at length about his time with Terry Anderson. They had been together for many years. Tom had found Terry's aggressive debating technique exhausting, and felt he could never win an argument. He was aware of his dependence on Terry. Yet a few days after Terry's departure Tom admitted he felt a kind of relief that Terry had gone. Sometimes when two people spend all of their time in each other's company, having nothing but themselves and their own quality of mind or spirit to entertain themselves, they can without perceiving it become exhausting to one another. But, as we explained to Tom, it is a matter of mutual survival. Terry needed to talk and needed someone to listen and Tom needed to hear someone speaking to him. The sharing was reciprocal.

The companionship we had shared in this cellar restored Tom's confidence. Now when the guards abused him for being CIA or called him a spy, Tom simply laughed it off. He would say 'Yes, I am the big chief CIA, all Lebanon, Syria, Israel.'

When a person leaves a room, he becomes the topic of conversation for those remaining. It is a human preoccupation. So it was with us.

These men with whom we had spent so much time and whom we had come to know with such intimacy had left a deep impression on us. That we talked about them in their absence was a measure of the mark they had left upon us. It was also a way of finding a point of balance in ourselves, understanding our friends correctly, and in so doing assuring ourselves that we were worthwhile and had meaning; that our perception and our understanding had not been twisted out of all recognition. To love someone and know that it is meaningful one must be critical of the object of one's love. Criticism gives it value. As it increases in value, our own sense of self-worth equally increases. Terry and Frank, our absent comrades, became the object of humorous derision, admiration, sympathy and sometimes pity. We had known them as part of ourselves. We had identified much in them with our own experience. To be cruelly critical would be like brutalizing ourselves. Inevitably some petty frustrations with our departed companions surfaced, but we were always able to restore a more reasonable and humane perspective. In this situation of absolute denial we needed to feed off one another. It only mattered that we gave as much as we took.

It was a few weeks after Terry Anderson was taken from us that Tom Sutherland's turn came. Like Anderson's it was without warning. One day he was with us, the next he was gone. John and I were alone again. We found ourselves discussing the Americans as a group, and their relations with each other as compared with our own. Our absent friends filled our discussions for many days. We talked a lot about how you would go about making a film of the experience we had undergone.

Our captors came to talk with us more often now. Perhaps with only two of us in the room, they felt safer. We were let off our chains for longer periods. With fewer people to talk to and the room less crowded we returned to our exercising. Knowing that the camera in the corner was an eye unblinkingly observing us, we would sometimes perform for our audience upstairs. It was a way of ridiculing them and of restoring our own sense of resistance, defiance and strength. John would occasionally stand with his face pressed close to the camera grimacing and making faces. On other occasions he would mimic the departed Americans.

We were to spend many weeks of expectation here. Our hopes at the ending of the Gulf war had not been lessened. As time went on and nothing seemed to be happening, we reassured one another by constantly repeating 'Another month, perhaps two.' Always our future was another month, perhaps two.

When it came, the manner of our removal was different from before. We knelt down; again our hands were chained to our ankles. We were carried in a bag and there was a car to be dumped into. We were driven for miles and miles, coming down to Beirut again. But there were no check points. Cars behind us, cars in front of us guaranteed our delivery back to the city. A blaring siren accompanied us throughout the journey. Never before had that happened. I thought then and I still believe that it was the Syrian Army that guaranteed our journey.

So we were hauled out of the boot, carried upstairs to a room, thanking God that we were still together. They chained me to one wall and John to another. This was all done in darkness. I reached out 'You okay?' 'Yes,' John replied. From nowhere a cigarette lighter flared. Throughout our noisy arrival, with the guards carrying in mattresses and blankets, another prisoner had been sitting, silent and invisible in the corner. The momentary flash revealed only a darkened silhouette. 'Who are you?' I demanded. A voice like a slowly returning echo declared, 'My name is Frank Reed.'

I could reach out at the end of my chain and tousle his head, the way people do a child or a dog. It was good to be with someone else. The next morning was a surprise and a confirmation. Frank had been there for about nine months on his own. He had been abused remorselessly. When the guards came in during the day they would kick him. Mazin, the guard who lay on top of me during that suffocating ride, who kissed me and took away the binding tapes, was here. He disliked Frank. He kicked him. He said to us: 'You all right? . . . This man touch you? . . . This man touch you?' The man that we were now living with was incapable of touching. We were chained well away from one another, barely within reach. I suppose they thought we would have sexual relations with one another. We were angry at the behaviour of our guards and their treatment of Frank. His constant physical humiliation left a deep scar on him.

He had known more periods of isolation than the rest of us and had lost resolve, lost his capacity to be himself. Though we would have some hours of light during the day, I thought as I watched Frank that much of him remained in the dark.

We talked to Frank about things that had happened in the outside world. But Frank had decided a long time ago to leave the reality of the situation. He was hurt deeply. The sudden novelty of our return was perplexing and confusing.

The belief that we would be sexually involved if we could touch one another made me sick and angry at the inadequacy of the people who chained us, at their small obsessive minds. The poison was not in the locks but in the mental chains of our captors. Touch was, to us, survival, defiance, self-assertion. They chained us away from touching, from reaching out to one another to take a hand and say 'Fuck it, come on, we'll beat it.'

When we were taken off the chains John and I exercised vigorously. Frank did not. We said 'C'mon get up, walk.' He would not walk. He believed he was the last American hostage. His sense of reality was much distorted, and his conversation and behaviour evidenced the huge toll the deprivations and brutality had taken on him. For long periods he would sit with a blanket over his head, lost in his own world. For him we were not there. When the guards came in during exercise periods he fell on the floor, and crawled to his corner. 'Get up, don't ever do that, get up, get up.' I lifted him to make him stand or sit. This is what happens to anyone left alone for too long and their life becomes nothing but abuse, I reflected. 'Get up, get up, never let these people see you crawling . . . Get up, get up, get up.' A man can be so destroyed that he crawls across the floor, frightened. It was crucifying to watch. I could not bear it. 'Get up, get up, don't do this . . . get up.'

I hoped that I was speaking to something deep in him. My Irish bravado did not help. John McCarthy, being calmer, said to the guards: 'Don't beat this man any more . . . bring your chiefs here. I want to speak with them.' The guards didn't like that sort of questioning of their own freedom. They loved a brave man but they were frightened of the challenge. Mazin knew that if the chiefs ever visited and we complained of his ruthless abuse there would be much trouble for him. John's firmness and assurance made Mazin fearful. Within days the atmosphere of brutality changed. Mazin, afraid of the consequences to himself, began treating Frank like a favourite uncle. Frank in response slowly returned to himself and to us.

Back to the Beginning

Slowly, as the months passed, we each of us sought to find a meeting place in our understanding. Humanization is a reciprocal thing. We cannot know ourselves or declare ourselves human unless we share in the humanity of another. Finding our way back from the animal condition imposed on us was no easy task. The worlds we created and in which we found a refuge were more alluring than the vacant reality of the world outside ourselves. We needed the stimulus of another person, his sympathy, his critical judgement to help guide us. We needed his assurance that the world was worth the effort. And this when there was no external stimulus, no window to look out of, no door to walk through; when there was not the colour and the noise of movement and of life. Then the idea of a return home was more than difficult. It was frequently undesired. There were no signposts and no lights by which to see the way.

I remembered one of the prison cells I had been kept in. I awoke early in the morning hearing the dawn call to prayer and suddenly jumped up screaming and swearing as I swept the ants from my flesh. Hundreds and hundreds seasonally invaded the cells in which we were kept. Like the giant Gulliver in a rage of frustration and cold sweat I would stamp and slap and crush them without mercy, without any thought of their separate existence. But after days of this I got tired of my anger. It exhausted me. The ants were inexhaustible. I began searching out where they entered the cell, blocking up small cracks and fissures with bits of wet tissue or broken matchsticks, but they would always find another point of entry. As I watched them pour into the cell through so many different places they became for me a form of entertainment. I watched them work. I watched how they would search out a crumb of bread four or five times their own size. They would trail and pull or push this piece of bread the full length of my tiny cell, scale a vertical wall, crawl along ridges until they found an exit point and take with them what they had found.

My fascination made friends of them. I was grateful for their fortitude, for their strength, for their resilience and instead of raging at them I would sit awaiting their return. I watched how they worked together. And how, if I had crushed one in the night by accident, the others would gather around and if there was life in it still, a comrade would lift this wounded companion and carry it across what for these tiny creatures must have seemed like miles, crawl up the vertical wall and search out an escape point through which they could take this maimed insect to be amongst its own. This incident became a symbol for me in this blank room with its three chained creatures. We cannot abandon the injured or the maimed, thinking to ensure our own safety and sanity. We must reclaim them, as they are part of ourselves.

The days in my last months of captivity were a coming back to reality for each of us. The half-man we had found when we first came there we understood and gently, without insistence, tried to lift that blanket from him, not with our hands but with our minds and with what compassion or affectionate criticism we could find.

Frank emerged from behind his blanket slowly, tenuously. As he did so, so did we. His coming back was a homecoming for us all, though we remained in that room, chained, barely able to reach out and touch one another's hands. It was a restoration of meaning for all of us.

John's strength, his defiance and resistance to the guards, his steely calm made them wary. John was in command. They became frightened. What if their chief should come to visit, if someone was ill, and what if John or I should speak of what had happened here to Frank. These violent men, who had taken their strength and manhood from a man unable to resist, were now cowering within themselves.

The beatings and the abuse were at an end. There were no more insidious insults. There was no more kicking or spitting. There was no more standing with us in the toilet and insisting that we could not stand to urinate because it was the way of Satan. Such abuse we would not listen to, but the idiocy that we had to endure was its own kind of punishment.

Things improved in this place, the food was better than it had ever been before. They gave us a television regularly, but we were never allowed to watch the news. Three times a week we would be offered a video film. Gratefully we would accept only to find ourselves bored stupid by Kung-Fu films or the usual gratuitous violence of western movies. Often we talked about how the violence of men like our guards was at least partly conditioned by the glut of American video violence, and how their twisted, obsessional concern with sexuality was in part a response to the slew of nudity in the western films they saw. In our own way we were subject to a violence and perversion conditioned by products of the West. We remembered how the guns that they had shown us were all of European manufacture.

The shadows that engulf a man until he loses his substantiality had begun to dissipate. A light that glowed and burned and grew within was extinguishing the power of the shadowy darkness. We were all emergent, men still hungry for a future, believing in that future and casting off all futility. We were each laughing again, telling stories, outrageous lies as big and as monstrous as mountains and laughing at sheer fantasy again. Mad schemes were designed and as we each described them and watched the fascination of our listeners we got carried away, and made our tales taller and more incredible.

There was a new atmosphere here, and one that boded well for us. Occasionally Mahmoud would come as a visitor to sit and talk with us and tell us about world events. We were never astounded by what he reported though the reality of some of these events was truly astonishing. The Berlin Wall had fallen in November 1989, but our minds could not be amazed by simply human things, for they had travelled into more amazing and awesome places.

Many months after we arrived here Frank was removed. We knew though we were not told that this time he had been released. Every night, I would crawl across the floor, putting my ear to the bottom of the door and listening to the news reports, my Arabic good enough to tell me that he really had been freed. His release was a boost to us.

We had long recognized that the guards were as much our prisoners as we were theirs, and they were now more prisoners than ever before. In many respects they had become our servants. If we asked for anything we were given it immediately. Medicine, a particular kind of food, coffee, hot chocolate – all were given to us. Only newspapers were refused. In the light of this, we became more confident. To treat us so royally, but yet to refuse magazines or newspapers, suggested strongly that something was happening which they did not want us to know about. That something, we were sure, was an impending end to our captivity.

After Frank left, another prisoner was moved into the room beside ours. For some days there was silence from this other person's room, then inevitably the knocking began. A man will risk his life or the better part of it to communicate. The knocking told us who it was, and we were not surprised. We had guessed as much beforehand. We returned the messages, tapping out our own identity and what news and information we could pass on. It was a slow, laborious process, but we knew how hungry Terry Waite must be for news. We had always known that he would be alone. The fact that he was in this apartment with us now further reinforced our hopes.

Daily we would be taken to the toilet, returned and exercised. In the afternoon the guards would come to unchain us, take us one at a time from the room, across the hall into the kitchen. We would sit on a chair in front of a window. The window would be opened and in would come the heat and light of the sun, blazing through our blindfolds. A radio was always playing in the kitchen. Often the guard Bilal, the one who had asked John to teach him to dance, would tune the radio to some western rock station and we would listen to old and familiar tunes. Occasionally we caught some quick news flash, half understanding it before the guards would flick to another station. There was much talk now with the guards, and jokes were traded.

John sat chained to his wall at one end of the large apartment room and I, chained to mine, at the other. We would take our socks, stuff them full of paper or some rag or shirt that we had torn up, wrap the sock around this and make ourselves a small ball. Chained to the wall we would viciously pass this ball back and forward, scoring points against each miss. The next morning during exercise we would bring out our secret ball and play soccer or volleyball, choking on the laughter.

'Hope for everything but expect nothing' had long been our motto. But now hope increased expectation, rather than limited it. We spoke little to one another about our possible release. We hoped we would both go together. We expected it would not happen like that. Yet we enjoyed one another's company too much to bear the thought of either of us going before the other.

It comes as all things that change a life must come: without warning. An afternoon visit, suddenly there are many men in the room. A guard kneels down, lifting me by the arm with the command 'Stand, Brian, stand.' I stand, wondering, not really expecting this to be the moment. I am unchained and led from the room and into another. On the floor is a mattress and I am made to sit on it and am chained again.

Slowly something is dawning on me. To move me to another room and rechain me is a separation that means something though I cannot allow myself to believe what it might be. Grasping hold of something and then having it instantaneously taken away had hurled many of us in the past into that abyss we all knew too well. But I sit in defiant silence. A man kneels in front of me, his hand gentle on my shoulder. It is the voice of one of the chiefs. Quietly he says 'Brian, you go home.' I am silent and unstunned. 'Home, you mean another place?' I ask, for I have heard these words before.

Again the hand at my shoulder and the voice. 'You go home, family, Dublin.' The sound of the word Dublin suggests that something is imminent. I am still amazingly calm. I ask 'What about my friend?' There is silence, voices mumble in Arabic. All of them leave the room. Ten minutes later two men return, they ask whether I want anything. That phrase I have heard ten thousand times before. 'I want to speak with my friend John. I want to speak with him now. I will not go without speaking.' My voice is rising in panic, realizing 'My God, it is over.'

They recognize my insistence, the loudness of my voice, the determination in it. A man kneels again in front of me, quietly he asks 'What do you want?' I answer, my voice slow, loud enough so that I hope John will hear. 'I want to speak with John, I will not go from this room until I speak with him.' The figure still squats in silence in front of me. After some minutes he leaves. I am given tea. I sit, the door is left wide open.

I know they have gone into the kitchen and are there talking. After half an hour two men come into the room. 'Brian,' a voice says. I sit silent, 'You douche, take shower.' I sit silent, wondering is this an order or an offer. Again I say to them 'Take me to John, I want to say goodbye.' My voice is more angry now than determined but it's a quiet anger. Again the chief kneels down in front of my blindfolded face. His hand is at my shoulder but not this time in a pat of affection; squeezing and gripping hard again. 'After douche, after some hours you talk with your friend.' I nod, not knowing whether to believe and accept or to face the pointlessness of argument.

I am left for those hours to think. I begin to believe what I have been told and suddenly there is something in me I cannot resolve. I know it is over and within hours or days I will not be wearing a blindfold. I will be unfettered. But I feel it build in me, the weight of my imprisonment. For how much freedom can there be for a man when he leaves one half of himself chained to the wall? I begin to try to order my thinking to see beyond the consequences of any action I can take. I can argue and fight and insist on staying until my friend is released. But if I don't go, how will my family and friends receive it? Perhaps even now they are sitting waiting for the final confirmation. Has their suffering been so little over the past four and a half years that I can refuse this, and thrust them back into their anguish? I think one moment that I am thinking only of myself and then that I am not. I am trying desperately to find a balance in my compassion. I weigh the scales and I move back and forth and I am caught in indecision. My hands stretched out to the man in the room next door and to my family far away. Which has the greater hold and where is the greater pull on me?

My mind flashes back over four and a half years, those memories percolating through my history and that of my friends. I am in a delirium of contradictory desire that will not resolve itself. Only I can make this choice and I am incapable. Great love has weakened me. I am again on that raft in an ocean, tossed by the turbulent tides of affection. I try to work out what I should do for I must choose and in what I choose make myself. I remember every moment of my time alone, my time with John and with those other captives. And I remember how we first met, our relationship, the kinds of needs I had of John and he of me. And how we sought always to give and take, thinking always of the other. And as I review it all, all that wonder, I see his face stare at mine. I had watched this man grow, become full and in his fullness enrich me. And I know that if in my defiance I walk back into that room and have myself chained, refusing to go home, I will have diminished him, for he is a bigger man than to succumb to the needs that isolation breeds. I cannot do this, I cannot belittle him. I know that in going free I will free him. He will not surrender, he has gone beyond it. I know that the deep bond our captivity has given us will be shattered if I return. Our respect for each other demands of each that we take our freedom when it comes.

And so I took it, feeling that my arm had been wrenched off my shoulder and was suddenly missing. I walked blindfold into the shower. I stood indifferent to its warm embrace, and soaped down my body. I was numb. They allowed me to take as long as I wished. But I had no wish to stand, only to be gone.

I sat on a chair and listened to the scissors clip my hair. Jokes were being cracked about me. Bilal the barber offered to give the hairs on my chest a trim. I smiled.

Curiously the guards did not come to talk with me as I sat out those remaining hours. I wondered if they understood my anguish or my resolution. I sat in silence, unmoving, concentrating my mind and trying telepathically to send a message across that small hallway and underneath the door to my friend waiting and wondering. I tried also to send messages to say to those who I knew sat at the edge of a terrible anxiety and of a chasm of hope that it was over. I was about to begin my beginning.

As I had first been taken, so I was being released. I sat in the back of a Mercedes, my head resting upon the lap of one of the guards I had known as Ali. His hand gently shielded my eyes. We drove through the back streets of the suburbs. It was a strange comfort to sit in a Mercedes. The car stopped. I could hear men outside talking. There was much snapping of magazines into guns, and an older man, perhaps in his mid-forties or fifties, entered the passenger seat. The previous passenger had left and not returned. Ali sat, his Kalashnikov beside his knee. The driver said something. Someone clipped a magazine into a gun and handed it to him. The older man barked an order and the car moved off. For fifteen minutes we drove and then stopped. The passenger got out. The door opened. Ali excitedly, quickly said to me 'Yallah, yallah, go, go . . . Good luck . . . good luck.' I emerged as I had never done before, clothed in trousers, shoes, socks, a T-shirt, a sweater, and my eyes unblindfolded yet still unseeing in the dark. The older man took me by the hand.

We walked forward slowly. In front of me, perhaps a hundred yards off, the lights of a single car flashed on and remained alight. The car in which we had arrived flashed its lights and they also remained lit. Along this path of light we walked, this man and I, hand in hand. In the light two men approached us, one carrying a Kalashnikov. We met. There was a long, low whitish wall to the right of me, beyond which the last lights of the city were burning. Voices spoke and exchanged greetings. I could not understand them. The man holding my hand placed my hand into the hands of the men who had came up to us. Nothing more was said. Heads were nodded. The deed was done. The man who had walked me like a child, his hand in mine, turned and walked slowly away.

I walked between the two men who had received me. 'You are

Syrian?' I asked. They looked at me. I asked again 'You are Syrian?'
One of them answered 'Syria,' and nodded his head. I turned like Lot's
wife to take one last look and saw nothing but the car's headlights. A
Syrian nudged me forward. I climbed into another car. In the back, as
in the car I had just left, sat a young man with a Kalashnikov. The pair
who had received me spoke some words, the motor started and the car
drove off. The passenger in front turned to me and with very feeble
English asked 'You . . . nationality?' I answered 'Irish.' He nodded,
said something to the driver, turned to me again and asked 'How
long?' 'Four and a half years,' I answered. The driver made a noise like
a low whistle. We moved on into the night. Did the night know what
had passed?

On through that darkness. There was silence in the vehicle. I
remember feeling extremely calm, resigned, unaffected by all that had
happened. The car careered through those back streets and was
suddenly in the heart of the city, and equally suddenly it stopped. Men
with guns were milling around it. The door was opened for me, I
stepped out. Faces stood and looked at me. I was ushered inside a
building, up a marble staircase and into a waiting room. I was left
there with two Syrians in plain clothes. They sat looking at me, then
the passenger in the car came back and I was ushered into a large room.
    At the head of the room was a huge polished desk and behind it a
Syrian in his fifties. He beckoned me to sit. He exchanged some words
with men who had come into the room after me. One of them went
out and returned with a young man in his twenties who bowed in
terror to the figure behind the desk. He spoke some words to him and
he turned to me bowing and asked me would I like anything? Did I feel
well? To which I answered 'Yes, I'm fine . . . I would like a coffee.'
My answer was translated for the man behind the desk and the coffee
was brought. He kept saying to me as I drank the coffee 'You strong.
Strong,' making the bicep in his arm jump. I knew how important
physical strength is to the Arab mind. I simply nodded and smiled,
bemused by the excitement and the silence around me. My nationality
and name were again confirmed. A telephone call was made to
Damascus. I heard my name again and the word 'Irish' spoken. The
receiver was placed back on the telephone. I was again asked if I would
like to eat. I thanked them and said 'No . . . a glass of water perhaps.'
Water was brought and I watched these men watch me as I finished
the glass.

Then we were off again. Back down the marble staircase and into the waiting car. The same driver, but a new passenger and another guard with his Kalashnikov sat in the back seat, and so we set off. Driving once again, up through the hill villages of Lebanon. This time there were no check points. The car travelled unmolested through the night. I asked the passenger if we were going to Syria. 'Yes, of course,' he answered in good English. On and on we drove. I sat quiet and calm watching the villages go about their evening life. There seemed more night life here than in the city of Beirut. I turned once more to the passenger in the front and said 'So this is the road to Damascus?' He answered quietly 'Yes.'

I spent two nights in Syrian Army Intelligence Headquarters. On arrival there I was brought to the Deputy Chief of Intelligence with the passenger who had driven from Beirut with me. While I sat in the office looking around its palatial furnishings and became aware of the poverty of the clothes in which I had been returned to life, I thought to myself how quickly our little vanities return to us. The two men chatted in Arabic and then asked me politely how I was and did I want anything? In the last few hours I had become excruciatingly bored with this expression. I didn't know what I wanted. An interpreter was brought. I spoke with him at length, the questions coming first from the intelligence officer, through my interpreter to me.

At first they were casual questions, then increasingly they were asking about who had held us, where we were held, did I recognize the captors, did I know anything about them. They were keen to know who I had been held with, who I had had contact with. At first I answered, but became increasingly aware of what was happening. This was another interrogation.

New clothes were sent for and I went into the security chief's own bedroom with the interpreter and the servant and another man whose function I did not know. I undressed, the interpreter saying 'We are all men here.' I smiled. I had little vanity about my body. I stripped and got into the cool linen and the cool cotton.

I returned from the room and saw laid out on the table a huge spread of food. A typical Arab feast. My stomach quietly revolted. I could not eat much of this; still all the different shapes and colours would be fun to play with. I sat and joined the men about me.

Another man was there. The deference with which the others

addressed him suggested that here was a man of some importance. The meticulousness of his English confirmed this and the depth of his questions reinforced it. We talked generally of what was happening in the world. The Syrians were anxious to speak of Iraq's invasion of Kuwait. Then as we relaxed in this general discussion of world events, questions about my captivity again arose. I answered at first without thinking, then as I returned some questions and they remained unanswered, I realized I was being debriefed. It was time to toss the ball in the air. I remembered that old Belfast colloquialism which had sustained us all, and become a catchphrase for us in our imprisonment: 'Say whatever you like, but whatever you say say nothing.'

At the end of our three-hour meal and curious conversation I was again addressed by the intelligence chief, this time directly in English. 'You are tired, perhaps you would like to sleep.' 'No, I am not tired. I want to go for a walk . . . I have not walked the streets for four and a half years.' There was astonishment on the faces of the men about the table. They looked questioningly at the security chief. He looked to each of them, then directly at me. He nodded to them, brushing away their fears. 'Okay it is fine,' he said. That night I was driven around the city of Damascus with two armed plainclothes security men on each side of me. Freedom comes slowly at first.

Nightmare

I know that nightmares have their source
Like the abstract has some social sense.
Time fluxes in the dark
Night stalking mind, closer than blood.
Dreams, words, things felt – not said,
Spaces on every side:
Bat's wings beat like heart
Or drum
Translating silence to insanity.

Daylight mind invades the dark
Thing to be fixed or set apart.
Conviction rejecting guilt
Condemned without crime.
Onlookers can't look in
Nor mind look out.
I huddle, insensible
As blank air
And fear the vertigo of the night
Seeing myself
Dropped
God knows where
From such a height.

Brian Keenan